Benziger Brothers

The Catholic national series: The New fifth reader

Benziger Brothers

**The Catholic national series: The New fifth reader**

ISBN/EAN: 9783742844927

Manufactured in Europe, USA, Canada, Australia, Japa

Cover: Foto ©Lupo / pixelio.de

Manufactured and distributed by brebook publishing software (www.brebook.com)

Benziger Brothers

**The Catholic national series: The New fifth reader**

The New fifth reader

# HARVARD COLLEGE LIBRARY

THE ESSEX INSTITUTE
TEXT-BOOK COLLECTION

. .

GIFT OF
GEORGE ARTHUR PLIMPTON
OF NEW YORK

JANUARY 25, 1924

THE DEFENSE OF THE BRIDGE OF ATHLONE.

THE CATHOLIC NATIONAL SERIES.

# THE NEW FIFTH READER.

NEW YORK, CINCINNATI, AND CHICAGO:
**BENZIGER BROTHERS,**
Printers to the Holy Apostolic See.

Copyright, 1894, by BENZIGER BROTHERS.

# CONTENTS.

| LESSON | | PAGE |
|---|---|---|
| | INTRODUCTION | 9 |
| 1. | PERCY WYNN'S FIRST DAY AT COLLEGE (I). *Rev. Francis J. Finn, S.J.* | 23 |
| 2. | PERCY WYNN'S FIRST DAY AT COLLEGE (II). " " | 26 |
| 3. | THE KING AND THE CHILD...*Eugene J. Hall* | 32 |
| 4. | HUNTING THE ELEPHANT IN AFRICA (I). *Sir Samuel White Baker* | 35 |
| 5. | HUNTING THE ELEPHANT IN AFRICA (II). " " | 39 |
| 6. | HUNTING THE ELEPHANT IN AFRICA (III). " " | 42 |
| 7. | THE HOSPITALITY OF THE SPANISH PEOPLE. *Lady Herbert* | 44 |
| 8. | LADY YEARDLY'S GUEST...*Margaret J. Preston* | 47 |
| 9. | IN A BALLOON..."*Household Words*" | 51 |
| 10. | CATHOLICITY AND AMERICAN LIBERTY. *Archbishop Hughes* | 55 |
| 11. | THE RIDE OF JENNIE MCNEAL...*Will Carleton* | 59 |
| 12. | THE POWER OF THE BLESSED SACRAMENT (I). *Rev. Michael Müller, C.SS.R.* | 64 |
| 13. | THE POWER OF THE BLESSED SACRAMENT (II). " " | 67 |
| 14. | THE POWER OF THE BLESSED SACRAMENT (III). " " | 71 |
| 15. | PANCRATIUS...*Eleanor C. Donnelly* | 75 |
| 16. | HUNTING THE HONEY-BEE...*John Burroughs* | 79 |
| 17. | JACQUES DUFOUR...*William W. Howe* | 83 |

## CONTENTS.

| LESSON | | PAGE |
|---|---|---|
| 18. The Cathedral of Seville and the Tomb of St. Ferdinand | ...Lady Herbert | 88 |
| 19. Thomas Hood | ...James T. Fields | 92 |
| 20. The Fishermen of Wexford | ...John Boyle O'Reilly | 96 |
| 21. A Military Stratagem (I) | ...John P. Kennedy | 100 |
| 22. A Military Stratagem (II) | " " | 105 |
| 23. A Military Stratagem (III) | " " | 110 |
| 24. Charity | ...Maurice Francis Egan | 114 |
| 25. The Search for Livingstone | ...Edward King | 116 |
| 26. Supposed Speech of John Adams | ...Daniel Webster | 121 |
| 27. The Galley Slave | ...Henry Abbey | 125 |
| 28. On Learning by Heart | | 128 |
| 29. A Ruffian in Feathers | ...Olive Thorne Miller | 131 |
| 30. The Yellow-hammer | ...Rev. F. W. Faber | 136 |
| 31. The Cruise of the Dolphin (I) | ...T. B. Aldrich | 140 |
| 32. The Cruise of the Dolphin (II) | " " | 142 |
| 33. The Norman Baron | ...Henry W. Longfellow | 146 |
| 34. Mrs. Caudle Wants Money for Clothes. | Douglas W. Jerrold | 149 |
| 35. John Hughes, First Archbishop of New York. | Rev. Dr. Henry A. Brann | 152 |
| 36. Evangeline | ...Henry W. Longfellow | 156 |
| 37. Bamboo (I) | ...A. R. Wallace | 161 |
| 38. Bamboo (II) | " " | 165 |
| 39. Erin's Flag | ...Rev. Abram J. Ryan | 169 |
| 40. Lost on the Floes (I) | ...Elisha Kent Kane | 172 |
| 41. Lost on the Floes (II) | " " | 176 |
| 42. Lost on the Floes (III) | " " | 179 |
| 43. The American Flag | ..Rev. Dr. Charles Constantine Pise | 183 |
| 44. The Escape of Harvey Birch | ...J. Fenimore Cooper | 185 |

## CONTENTS.

| LESSON | | PAGE |
|---|---|---|
| 45. THE LAST OF THE SIGNERS.... | ..........George Lippard | 190 |
| 46. THE OLD CONTINENTALS................ | Guy H. McMaster | 193 |
| 47. QUAIL ................................................ | | 195 |
| 48. THE BLUE AND THE GRAY........... | Francis Miles Finch | 198 |
| 49. IS A TURTLE FISH OR GAME?.......... | Alexander Hunter | 201 |
| 50. MARCO BOZZARIS..................... | Fitz-Greene Halleck | 204 |
| 51. TEACHING TO THINK............. | Daniel Pierce Thompson | 207 |
| 52. A CHRISTIAN MARTYR (I).............. | Cardinal Wiseman | 212 |
| 53. A CHRISTIAN MARTYR (II)............. | "         " | 217 |
| 54. A BOY ON A FARM............. | Charles Dudley Warner | 223 |
| 55. THE BAREFOOT BOY.................. | John G. Whittier | 225 |
| 56. THE HURRICANE...................... | John J. Audubon | 229 |
| 57. THE ROYAL SCHOLAR................... | Francis Palgrave | 233 |
| 58. DEATH OF THE FLOWERS.......... | William Cullen Bryant | 238 |
| 59. AN OLD-FASHIONED GIRL............... | Louisa M. Alcott | 240 |
| 60. MY GARDEN ACQUAINTANCE......... | James Russell Lowell | 244 |
| 61. VENERABLE JOAN OF ARC........ | Rev. Dr. John Lingard | 248 |
| 62. THE CATARACT OF LODORE................. | Robert Southey | 254 |
| 63. BENEATH THE FALLS OF NIAGARA........... | John Tyndall | 259 |
| 64. RIP VAN WINKLE (I).................. | Washington Irving | 264 |
| 65. RIP VAN WINKLE (II)................ | "         " | 268 |
| 66. RIP VAN WINKLE (III)............... | "         " | 271 |
| 67. WHAT I LIVE FOR.................... | G. Linnæus Banks | 274 |
| 68. BOOKS............................... | Maurice Francis Egan | 276 |
| 69. THE POOR FISHER-FOLK...................... | ............. | 278 |
| 70. RIENZI'S ADDRESS TO THE ROMANS... | Mary Russell Mitford | 283 |
| 71. THE CLOTHING OF SOME ANIMALS.... | Francis T. Buckland | 285 |
| 72. AN APRIL DAY................................. | Chaucer | 290 |
| 73. THE SEVEN SLEEPERS...................... | Baring Gould | 292 |

## CONTENTS.

| LESSON | | PAGE |
|---|---|---|
| 74. The Ride of Collins Graves....... | John Boyle O'Reilly | 296 |
| 75. The Bold Dragoon................................. | | 300 |
| 76. The Meeting with the Master....... | Miles Gerald Keon | 301 |
| 77. Electricity (I).................... | Arabella B. Buckley | 306 |
| 78. Electricity (II).................... | " " | 310 |
| 79. Miracles.......................... | Cardinal Newman | 314 |
| 80. Paradise and the Peri................. | Thomas Moore | 316 |
| 81. A Hundred Years of American Independence. | Richard O'Gorman | 321 |
| 82. The Chariot Race (I).................... | Lewis Wallace | 327 |
| 83. The Chariot Race (II)................... | " " | 331 |
| 84. The Chariot Race (III)................. | " " | 335 |
| 85. A Winter's Night.................... | John G. Whittier | 338 |
| 86. How Certain Plants Capture Insects........ | Asa Gray | 341 |
| 87. The Massacre of Cawnpore........... | Justin McCarthy | 344 |
| 88. An Iceberg............................. | Louis L. Noble | 348 |
| 89. Elegy Written in a Country Churchyard (I). | Thomas Gray | 351 |
| 90. Elegy Written in a Country Churchyard (II). | " " | 354 |
| 91. Sancho Panza's Government.................. | Cervantes | 357 |
| 92. Storming the Heights of Abraham (I). | Francis Parkman | 360 |
| 93. Storming the Heights of Abraham (II). | " " | 366 |
| 94. Sowing and Reaping............. | Adelaide Anne Procter | 372 |
| 95. The Necessity of Government........ | John C. Calhoun | 373 |
| 96. How they Kept the Bridge at Athlone. | A. M. Sullivan | 375 |
| 97. A Ballad of Athlone.................. | Aubrey De Vere | 380 |
| 98. The Last Days of Colonel Newcome. | William Makepeace Thackeray | 381 |

# INTRODUCTION.

A good reader conveys fully and clearly to his hearers the ideas and feelings of a writer.

No one can read well who does not thoroughly understand what he reads; hence the necessity of studying each lesson until not only the meaning of the words in the lesson is perfectly understood, but also the nature and character of the whole lesson. A reader must enter fully into the feelings and sentiments of a writer before he can render them well.

RULE.—Let the pupil study the lesson, and become acquainted with its subject, before he attempts to read it aloud. Difficult lessons should first be read and explained by the teacher.

[*Italics* are used in the examples to show the part of the word or sentence to which the rule applies.]

## ARTICULATION.

ARTICULATION is the distinct utterance of the elementary sounds in syllables and words.

RULE.—Articulate distinctly each syllable.

The first step toward becoming a good reader is a correct articulation. A public speaker, possessed of only a moderate voice, if he articulate correctly, will be better understood, and heard with greater pleasure, than one who vociferates without judgment. The voice of the latter may, indeed, extend to a considerable distance, but the sound is dissipated in confusion. Of the former voice, the smallest vibration is perceived at the utmost distance to which it reaches; hence it has often the appearance of penetrating even further than one which is loud, but badly articulated.

## PHONIC CHART.

### Vowel Sounds.

| | | | |
|---|---|---|---|
| ā long, | as in ale. | ĭ short, | as in in. |
| ă short, | " " at. | ō long, | " " old. |
| ä Italian, | " " arm. | ŏ short, | " " on. |
| ạ broad, | " " all. | ǫ intermediate, | " " do. |
| à intermediate, | " " ask. | ū long, | " " use. |
| â before r, | " " air. | ŭ short, | " " up. |
| ē long, | " " eve. | ụ intermediate, | " " put. |
| ĕ short, | " " end. | oi, oy, | " " oil, toy. |
| ẽ intermediate, | " " her. | ou, ow, | " " out, now. |
| ī long, | " " ice. | | |

### Consonants.

| | | | | | |
|---|---|---|---|---|---|
| b, | as in băd. | l, | as in lĭp. | s, | as in sạlt. |
| d, | " " dŏt. | m, | " " măt. | sh, | " " shē. |
| f, | " " fŭn. | n, | " " nō. | t, | " " tĭn. |
| h, | " " hŏt. | ng, | " " sĭng. | th, | " " thĭn. |
| j, | " " joy. | p, | " " păn. | v, | " " văt. |
| k, | " " kĭn. | r, | " " rŏt. | w, | " " wâit. |

y, as in yē.    z, as in zōne.

## EQUIVALENT SOUNDS.

| Vowels. | | | | Consonants. | | | |
|---|---|---|---|---|---|---|---|
| ạ, | like ŏ, | as in | whạt. | ç, | like s, | as in | çēde. |
| a, | " ĕ, | " " | any. | ẹ, | " k, | " " | eạt. |
| ê, | " ā, | " " | thêre. | ch, | | " " | chĭld. |
| ẹ, | " ā, | " " | prey. | çh, | " sh, | " " | çhāiṣe. |
| e, | " ĭ, | " " | pretty. | ch, | " k, | " " | chôrd. |
| ī, | " ē, | " " | pŏlīçe. | ğ, | | " " | ğĕt. |
| ĭ, | " ē, | " " | vĭrgin. | ġ, | " j, | " " | ġĕm. |
| ȯ, | " ŭ, | " " | sȯn. | gh, | " f, | " " | roŭgh. |
| ọ, | " ȯȯ, | " " | wọlf. | ṇ, | " ng, | " " | fĭṇger. |
| ô, | " ạ, | " " | fôrm. | ph, | " f, | " " | phāṣe. |
| ōō, | | " " | mōōn. | qu, | " k, | " " | pīque. |
| ŏŏ, | | " " | fŏŏt. | qu, | " kw, | " " | quāil. |
| ụ, | " ōō, | " " | rụde. | s, | | " " | same. |
| û, | " ē, | " " | ûrge. | ṣ, | " z, | " " | rōṣe. |
| u, | " ĕ, | " " | bury. | th, | | " " | thĭng. |
| u, | " ĭ, | " " | busy. | th, | | " " | thē. |
| ȳ, | " ī, | " " | flȳ. | wh, | " hw, | " " | whạt. |
| y̆, | " ĭ, | " " | my̆th. | x̣, | " ġz, | " " | ĕx̣ĭst. |
| y, | " ē, | " " | myrrh. | z, | " zh, | " " | āzūre. |

i, like consonant y, as in onion.

ce, ci, sci, se, si, s, ti, like sh, as in ŏcean, vĭcious, cŏnscious, nạuseous, session, sụre, nation.

A common error in articulation is the slurring or blending of final and initial letters. Care should be taken to bring out the full sound of each word, as if it stood alone, without *overdoing* the matter.

### EXERCISE.

Sees him; must tell; his cry; would you; sixth day; next time; most people; hands him; costs more; made you; folds his; sifts sand; fields lie; and end; lasts till; some mice; must spin; Arctic ocean; facts are; assists.

## ACCENT.

ACCENT is a peculiar stress or effort of the voice upon certain syllables of words, which distinguishes them from the others by a greater distinctness and loudness of pronunciation.

In every word of more than one syllable, one of the syllables is pronounced with particular force, and this is called the *accented* syllable. Many polysyllabic words have two accents, a *primary* and a *secondary*, differing only in degree, the *primary* being uttered with a greater stress of voice than the *secondary*.

No definite rule can be given in regard to the placing of the accent. The proper pronunciation of words, which includes correct accentuation, can be acquired only by careful attention to the language of correct speakers, and by the use of a good dictionary.

## EMPHASIS.

EMPHASIS is a particular force or stress of voice given to one or more words of a sentence, or to a whole sentence; it is to the word or sentence what the accent is to the syllable.

There are several modes by which a word or words may be emphasized:

1. By *tone*, varying in degree according to the importance of the word or words.
2. By a *change in the inflection*.

3. By *time*, in which prominence is marked by a prolongation of the sound of the word or by an abridgment of it.

4. By a *pause*.

The only rule that can be given for distinguishing the words that should receive emphasis is to place it on those that directly convey the meaning or denote the contrast: the parts of a sentence charged with the greatest degree of sense should be pronounced with the greatest prominence.

The emphasis must, according to the intention of the speaker, be put upon that word which signifies the point.

Example: "Is it true that you have seen an officer from the court to-day who told you the bad news?"

If the inquirer merely wants to know whether *I* or some *other* person has seen the court officer, the emphasis falls on *you*. If he only wants to know from whom I received the news, he will emphasize *officer*. If he wants to know whether the news may be depended on, *court* will be the emphatic word. If he wishes to learn when I heard the news, he will put the emphasis on *to-day*. If he knows that I have seen the officer, and merely wants to learn whether I have heard any *news*, he will emphasize *news*. If he merely wants to know whether the news I heard was *bad*, he will put the emphasis on the word *bad*.

Emphasis, generally, may be divided into two kinds, *Emphasis of Sense* and *Emphasis of Feeling*.

Emphasis of Sense determines the meaning, and by a change of its position a sentence may be made to convey very different meanings; as,

Is *your* friend very sick?
(Meaning your friend, and not another person's friend.)
Is your *friend* very sick?
(Meaning your friend, not your brother or other relative.)
Is your friend *very* sick?
(Meaning is your friend very sick or only slightly ill.)

Emphasis of Feeling is suggested and governed by emotion: although not strictly necessary to the sense, it is, in the highest degree, expressive of sentiment: as,

Then must the Jew be *merciful*.
On what compulsion *must* I? tell me that.

## INFLECTION.

INFLECTION is the rise or fall of the voice in speaking or reading.

In the *rising inflection*, which is marked with the acute accent ('), the voice rises from the general pitch to the highest tone required; but in the *falling inflection*, marked by the grave accent (`), the voice begins above the general pitch and falls back to it. In the *circumflex*, which is a union of the *rising* and *falling inflections*, the voice does not rise or fall *directly*, but in a sort of curve. There are two kinds of *circumflex* inflections: the *rising circumflex*, marked ⌣, which begins with the *falling* and ends with the *rising inflection*, and the *falling inflection*, marked ⌢, which begins with the *rising* and ends with the *falling inflection*.

RULE I.—The general rule is, that the ideas which are complete, certain, or positive, take the Falling Inflection, while those that are incomplete, doubtful, or negative, take the Rising Inflection; as,

I know this to be the case`.
I think I shall be there`.

RULE II.—The Rising Inflection is generally used in questions that can be answered by *yes* or *no*; while the answers, when positive, take the Falling Inflection; as,

Do you attend school'? Yes`, I do`.

INTRODUCTION. xv

>Are you going home to-day´?
>Yes`, or at the latest to-morrow`.

>Where is the Earl of Holderness`?
>The noble earl is dead`.

**Rule III.**—Questions which cannot be answered by *yes* or *no*, together with their answers, generally take the Falling Inflection; as,

>Whose image and superscription hath it`?
>They, answering, said to him: Cæsar's`.

**Rule IV.**—In Contrasts or Comparisons, the first part usually takes the Rising, the second part the Falling Inflection; as,

>He follows him through thick´ and thin`.

>As fire is opposed to water´, so vice is to virtue`.

>And there are bodies celestial´, and bodies terrestrial`.

**Rule V.**—When in Contrasts or Comparisons one part is affirmed and the other denied, the affirmative takes the Falling, and the negative the Rising Inflection, no matter in which order they are; as,

>This is not winter´, it is summer`.
>This is summer`, not winter´.
>This is no accident´, it is God's curse`.
>This is God's curse`, it is no accident´.

**Rule VI.**—The Circumflex is used to express wonder, contempt, ridicule, mockery; in these cases the Rising Circumflex is used for the Rising Inflection, and the Falling Circumflex for the Falling Inflection; as,

>O uprĭght judge! Mark̑, Jew!—a leaȓned judge!

## MODULATION.

MODULATION refers to *pitch, force, quantity*, and *quality* of the voice in speaking and reading.

The proper modulation of the voice contributes very much to good reading; it constitutes in a great measure what is called expressive reading, and is particularly effective for the expression of all kinds of feelings and emotions.

It is necessary to study carefully the general character of each lesson:—is it joyful, sad, or merely narrative? is it poetry, and what kind? or is it a dialogue? As it is one or the other, so must we adapt to it the pitch, force, quantity, and quality of the voice.

RULE.—Pitch, force, quantity, and quality of the voice are intimately connected, and should always correspond to the nature of the subject.

## PITCH.

PITCH is the prevailing or governing note, and that in which sentences are generally begun. It may be high, medium, or low.

The pitch is entirely different from loudness or softness. As in music a sound may be loud or soft whether the note be high or low, so in speaking or reading the voice may be loud or soft, whether the pitch be high or low.

Much of the ease and beauty of reading depends upon the pitch that is taken. Every reader must take the pitch that is best suited to his voice, for only by doing so will he be enabled to speak with ease and effect. If the pitch is chosen too high or too low, the reader will soon be wearied and tired out. It should vary with, and be appropriate to, the character of the subject.

Care must be taken to avoid a sing-song tone, or a mere rise and fall of the voice without regard to the sense of the words, an error very common, especially in reading poetry.

1. A *medium pitch* is used for merely narrative and descriptive subjects; where there is no excitement, where reason predominates over feeling; as,

Taking balloons as they are, "for better, for worse," let us for once have a flight in the air.

2. A *high pitch* is used in expressing excitement, joy, and other strong and sudden feelings; as,

"Ben Hur! Ben Hur!" they shouted.

3. A *low pitch* is used in expressing sadness, feelings which are deep and intense and of a more lasting character; as,

They wrenched at the planks 'mid a hail of fire:
*They fell in death, their work half done.*

**RULE.**—The pitch should in all cases be chosen within the natural compass or range of the voice.

## FORCE.

FORCE refers to the strength and power of the voice, and embraces every variation from a whisper to a shout.

The main purpose of all speech is to be understood, and neither more nor less *force* should be used than is necessary to accomplish this with *effect*. There are three degrees of *force—loud, moderate,* and *gentle.*

1. *Moderate force* is used in ordinary conversation, narration, or description; as,

Are you on your way to school now?

2. *Gentle force* is used to express tenderness, sadness, caution, secrecy, etc.; as,

Sow with a generous hand;
Pause not for toil and pain;

> Weary not through the heat of summer,
> Weary not through the cold spring rain;
> But wait till the autumn comes
> For the sheaves of golden grain.

3. *Loud force* is used in command, exultation, denunciation; as,

> "Harvey Birch!—take him, dead or alive!"

RULE.—Use sufficient force to make yourself understood by your audience, but be careful not to strain the voice or to lose control of it.

## QUANTITY.

QUANTITY, or TIME, refers to the length or shortness of the sound, or the movement of the voice, as *slow*, *medium*, or *quick*.

A distinct articulation is the basis of all good reading, which should never be so *quick* as to render the words or sentences unintelligible. On the other hand, if the *time* be too *slow*, the reading becomes tiresome to both reader and hearers; to produce the desired effect, the *quantity* or *time* in reading should be suited to the subject.

1. *Medium Time* is used in ordinary narration or description; as,

The bell began to ring for morning chapel; he got up and went toward his gown, groping toward it as though he could hardly see, and put it over his shoulders, and would go out, but he would have fallen in the court if the good nurse had not given him her arm.

2. *Slow Time* is used in the expression of feelings of solemnity, awe, reverence, etc.; as,

> I would not spend another such a night,
> Though 'twere to buy a world of happy days,—
> So full of dismal terror was the time!

3. *Quick Time* is used to express sudden fear, anger, joy, humor; as,

.... Quick! be quick, be quick, I say!
They come! they come! Away! away!

**Rule.**—The Quantity, or Time, should never be too quick to interfere with distinct articulation, nor so slow as to grow wearisome to the hearers.

## QUALITY.

Quality of the voice refers to the tone or general character of the sound, as smooth, round, deep, harsh, acute, whispered.

By the quality of the voice we can, at once, recognize the cry of pain, the utterance of grief or joy, the command or threat, even though the words in which they are conveyed be unknown to us.

In reading dialogues or dramatic compositions, where two or more persons are represented as speaking, particular attention to the *quality* of the voice must be paid to render the *personation* effective.

The same person may also use different tones, as, for example, in the lesson "A Military Stratagem," the words of Horse Shoe Robinson:

"If I find any trouble in taking you, all five, safe away from this house, I will thin your numbers with your own muskets,"

should be read in a *stern, threatening tone*, while further on in the same lesson, the lines:

"By your leave, my pretty gentleman, you will lead, and I'll follow. It may be a new piece of drill to you, but the custom is to give the prisoners the post of honor,"

requires a *jocular, sarcastic tone.*

## PAUSES.

A PAUSE is a suspension of the voice in speaking or reading. The most important pauses are indicated by punctuation-marks; in many cases, however, where punctuation-marks are not used, a pause is required to give the meaning clearly and effectively.

RULE I.—Emphatic words should generally be followed by a pause; as,

Sink or swim, | survive or perish, | I give my hand and heart to this vote. We NEVER | shall submit.

RULE II.—Emphatic words should be preceded by a pause, when at the close of a sentence or when such a word is an adjective immediately following the noun it qualifies; as,

For breast-high, threatening, from the sea uprose | a Human Shape!

Many a carol, | old and saintly,
Sang the minstrel and the waits.

RULE III.—The subject of a sentence, if compound, requires a pause; as,

In the pauses of the shower, | you heard the rumbling of the earth beneath and the groaning waves of the tortured sea.

So Martin the bishop, and Antipater the governor | ordered the young men to be brought before them.

RULE IV.—Between parts of a sentence not following in the natural order (inverted sentences) a pause is required; as,

Who risked what they risked, free from strife,
And its promise of glorious pay | his life!

Strongly built were the houses | with frames of oak and of hemlock.

**RULE V.**—Between the parts of sentences which are connected by a relative pronoun, a conjunction, or an infinitive, a pause is required; as,

Of the noble fifty-six | who, in the Revolution, stood forth undismayed by the ax or gibbet he alone remains.

". . . . We'll be glad to-morrow,"
The mother half-musing said,
As she looked at the eager workers,
And laid on a sunny head
A touch | as of benediction.

And then, with a voice whose yearning
The father could scarcely stem,
He said, | to the children pointing, |
"I want him to be like *them*."

**RULE VI.**—In elliptical phrases, the ellipsis should be marked by a pause; as,

You are forever young, and gentle, and pure; | a part of my own childhood that time cannot wither; | always a little boy.

# NEW FIFTH READER.

## LESSON I.

2. sär căs′ tĭc; *a.* bitterly severe.
3. wḗa′ zn̆; *a.* thin; sharp.
3. lĭe̱ṵ; *n.* place; stead.
3. glōa̱t′ ing; *v.* gazing on with malice.
5. ăs sĕnt′ ed; *v.* admitted as true.
6. cŏm plȳ′; *v.* consent.
6. mĕn′ a çĭng; *a.* threatening.
8. dĭnt; *n.* force.

REMARK.—Where there is more than one definition of a word the first definition gives the sense in which it is used in the Lesson.

The number preceding the word defined refers to the paragraph in which the word occurs.

### Percy Wynn's First Day at College. Part I.

1. "Say, young fellow, what are you moping here for?" The person thus rudely addressed was a slight, delicate, fair-complexioned child, whose age, one could perceive at a glance, must have been something under fourteen. Previous to this interruption, he had been sitting solitary on a bench in a retired corner of the college playground.

The boy's lips trembled, but he made no answer. He seemed, indeed, at a loss for words.

"Well, at least tell us what's your name," pursued Charlie Richards, the boy who put the question.

"Percy Wynn, sir."

2. His voice was clear and musical. The name evoked a low, derisive chuckling from the crowd.

"Percy Wynn! Percy Wynn!" repeated Richards in a tone intended to be sarcastic. "Why, it's a very, very pretty name. Don't you think so yourself?"

"Oh yes, indeedy!" answered Percy very seriously, whereupon there was a shout of laughter from the boys. As Percy perceived that his questioner had been mocking him, the blood rushed to his face, and he blushed scarlet.

3. "My! look how he blushes—just like a girl," cried Martin Peters, a thin, puny, weazen-faced youth, who in lieu of strength employed a bitter tongue.

There was another laugh; and as poor Percy realized that the eyes of nearly a dozen boys were feeding and gloating upon his embarrassment, he blushed still more violently, and arising, sought to make his way through them and escape their unwelcome company.

4. But Richards rudely clutched his arm.

"Hold on, Percy."

"Oh, please do let me go. I desire to be alone."

"No, no; sit down. I want to ask you some more questions." And Richards roughly forced him back upon the bench.

"Now, Percy, do you know where you're going to sleep to-night?"

"Yes, sir; over there in that—that—dormitory, I think the prefect said it was. He showed me my bed a little while ago."

"Very well; now you're a newcomer, and don't know the customs of this place. So I want to tell you something. To-night, just as soon as you get in bed—and, by the way, you must hurry up about it—you must say in a loud, clear tone, 'Put out the lights, Mr. Prefect; I'm in bed.'"

5. The listeners and admirers of Richards forced their faces into an expression of gravity. They were inwardly tickled: lying came under their low standard of wit.

"Oh, indeed!" said Percy. "Excuse me, sir, but can't you get some one else to say it?"

"No, no; you must say it yourself. It's the custom for newcomers to do it the first night they arrive."

"But, dear me!" exclaimed Percy, "isn't it a funny custom?"

"Well, it *is* funny," Richards assented, "but it's got to be done all the same."

"Very well, then; I suppose I must do it."

"Now, do you remember what you are to say?"

"'Put out the lights, Mr. Prefect; I'm in bed.'"

"That's it exactly; you've learned your lesson well."

6. "Now there's another thing to be done. You must turn a handspring right off."

"Turn what?" asked Percy in a puzzled tone.

"Look," and Richards suited the action to the word.

"Oh, upon my word," protested Percy in all earnestness, "I can't."

"No matter; you can try."

"Oh, please do excuse me, sir, this time, and I'll practice at it in private," pleaded Percy. "And when I've learned it, I'll be ever so glad to comply with your wishes."

"Whew!" exclaimed John Sommers, "he's been reading up a dictionary!"

"Oh, indeed I haven't," protested Percy.

"Come on," Richards urged in a tone almost menacing, "you must try. Hurry up, now; no fooling."

7. Percy could endure his awkward position no longer. Bursting into tears, he arose and again attempted to make his way through his tormentors.

Richards caught him more rudely than upon the first occasion, and with some unnecessary and brutal violence flung him back upon the bench. "See here, young fellow," he said angrily, "do you want to fight? or are you going to do what you're told?"

8. "Of course he doesn't want to fight, and he'd be a fool to do anything *you* tell him," said a newcomer on the scene, who brought himself through the thick of the crowd by dint of vigorous and unceremonious elbowing. "See here, Richards, it's mean of you to come here with your set and tease a new boy. Let him alone." And Master Thomas Playfair seated himself beside the weeping boy, and stared very steadily and indignantly into Richards' face. The bully's eyes lowered involuntarily, he hesitated for one moment, then, abashed, turned away.

In this and similar Lessons the number in parenthesis refers to the paragraph or stanza in which the word, sentence, or expression occurs.

**Explain** the expressions: "at a loss for words" (1); "pursued Richards" (1); "evoked a low, derisive chuckling" (2); "employed a bitter tongue" (3); "feeding and gloating upon his embarrassment" (3); "could endure his awkward position no longer" (7); "the bully's eyes lowered involuntarily" (8).

## LESSON II.

1. re̅' as sur' ing; *a.* restoring courage to.
7. sym' pa thĕt' ic; *a.* exhibiting pity and tenderness toward one in trouble.
7. bois' tĕr ous ness; *n.* noise; violence; disorder.
10. ĕx prĕss' Ive; *a.* serving to express, utter, or represent.
10. ăn' I mā' tion; *n.* liveliness.
10. ăb sôrbĕd'; *v.* engaged, or engrossed wholly.
10. re fĕc' tó rў; *n.* a room where meals are eaten.

### Percy Wynn's First Day at College. Part II.

1. For a few moments there was a silence, broken only by the sobs of Percy. Tom's right hand, meanwhile, was deep in his jacket-pocket. Presently, when Percy had become calmer, it emerged filled.

"Here, Percy, take some candy."

Tom had a way of offering candy which was simply

TOM PLAYFAIR INTERFERES ON BEHALF OF PERCY WYNN.

irresistible. No long speech could have had so reassuring an effect. Percy accepted the candy, and brightened up at once; put a caramel in his mouth, then drawing a dainty silk handkerchief from his breast-pocket, he wiped his eyes and broke into a smile which spoke volumes of gratitude.

2. "That's good," said Tom, encouragingly. "You're all right now. My name's Tom Playfair, and I come from St. Louis. I know your name already, so you needn't tell me it. Are you a Chicago boy?"

"No, sir, I'm from Baltimore."

"See here," said Tom, "do you want me to run away?"

"No, indeedy!" said Percy, smiling, shaking back his long golden locks, and opening his eyes very wide. "Why, are you afraid of Baltimore boys?"

"It isn't that," Tom made answer. "But if you say 'sir' to me, I'll run away. Call me Tom and I'll call you Percy."

"Very well, Tom, I will. And I am very happy to make your acquaintance."

3. Tom was startled, and for a moment paused, not knowing what manner of reply to make to this neatly-worded compliment.

"Well," he said at length, "let's shake hands, then."

To his still greater astonishment, Percy gravely arose and with a graceful movement of his body, which was neither a bow nor a curtsy, but something between the two, politely took his hand.

"Well, I never!" gasped Tom. "Where in the world did you come from?"

"From Baltimore, Maryland," said Percy. "I thought I had just told you."

"Are all the boys there like you?"

"Well, indeed, Tom, I really don't know. I wasn't acquainted with any boys, you know. Mamma said they were too rough. And "—here Percy broke almost into a sob—" they *are* rough, too. You're the only one of the boys I've met so far, Tom, that's been kind to me."

4. Tom whistled softly.

"Didn't know any boys?"

"Not one."

"Well, then, who on the round earth did you play with?"

"Oh, with my sisters, Tom. I have ten sisters. The oldest is eighteen, and the youngest is six. Kate and Mary are twins. And oh, Tom, they are *all* so kind and nice. I wish you knew them; I'm sure you'd like them immensely."

5. Tom had his doubts. In his unromantic way, he looked upon girls as creatures who were to be made use of by being avoided.

"Did you play games with your sisters, Percy?"

"Oh yes, indeedy! And, Tom, I can dress a doll or sew just as nicely as any of them. And I could beat them all at the skipping-rope. Then we used to play 'Pussy wants a corner,' and 'Hunt the slipper,' and 'Grocery-store,' and I used to keep the grocery and they were the customers—and oh, we did have such times! And then at night mamma used to read to us, Tom—such splendid stories, and sometimes beautiful poems, too. Did you ever hear the story of Aladdin and the Wonderful Lamp?"

"I believe not," said Tom modestly.

"Or Ali Baba and the Forty Thieves?"

Tom again entered a negative.

6. "Oh, they're just too good; they're charming. I'll

tell them to you, Tom, some day, and a good many more. I know ever so many."

"I like a good story," said Tom, "and I'm sure I'll be very glad to listen to some of yours."

"Oh yes, indeedy! But, Tom, do you know why I've come here? Our family has given up housekeeping. Poor, dear mamma has fallen into very delicate health, and has gone to Europe with papa for a rest. Papa has given up business, and intends, when he returns, to settle in Cincinnati. He has sent all my sisters to the school of the Sacred Heart there, except the oldest and the two youngest, who are staying with my aunt who lives on Broadway. But they've promised to write to me every day. They're going to take turns. Do your sisters write to you regularly, Tom?"

"I haven't any sister," Tom answered, smiling. But there was just a touch of sadness in the smile.

"What! not a single one?"

Percy's expression was one of astonishment.

"Not one."

7. Astonishment softened into pity.

"Oh, poor boy!" he cried, clasping his hands in dismay. "How did you manage to get on?"

"Oh, I've pulled through. My mamma is dead too," said Tom, still more sadly.

The deep sympathy which came upon Percy's face at this declaration bespoke a tender and sympathetic heart. He said nothing, but clasped Tom's hand and pressed it warmly.

"Well, you *are* a good fellow!" broke out Tom, putting away his emotion under cover of boisterousness, "and I'm going *to make a boy out of you.*"

"A boy!" Percy repeated.

"Yes, a boy—a real boy."

"Excuse me, Tom; but may I ask what you consider me to be now?"

8. Tom hesitated.

"You won't mind?" he said doubtfully.

"Oh, not from you, Tom; you're my friend."

"Well," said Tom, haltingly, "you're—well, you're just a little bit queer, odd—*girlish*—that's it."

Percy's eyes opened wide with astonishment.

"You don't say! Oh, dear me! But, Tom, it's so funny that I never heard I was that way before. My mamma and my sisters never told me anything about it."

"Maybe they didn't know any boys."

"Oh yes, they did, Tom. They knew *me*."

9. Percy considered this convincing.

"Yes; but you're not like other boys. They couldn't judge by you."

"Excuse me!" said Percy, still in great astonishment.

"You're not like other boys; not a bit."

"But I've *read* a great deal about boys. I've read the Boyhood of Great Painters and Musicians, and about other boys too, but I can't remember them all now. Then I've read Hood's

> "'Oh, when I was a little boy
> My days and nights were full of joy.'

Isn't that nice, Tom? I know the whole poem by heart."

10. It was now Tom's turn to be astonished.

"You don't mean to say," he said in a voice expressive almost of awe, "that you read poetry-books?"

"Oh yes, indeedy!" answered Percy with growing animation; "and I like Longfellow ever so much—he's a dear poet—don't you?"

Just then the bell rang for supper. Tom, absorbed in wonder, brought his new friend to the refectory, and, during the meal, could scarcely refrain from smiling, as he noticed with what dainty grace our little Percy took his first meal at St. Maure's.

11. That night Mr. Middleton was quietly reading in the dormitory while the boys were slipping into bed, when a clear, sweet voice broke the stillness.

"Put out the lights, Mr. Prefect; I'm in bed."

Mr. Middleton arose from his chair, and swept the whole length of the dormitory with his eye. There was a general smile, but no loud laughter. Poor little Percy, dreadfully alarmed at the sound of his own voice breaking upon the silence, shut his eyes tight. Of course, he could scarcely *hear* the smiles, and so, as everything was quiet, he had no reason to think that his proceedings had been in any wise irregular. And thus very soon the singular child fell asleep, with those sacred names upon his lips which a fond mother, bending nightly over the bedside of her child, had taught him to utter in all confidence, innocence, and love.

Rev. Francis J. Finn, S.J.

**Explain** the expressions: "had a way of offering candy which was simply irresistible" (1); "a smile which spoke volumes of gratitude" (1); "entered a negative" (5); "Astonishment softened into pity" (7); "putting away his emotion under cover of boisterousness" (7); "considered this convincing" (9); "absorbed in wonder" (10); "broke the stillness" (11).

My God and Father, while I stray
Far from my home, on life's rough way,
Oh, teach me from my heart to say,
    Thy will be done!
Renew my will from day to day;
Blend it with Thine, and take away
All that now makes it hard to say,
    Thy will be done!

## LESSON III.

2. thrŏng; *n.* a great crowd.
9. ĕarl' dŏm; *n.* the dignity of an earl.
13. aught (*awt*); *n.* anything.
14. brawn' ў; *a.* muscular; robust; strong.
14. craft' ў; *a.* shrewd; cunning.
15. hĕr' ĭt aġe; *n.* that which is inherited.
16. gāĭn sāy'; *v.* deny.
17. casques (*kasks*); *n.* helmets.

### The King and the Child.

1. The sunlight shone on the walls of stone
   And towers sublime and tall;
   King Alfred sat upon his throne
   Within his council hall.

2. And glancing o'er the splendid throng,
   With grave and solemn face,
   To where his noble vassals stood,
   He saw a vacant place.

3. "Where is the Earl of Holderness?"
   With anxious look he said.
   "Alas, O King!" a courtier cried,
   "The noble Earl is dead!"

4. Before the monarch could express
   The sorrow that he felt,
   A soldier with a war-worn face
   Approached the throne and knelt.

5. "My sword," he said, "has ever been,
   O King! at thy command,
   And many a proud and haughty Dane
   Has fallen by my hand.

6. "I've fought beside thee in the field,
    And 'neath the greenwood tree;
  It is but fair for thee to give
    Yon vacant place to me."

7. "It is not just," a statesman cried,
    "This soldier's prayer to hear;
  My wisdom has done more for thee
    Than either sword or spear.

8. "The victories of the council hall
    Have made thee more renown
  Than all the triumphs of the field
    Have given to thy crown.

9. "My name is known in every land,
    My talents have been thine;
  Bestow this Earldom, then, on me,
    For it is justly mine."

10. Yet, while before the monarch's throne
    These men contending stood,
  A woman crossed the floor who wore
    The weeds of widowhood.

11. And slowly to King Alfred's feet
    A fair-haired boy she led—
  "O King! this is the rightful heir
    Of Holderness," she said.

12. "Helpless he comes to claim his own,
    Let no man do him wrong,
  For he is weak and fatherless,
    And thou art just and strong."

13. "What strength of power," the statesman cried,
   "Could such a judgment bring?
   Can such a feeble child as this
   Do aught for thee, O King,

14. "When thou hast need of brawny arms
   To draw thy deadly bows,
   When thou art wanting crafty men
   To crush thy mortal foes?"

15. With earnest voice the fair young boy
   Replied: "I cannot fight,
   But I can pray to God, O King!
   And Heaven can give thee might!"

16. The King bent down and kissed the child;
   The courtiers turned away.
   "The heritage is thine," he said,
   "Let none thy right gainsay.

17. "Our swords may cleave the casques of men,
   Our blood may stain the sod,
   But what are human strength and power
   Without the help of God!"

Eugene J. Hall.

Who are the persons described in the poem? Who was the first to claim the vacant place (4)? What reasons did he urge for his claim (5, 6)? Who was the next to make a claim (7)? Why did he think that he should have the place (8, 9)? Who was the third to claim it (10)? For whom did she claim it (11)? Why (12)? What objection was made to the boy's appointment (13, 14)? What did the boy say (15)? What did the King decide (16, 17)? What is the moral of the poem?

## LESSON IV.

1. ağ ga ġēęrş'; n. mounted native hunters.
2. trŭmp'ĕt ing; v. making a peculiar cry.
3. cŏv'ẽrt; n. hiding-place; that which covers.
3. jŭṇ glę; n. land mostly covered with trees, brush-wood, etc.
3. stạlkẹd; v. walked slowly; approached by stealth.
6. ăl tẽr' natę lỷ; adv. by turns.
8. cōụrsę; n. hunt; chase.
10. dĕx tẽr' I tỷ; n. activity; skill.
11. In vā' rĭ á blỷ; adv. without change.

### Hunting the Elephant in Africa. Part I.

1. The aggageers reported the fresh tracks of a herd, and they begged me to lose no time in accompanying them, as the elephants might retreat to a great distance. There was no need for this advice; in a few minutes my horse Tétel was saddled, and my servants with spare rifles were in attendance. The aggageers were quickly mounted. It was a sight most grateful to a sportsman to witness the start of these hunters, who with their sabres slung from the saddle-bow, as though upon an every-day occasion, now left the camp with these simple weapons only, to meet the mightiest animal of the creation in hand-to-hand conflict.

2. Tracking was very difficult; as there was a total absence of rain, it was next to impossible to distinguish the tracks of two days' date from those most recent upon the hard and parched soil. The greater part of the day passed in useless toil, and after fording the river backward and forward several times, we at length arrived at a large area of sand in a bend of the stream, that was evidently overflowed when the river was full; this surface of many acres was backed by a large forest.

3. Upon arrival at this spot, the aggageers, who appeared

to know every inch of the country, declared that, unless the elephants had gone far away, they must be close at hand, within the forest. We were speculating upon the direction of the wind, when we were surprised by the sudden trumpeting of an elephant, that proceeded from the forest, already declared to be the covert of the herd. In a few minutes, a fine, large elephant marched majestically from the jungle upon the large area of sand, and proudly stalked directly toward the river.

4. At that time we were stationed under cover of a high bank of sand that had been left by the retiring river in sweeping round an angle; we immediately dismounted and remained well concealed. The question of attack was quickly settled; the elephant was quietly stalking toward the water, which was about three hundred paces distant from the jungle; this intervening space was heavy, dry sand, that had been thrown up by the stream in the sudden bend of the river. I proposed that we should endeavor to stalk the elephant, by creeping along the edge of the river, under cover of a sand-bank about three feet high, and that, should the rifles fail, the aggageers should come on at full gallop, and cut off its retreat to the jungle; we should then have a chance for the swords.

5. Accordingly I led the way, followed by my head man with a rifle, while I had my large gun, which I called "Baby," that carried a half-pound explosive shell. Florian accompanied us. Having the wind fair, we advanced quickly for about half the distance, at which time we were within a hundred and fifty yards of the elephant, which had just arrived at the water and had commenced drinking.

6. We now crept cautiously toward it; the sand-bank had decreased to a height of about two feet, and afforded very little shelter. Not a tree nor bush grew upon the

surface of the barren sand, which was so deep that we sank nearly to the ankles at every footstep. Still we crept forward, as the elephant alternately drank and then spouted the water in a shower over its colossal form; but just as we had arrived within about fifty yards, it happened to turn its head in our direction, and immediately perceived us.

7. It raised its enormous ears, gave a short trumpet, and for an instant wavered in its determination whether to attack or fly; but as I rushed toward it with a shout, it turned toward the jungle, and I immediately fired a steady shot at its shoulder with the "Baby."

8. The only effect of the shot was to send it off at a great speed toward the jungle; but at the same moment the three aggageers came galloping across the sand like greyhounds in a course, and wisely keeping on a line with the jungle, they cut off its retreat, and turning toward the elephant, they confronted it, sword in hand.

9. At once the furious beast charged straight at the enemy; but now came the very gallant but foolish part of the hunt. Instead of leading the elephant by the flight of one man and horse, according to their usual method, all the aggageers at the same moment sprung from their saddles, and upon foot, in the heavy sand, they attacked the elephant with their swords.

10. In the way of sport, I never saw anything so magnificent, or so absurdly dangerous. The elephant was mad with rage, and, nevertheless, it seemed to know that the object of the hunters was to get behind it. This it avoided with great dexterity, turning as it were upon a pivot with extreme quickness, and charging headlong, first at one, and then at another of its assailants, while it blew clouds of sand in the air with its trunk and screamed with

fury. Nimble as monkeys, nevertheless the aggageers could not get behind it. In the folly of excitement, they had forsaken their horses, which had escaped from the spot.

11. The depth of the loose sand was in favor of the elephant, and was so much against the men that they avoided his charges with extreme difficulty. It was only by the determined pluck of all three that they alternately saved one another, as two invariably dashed in at the flanks when the elephant charged the third, upon which the wary animal immediately gave up the chase, and turned round upon its pursuers.

12. During this time I had been laboring through the heavy sand, and shortly after I arrived at the fight, the elephant charged directly through the aggageers, receiving a shoulder-shot from one of my large rifles, and at the same time a slash from the sword of one of the men, who, with great dexterity and speed, had closed in behind it just in time to reach its leg.

13. Unfortunately, he could not deliver the cut in the right place, as the elephant, with increased speed, completely distanced the aggageers; it charged across the deep sand, and reached the jungle. We were shortly upon its tracks, and, after running about a quarter of a mile, it fell dead in a dry water-course. Its tusks, like those of the generality of Abyssinian elephants, were exceedingly short, but of good thickness.

**Explain** the expressions: "in useless toil" (2); "The question of attack was quickly settled" (4); "Having the wind fair" (5); "In the folly of excitement" (10); "completely distanced the aggageers" (13).

"Bad habits gather by unseen degrees,
As brooks make rivers, rivers run to seas."

## LESSON V.

2. skĭrt; v. to run along the edge of.
2. ĭm pĕn´ e tra blĕ; a. not to be entered.
3. ĭm plĭç´ ĭt; a. complete; undoubted.
7. lōōm´ ĭng; v. rising; appearing above the surface.

### Hunting the Elephant in Africa. Part II.

1. Some of our men, who had followed the runaway horses, shortly returned and reported that during the fight they had heard other elephants trumpeting in the dense jungle near the river. A portion of thick forest of about two hundred acres, upon this side of the river, was a tempting covert for elephants, and the aggageers, who were perfectly familiar with the habits of the animals, positively declared that the herd must be within this jungle.

2. Accordingly we proposed to skirt the margin of the river, which, as it made a bend at right angles, commanded two sides of a square. Upon reaching the jungle by the river side, we again heard the trumpeting of an elephant, and about a quarter of a mile distant we observed a herd of twelve of these animals, shoulder-deep in the river, which they were in the act of crossing to the opposite side, to secure themselves in an almost impenetrable jungle of thorny hedge.

3. The aggageers advised that we should return to the ford that we had already crossed, and by repassing the river we should most probably meet the elephants, as they would not leave the thick jungle until the night. Having implicit confidence in their knowledge of the country, I followed their directions, and we shortly afterward recrossed the ford, and arrived upon a dry portion of the river's bed, banked by a dense thicket.

4. Jali, my Arab sword-hunter, now took the management of affairs. We all dismounted and sent the horses to a considerable distance, lest they should, by some noise, disturb the elephants. We soon heard a cracking in the jungle on our right, and Jali assured us that, as he had expected, the elephants were slowly advancing along the jungle on the bank of the river, and would pass exactly before us.

5. We waited patiently in the bed of the river, and the cracking in the jungle sounded closer as the herd evidently approached. The strip of thick, thorny covert that fringed the margin was in no place wider than half a mile; beyond that the country was open and park-like, but at this season it was covered with parched grass, from eight to ten feet high: the elephants would, therefore, most probably remain in the jungle until driven out.

6. In about a quarter of an hour we heard by the noise in the jungle, about a hundred yards from the river, that the elephants were directly opposite us. I accordingly instructed Jali to creep quietly, by himself, into the bush, and to bring me information of their position. In three or four minutes he returned; he declared it would be impossible to use the sword, as the jungle was so dense that it would check the blow, but that I could use the rifle, as the elephants were close to us—he had seen three standing together, between us and the main body of the herd.

7. I told Jali to lead me directly to the spot, and, followed by Florian and the aggageers, with my gun-bearers, I kept within a foot of my little guide, who crept gently into the jungle. We advanced stealthily, until Jali stepped quietly to one side and pointed with his finger; I immediately observed two elephants looming up through the thick bushes about eight paces from me.

8. Determined to try fairly the forehead-shot, I kept my ground and fired a quicksilver-and-lead bullet from one of the large rifles. It struck in the centre of the beast's forehead. The only effect was to make it stagger backward, when, in another moment, with its immense ears thrown forward, it rushed on. I fired my remaining barrel a little lower than the first shot.

9. Checked in its rush, it backed toward the dense jungle, throwing its trunk about and trumpeting with rage. Snatching a rifle from one of my trusty men, I ran straight at it, took a most deliberate aim at the forehead, and once more fired. The only effect was a decisive charge; but before I fired my last barrel, Jali rushed in, and with one blow of his sharp sword severed the sinew of the hind leg. That instant the animal was utterly helpless. I had fired three shots so closely together that they occupied a space in its forehead of about three inches, and all had failed to kill. There could no longer be any doubt that the forehead-shot at an African elephant could not be relied upon, although so fatal to the Indian species.

**Explain** the expressions: "a tempting covert" (1); "a bend at right angles" (2); "fringed the margin" (5). There is a marked difference in the appearance of the Indian elephant and the African species: the former has a comparatively high oblong head with a concave forehead, whilst the latter has a round head and a convex forehead. The ears of the African elephant are much the larger, covering the whole shoulder and descending on the legs (9).

---

My son, keep the commandments of thy father, and forsake not the law of thy mother. Bind them in thy heart continually, and put them about thy neck. When thou walkest, let them go with thee: when thou sleepest, let them keep thee, and when thou awakest talk with them; because the commandment is a lamp, and the law a light, and reproofs of instruction are the way of life.—*Proverbs* vi. 20–23.

## LESSON VI.

4. reel ; *v.* stagger.
5. re-coil' ; *n.* the starting back of a gun when discharged.
6. băg'ging ; *v.* capturing.
7. çĭr-cŭm' fẽr-ĕnçe ; *n.* the line that goes round a circular figure ; the space included in a circle.

### Hunting the Elephant in Africa. Part III.

1. I now reloaded my rifles, and the aggageers quitted the jungle to remount their horses, as they expected the herd had broken cover on the other side of the jungle, in which case they intended to give chase, and if possible to turn the elephants back into the covert and drive them toward the guns. We accordingly took our stand in the small, open glade, and I lent Florian one of my double rifles, as he was provided with only one single-barreled elephant-gun.

2. About a quarter of an hour passed in suspense, when we suddenly heard a chorus of wild cries of excitement on the other side of the jungle, raised by the aggageers who had headed the herd and were driving them back toward us. In a few minutes a tremendous crashing in the jungle, accompanied by the occasional shrill scream of a savage elephant, and the continued shouts of the aggageers, assured us that the beasts were bearing down exactly in our direction; they were apparently followed, even through the dense jungle, by the wild and reckless Arabs.

3. I called my men close together, and told them to stand fast, and to hand me the guns quickly; and we eagerly awaited the onset that rushed toward us like a storm. On they came, tearing everything before them. For a moment the jungle quivered and crashed; a second

later and the herd, headed by an immense elephant, thundered down upon us.

4. The great leader came straight at me, and was received with shots right and left in the forehead from a large rifle as fast as I could pull the triggers. The shock made it reel backward for an instant and fortunately turned it and the herd likewise. My second rifle was rapidly handled, and I made a quick shot with both barrels at the temples of two fine elephants, dropping them both stone-dead.

5. At this moment the "Baby" was pushed into my hand by another of my men, just in time to take the shoulder of the last of the herd, which had already charged headlong after its comrades, and was disappearing in the jungle. Bang! went the "Baby"; round I spun like a weathercock, with the blood pouring from my nose, as the recoil had driven the sharp top of the hammer deep into the bridge. My "Baby" not only screamed, but kicked viciously. However, I knew that the elephant must be dead, as the half-pound shell had been aimed directly behind the shoulder.

6. We had done pretty well. I had been fortunate in bagging four from this herd, in addition to the single one in the morning; total, five. Florian had killed one, and the aggageers one; total, seven elephants. One that I had wounded in the shoulder had escaped, and two that had been wounded by Florian.

7. Having my measuring-tape in a game-bag, that was always carried by one of the men, I measured accurately one of the elephants that had fallen, with the legs stretched out, so that the height to the shoulder could be exactly taken:—From foot to shoulder, in a direct line, nine feet one inch; circumference of foot, four feet eight inches. We now left the jungle and found our horses waiting for

us in the bed of the river by the waterside, and we rode toward our camp, well satisfied with the day's work.

SIR SAMUEL WHITE BAKER.

**Explain** the expressions: "broken cover" (1); "bearing down" (2); "awaited the onset" (3); "the great leader came straight at me" (4).

**Sir Samuel White Baker**, the African traveler and explorer, was born in England in 1821, and died December 30, 1893. He was educated as an engineer, and at an early age went to Ceylon. His love of field-sports and of adventure led him to undertake a journey of exploration on the Upper Nile. In 1862, accompanied by his wife, he reached Khartoum, in Africa, and then ascended the White Nile. On March 14, 1864, after a perilous journey, he reached a vast inland sea, to which he gave the name of Albert 'Nyanza. For this he was knighted. He wrote many books of travel and adventure, the principal ones being "The Albert 'Nyanza" and "The Nile Tributaries of Abyssinia."

## LESSON VII.

1. hŭnt' ĭng-bŏx; n. a temporary residence for the purpose of hunting.
2. cŏr' rĭ dōr; n. a gallery or passage-way.
2. plăĭds; n. narrow woolen garments or pieces of cloth worn round the waist or on the shoulders, and reaching to the knees or feet.
3. ĭn tẽr sĕct' ed; v. divided into parts.
3. cu ré (kṳ rā'); n. a French word meaning *pastor*.
4. ĕs cṳ' rĭ ạl; n. a palace of the kings of Spain.
4. ĕm bŏs' omẹd; v. half concealed.
7. ĭn' no vā' tions; n. unreasonable changes or alterations.

### The Hospitality of the Spanish People.

1. The moon was bright and beautiful, and enabled the travelers to see the royal hunting-box and woods, and the rest of the fine scenery through which they passed, so that the journey was far less intolerable than usual, as is often the case when a thing has been much dreaded beforehand. At four o'clock in the morning they were turned out,

shivering with cold, at a wayside station, where they were to take the train to Avila; but, to their dismay, were told, by a sleepy porter, that the six o'clock train had been taken off, and that there would be none till ten the next morning, so that all hopes of arriving at Avila in time for church (and this was Sunday) were at an end.

2. The station had no waiting-room, only a kind of corridor with two hard benches. Establishing the children on these, for the moment, with plaids and shawls, one of the party went off to some cottages at a little distance off, and asked in one of them if there were no means of getting a bedroom and some chocolate. A very civil woman got up and volunteered both; so the tired ones of the party were able to lie down for a few hours' rest in two wonderfully clean little rooms, while their breakfast was preparing. The question now arose for the others: "Was there no church anywhere near?" It was answered by the people of the place in the negative. "The station was new; the cottages had been run up for the accommodation of the porters and people engaged on the line; there was no village within a league or two."

3. Determined, however, not to be baffled, one of the party inquired of another man, who was sleepily driving his bullocks into a neighboring field, and he replied that "over the mountains, to the left, there was a village and a curé; but that it was a long way off, and that he only went on great festivals." It was now quite light; the lady was strong and well, and so she determined to make the attempt to find the church. Following the track pointed out to her by her informant, she came to a wild and beautiful mountain-path, intersected by bright, rushing streams, crossed by stepping-stones, the ground perfectly carpeted with wild narcissus and other spring flowers.

4. Here and there she met a peasant tending his flocks of goats, and always the courteous greeting of "God be with you!" or "God guard you!" as heartily given as returned. At last, on rounding a corner of the mountain, she came on a beautiful view, with the Escurial in the distance to the left; and to the right, embosomed as it were in a little nest among the hills, a picturesque village, with its church tower and rushing stream and flowering fruit-trees, toward which the path evidently led. This sight gave her fresh courage, for the night journey and long walk, undertaken fasting, had nearly spent her strength.

5. Descending the hill rapidly, she reached the village green just as the clock was striking six, and found a group of peasants, both men and women, sitting on the steps of the picturesque stone cross in the centre, opposite the church, waiting for the Curé to come out of his neat little house close by, to say the first Mass. The arrival of the lady caused some astonishment; but, with the inborn courtesy of the people, one after the other rose and came forward, not only to greet her, but to offer her chocolate and bread. She explained that she had come for Communion, and would go into the church.

6. The old, white-haired clerk ran into the house to hasten the curé, and soon a kind and venerable old man made his appearance, and asked her if she wished to see him first in the confessional. He could scarcely believe she had been in Segovia only the night before. Finding that she was hurried to return and catch the train, he instantly gave her both Mass and Communion, and then sent his housekeeper to invite her to breakfast, as did one after the other of the villagers.

7. Escaping from their hospitality with some difficulty, on the plea of the shortness of the time and the length of

the way back, the English lady accepted a little loaf, for which no sort of payment would be heard of, and walked, with a light heart, back to the station, feeling how close is the religious tie which binds Catholics together as one family, and how beautiful is the hearty, simple hospitality of the Spanish people when untainted by contact with modern innovations and so-called progress. There was not a time during the four months that our travelers spent in this country when this natural, high-bred courtesy was not shown.   LADY HERBERT.

## LESSON VIII.

1. stŭb' blĕd; *a.* covered with the stumps of wheat and other grain left in the ground.
1. Yūlę; *n.* Christmas.
3. rough-hewn; *a.* roughly cut.
4. un blĕnch' ing; *adv.* not drawing back through fear.
5. gŭt' tûr ăl; *a.* hoarse; formed in the throat.
7. chāfęd; *v.* rubbed.
7. yĕàrn' ing; *n.* longing desire.
8. pá pōōsę'; *n.* a young child, so called by the North American Indians.
10. wạm' pŭm; *n.* ornaments made of small shells.
12. Im pēạch'; *v.* bring discredit on; call in question.

### Lady Yeardly's Guest.

1. 'Twas a Saturday night, midwinter,
  And the snow with its sheeted pall
Had covered the stubbled clearings
  That girdled the rude-built "Hall."
But high in the deep-mouthed chimney,
  'Mid laughter and shout and din,
The children were piling yule-logs
  To welcome the Christmas in.

2. "Ah, so! We'll be glad to-morrow,"
  The mother half musing said,

As she looked at the eager workers,
   And laid on a sunny head
A touch as of benediction,—
   " For heaven is just as near
The father at far Patuxent
   As if he were with us here.

3. " So choose ye the pine and holly,
   And shake from their boughs the snow;
We'll garland the rough-hewn rafters,
   As they garlanded long ago,—
Or ever Sir George went sailing
   Away o'er the wild sea foam,—
In my beautiful English Sussex,
   The happy old walls at home."

4. She sighed. As she paused, a whisper
   Set quickly all eyes a-strain:
" See! See!" and the boy's hand pointed,—
   " *There's a face at the window-pane!* "
One instant a ghastly terror
   Shot sudden her features o'er;
The next, and she rose unblenching,
   And opened the fast-barred door.

5. " Who be ye that seek admission?
   Who cometh for food and rest?
This night is a night above others
   To shelter a straying guest."
Deep out of the snowy silence
   A guttural answer broke:
" I come from the great Three Rivers,
   I am chief of the Roanoke."

6. Straight in through the frightened children,
   Unshrinking, the red man strode,
And loosed on the blazing hearthstone,
   From his shoulder, a light-borne load;
And out of the pile of deer-skins,
   With look as serene and mild
As if it had been his cradle,
   Stepped softly a little child.

7. As he chafed at the fire his fingers,
   Close pressed to the brawny knee,
The gaze that the silent savage
   Bent on him was strange to see.
And then, with a voice whose yearning
   The father could scarcely stem,
He said,—to the children pointing,—
   "I want him to be like *them!*

8. "They weep for the boy in the wigwam:
   I bring him a moon of days,
To learn of the speaking paper,
   To hear of the wiser ways
Of the people beyond the water,
   To break with the plow the sod,—
To be kind to papoose and woman,—
   To pray to the white man's God."

9. "I give thee my hand!" and the lady
   Pressed forward with sudden cheer;
"Thou shalt eat of my English pudding.
   And drink of my Christmas beer.—
My sweethearts, this night, remember,
   All strangers are kith and kin,

This night when the dear Lord's mother
    Could find no room at the inn!"

10. Next morn from the colony belfry
    Pealed gayly the Sunday chime,
And merrily forth the people
    Flocked, keeping the Christmas time.
And the lady, with bright-eyed children
    Behind her, their lips a-smile,
And the chief in his skins and wampum,
    Came walking the narrow aisle.

11. Forthwith from the congregation
    Broke fiercely a sullen cry:
"*Out! out! with the crafty red-skin!
    Have at him! A spy! A spy!*"
And quickly from belts leaped daggers,
    And swords from their sheaths flashed bare,
And men from their seats defiant
    Sprang, ready to slay him there.

12. But, facing the crowd with courage
    As calm as a knight of yore,
Stepped bravely the fair-browed woman
    The thrust of the steel before;
And spake with a queenly gesture,
    Her hand on the chief's brown breast:
"*Ye dare not impeach my honor!
    Ye dare not insult my guest!*"

13. They dropped at her word their weapons,
    Half-shamed as the lady smiled,
And told them the red man's story,
    And showed them the red man's child;

And pledged them her broad plantations,
That never would such betray
The trust that a Christian woman
Had shown on a Christmas Day!

MARGARET J. PRESTON.

What time of the year is the incident related in the poem supposed to have happened? What is meant by "laid on a sunny head a touch as of benediction" (2)? "Or ever" means "before" (3). Was the mother frightened when the boy said, "There's a face at the window-pane"? What did she do? Who entered when she threw open the door? What did the Indian do when he entered? What did he say he wanted? What is meant by "a moon of days" (8)? By "the speaking paper" (8)? How did the lady receive the chief? What happened when the lady, her children, and the Indian went to church on Christmas? What did the lady do? What did she say (12)? How did the congregation act?

## LESSON IX.

6. sī' mŭl tā' ne ŏus lў; *adv.* at the same time.
6. fōre shŏrt' ĕnĕd; *v.* represented as seen slanting.
12. păr' a çhūtē; *n.* a contrivance shaped somewhat like a large umbrella, by means of which anything may be sent down slowly from a balloon.
13. vălvē; *n.* a lid or cover.

14. ā' er o naŭt'; *n.* a balloonist.
14. spĕç' I fīēs; *v.* mentions so as to distinguish from other things.
15. grăp' nĕl-I rŏn; *n.* an anchor with four or five claws, used to hold small vessels.
15. smŏçk'-frŏçks; *n.* coarse linen shirts worn over the coat by farm laborers.

### In a Balloon.

1. It would appear that in almost every age, from time immemorial, there has been a strong feeling in certain ambitious mortals to ascend among the clouds. Taking balloons as they are, "for better, for worse," let us for once have a flight in the air.

2. The first thing you naturally expect is some extraordinary sensation in springing high up into the air, which

takes away your breath for a time. But no such thing occurs. The extraordinary part is, that you experience no sensation at all, so far as motion is concerned.

3. A very amusing illustration of this is given in a letter published by a well-known author, shortly after his ascent. "I do not despise you," says he, "for talking about a balloon going up, for it is an error which you share in common with some millions of our fellow-creatures; and I, in the days of my ignorance, thought with the rest of you. I know better now. The fact is, we do not *go up* at all; but at about five minutes past six, on Friday evening, Vauxhall Gardens, with all the people in them, *went down!*"

4. Feeling nothing of the ascending motion, the first impression that takes possession of you, in "going up" in a balloon, is the quietude—the silence, that grows more and more entire. The restless heaving to and fro of the huge inflated sphere above your head (to say nothing of the noise of the crowd), the flapping of ropes, the rustling of silk, and the creaking of the basket-work of the car,—all have ceased. There is a total cessation of all atmospheric resistance. You sit in a silence which becomes more perfect every second. After the bustle of many moving objects, you stare before you into blank air.

5. So much for what you first feel; and now, what is the first thing you do? In this case we all do the same thing: we look over the side of the car. We do this very cautiously, keeping a firm seat; and then, holding on by the edge, we carefully protrude the peak of our traveling-cap, and then the tip of the nose, over the edge of the car, upon which we rest our mouth.

6. Everything below is seen in so new a form, so flat compressed, and so simultaneously,—so much too-much-

at-a-time,—that the first look is hardly so satisfactory as could be desired. But soon we thrust the chin fairly over the edge, and take a good stare downward; and this repays us much better. Objects appear under very novel circumstances from this vertical position. They are stunted and foreshortened, and rapidly flattened to a map-like appearance; they get smaller and smaller, and clearer and clearer.

7. Away goes the earth, with all its objects—sinking lower and lower, and everything becoming less and less, but getting more and more distinct and defined as it diminishes in size. But, besides the retreat toward minuteness, the objects flatten as they lessen: men and women are five inches high, then four, three, two, one inch, and now a speck. The great city is a board set out with toys, its public edifices turned into baby-houses.

8. As for the Father of Rivers, he becomes a duskygray, winding streamlet; and his largest ships are no more than flat, pale decks, all the masts and rigging being foreshortened to nothing. We soon come now to the shadowy, the indistinct; and then all is lost in air. Floating clouds fill up the space beneath.

9. How do we feel, all this time? "Calm, sir,—calm and resigned." Yes, and more than this. After a little while, when you find nothing happens, and see nothing likely to happen, a delightful serenity takes the place of all other sensations.

10. To this the extraordinary silence, as well as the pale beauty and floating hues that surround you, is chiefly attributable. The silence is perfect,—a wonder and a rapture. We hear the ticking of our watches,—tick! tick!— or is it the beat of our own hearts? We are sure of the watch; and now we think we can hear both.

11. Two other sensations must by no means be forgotten. You become very cold and desperately hungry. Of the increased coldness which you feel on passing from a bright cloud into a dark one the balloon is quite as sensitive as you; and probably much more so, for it produces an immediate change of altitude.

12. We are now nearly three miles high! We may assume that you would not like to be "let off" in a parachute, even on the improved principle; we will therefore prepare for descending with the balloon.

13. The valve-line is pulled: out rushes the gas from the top of the balloon; you see the flag fly upward. Down through the clouds you sink, faster and faster, lower and lower. Now you begin to see dark masses below: there's the dear old earth again! The dark masses now discover themselves to be little forests, little towns, tree-tops, house-tops. Out goes a shower of sand from the ballast-bags, and our descent becomes slower; another shower, and up we mount again in search of a better spot to alight upon.

14. Our guardian aëronaut gives each of us a bag of ballast, and directs us to throw out its contents when he calls each of us by name, and in such quantities only as he specifies. Moreover, no one is suddenly to leap out of the balloon when it touches the earth, partly because it may cost him his own life or limbs, and partly because it would cause the balloon to shoot up again with those who remained, and so make them lose the advantage of the good descent already gained, if nothing worse happened.

15. Meantime the grapnel-iron has been lowered, and is dangling down at the end of a strong rope a hundred and fifty feet long. It is now trailing over the ground. Three bricklayers are in chase of it. It catches upon a bank; it

NEW FIFTH READER. 55

tears its way through. Now the three bricklayers are joined by a couple of fellows in smock-frocks, a policeman, five boys, followed by three little girls, and last of all a woman with a child in her arms, all running, shouting, screaming, and yelling, as the grapnel-iron and rope go trailing and bobbing over the ground before them. At last the iron catches upon a hedge—grapples with its roots; the balloon is arrested, but struggles hard: three or four men seize the rope, and down we are hauled and held fast.

The "Vauxhall Gardens" are a pleasure-resort in London (3). The "Father of Rivers" here referred to is the Thames (*těmz*), the Lesson being taken from "Household Words," an English magazine which for many years was edited by Charles Dickens (8).

Let the pupils tell in their own words, from what they have seen, if possible, or from what they have read, all they know about balloons and balloon-ascensions.

## LESSON X.

1. dăl'lỹ; *v.* linger.
1. trăv'ẽrsệ; *v.* wander over; cross in traveling.
1. ŏb lĭt'ẽr ăt ĕd; *v.* blotted out.
2. sỹm bŏl'ĭc; *a.* expressing by resemblance.
4. pälm; *n.* a token of success or triumph.

7. pā' pĭsts; *n.* an offensive name given to Catholics by Protestants.
8. mo lĕst'; *v.* to trouble.
8. mu nĭf'i çençệ; *n.* liberality; generosity.
8. ĭn tŏl'ẽr ançệ; *n.* refusal to allow to others the enjoyment of their opinions.

### Catholicity and American Liberty.

1. In passing so rapidly on the direct line of my subject, I have been obliged to leave unnoticed innumerable incidents, many of which possess attraction enough to have made one turn aside and dally by the way. For instance, the missionary labors of the Jesuits and other apostles of the cross, who, thirsting not for gold, but for

souls, had not ceased to traverse this country, in every direction, from the earliest period. Time has, to a great extent, obliterated their footsteps on the soil; but the reason is, in part, that the Indian tribes, among whom they labored, are gone—shrinking away into the deeper or more distant wilderness.

2. The memory of the illustrious Jesuit Fathers, who labored for their conversion, has accompanied their descendants even to their present remotest hunting-grounds. But it has become comparatively weak, and is now reduced to a symbolic term, which they cherish with great affection, and express in their words " black-gown," or " robe noir." Two hundred years ago the poor Franciscans trod the golden sand of California beneath their bare feet, without noticing or appreciating its value. They looked more to heaven than to earth; and it would have been almost out of keeping with their character to make the discovery which has recently startled the minds and whetted the cupidity of the world.

3. Two hundred years ago Father Le Moyne, laboring among the Onondagas of this State, discovered the salt springs which abound near Salina and Syracuse.

\* \* \* \* \* \* \* \*

Neither the descendants of the Virginia Colonists nor those of the Pilgrim Fathers have allowed their ancestors to pass away " unwept, unhonored, and unsung." They are proud of being the descendants of such parentage. Nor need a Catholic be ashamed if he is told that he was born near the site of old St. Mary's in Maryland. As a colony and as a State she has had her distinguished men.

4. Of the primitive colony of Catholic Maryland, what shall I say? Of course I shall invite your attention to those features which show that if civil, but especially re-

ligious, liberty be a dear and justly cherished privilege of the American people, the palm of having been the first to preach and practice it is due, beyond all controversy, to the Catholic colony of Maryland. The history of the whole human race had furnished them with no previous example from which they could copy, although Catholic Poland had extended a measure of toleration to certain Protestants of Germany which had been denied them by their own brethren in their own country.

5. George Calvert, known as Lord Baltimore, was the projector of the Catholic colony of Maryland, although it was actually settled under the leadership of his brother Leonard Calvert, "who," says Bancroft, "together with about two hundred people, most of them Roman Catholic gentlemen and their servants, sailed for the Potomac early in 1634." Their landing is described as having taken place on the 27th of March. On the spot on which they landed, and in their first humble village of St. Mary's, the historian goes on to state that—" there religious liberty obtained a home, its only home in the wide world."

6. From the impartial pen of a Protestant historian, a native of New England, of whose reputation the whole country may well be proud—I mean the Hon. George Bancroft,—I give the following character of Lord Baltimore:

7. "Calvert deserves to be ranked among the most wise and benevolent lawgivers of all ages. He was the first in the history of the Christian world to seek for religious security and peace by the practice of justice, and not by the exercise of power ; to plan the establishment of popular institutions with the enjoyment of liberty of conscience ; to advance the career of civilization by recognizing the rightful equality of all Christian sects. The asylum

of Papists was the spot where, in a remote corner of the world, on the banks of rivers which, as yet, had hardly been explored, the mild forbearance of a proprietary adopted religious freedom as the basis of the State."

8. He goes on further to remark that at that period " every other country in the world had persecuting laws ; 'I will not,'—such was the oath of the Governor of Maryland,—' I will not, by myself or any other, directly or indirectly, molest any person professing to believe in Jesus Christ, for or in respect of religion.' Under the mild institutions and munificence of Baltimore, the dreary wilderness soon bloomed with the swarming life and activity of a prosperous settlement; the Roman Catholics, who were oppressed by the laws of England, were sure to find a peaceful asylum in the quiet harbor of the Chesapeake ; and there, too, Protestants were sheltered against Protestant intolerance."

ARCHBISHOP HUGHES.

What is said of the motive which caused the Jesuits and other apostles of the cross to wander over this country (1) ? The discovery here referred to is that of gold in California; this was made about the time the address which forms this lesson was delivered (2). Who discovered the salt springs in the State of New York (3) ? The quotation "unwept, unhonored, and unsung" is from a poem by Sir Walter Scott (3). Who was George Calvert (5) ? Under whose leadership was Maryland actually settled (5) ? Who was George Bancroft (born 1800 ; died 1891) (6) ? Tell in your own words what he has said of Calvert and the settlement of Maryland.

The Onondagas (ŏn'ǫn dạ'gạs) were Indians (3).

---

### FALSEHOOD.

Let falsehood be a stranger to thy lips.
Shame on the policy that first began
To tamper with the heart to hide its thoughts !
And double shame on that inglorious tongue
That sold its honesty and told a lie !

## LESSON XI.

1. văl'or ŏŭs; *a.* brave; showing courage.
2. nĕū'trąl; *a.* not belonging to either side.
5. fī'ĕr ў; *a.* fierce.
5. wĕąl; *n.* welfare; prosperity; happiness.
7. vŏl'lĕў; *n.* a flight of shot, arrows or other missiles.
11. ĕ'ĕn; *adv.* an abbreviation for *even.*
11. ärch; *a.* roguish.
11. cōr'p̧ş; *n.* a part of an army; a body of men.

### The Ride of Jennie McNeal.

1. Paul Revere was a rider bold—
Well has his valorous deed been told;
Sheridan's ride was a glorious one—
Often it has been dwelt upon.
But why should men do all the deeds
On which the love of a patriot feeds?
Hearken to me, while I reveal
The dashing ride of Jennie McNeal.

2. On a spot as pretty as might be found
In the dangerous length of the Neutral Ground,
In a cottage cozy, and all their own,
She and her mother lived alone.
Safe were the two, with their frugal store,
From all of the many who passed their door;
For Jennie's mother was strange to fears,
And Jennie was large for fifteen years;
With fun her eyes were glistening,
Her hair was the hue of a blackbird's wing.
And while the friends who knew her well
The sweetness of her heart could tell,
A gun that hung on the kitchen wall
Looked solemnly quick to heed her call;

And they who were evil-minded knew
Her nerve was strong and her aim was true;
So all, kind words and acts did deal
To generous, black-eyed Jennie McNeal.

3. One night, when the sun had crept to bed,
And rain-clouds lingered overhead,
And sent their pearly drops for proof
To drum a tune on the cottage roof,
Close after a knock at the outer door,
There entered a dozen dragoons or more.
Their red coats, stained by the muddy road,
That they were British soldiers showed;
The captain his hostess bent to greet,
Saying: "Madam, please give us a bit to eat:
We will pay you well, and if may be,
This bright-eyed girl for pouring our tea;
Then we must dash ten miles ahead,
To catch a rebel colonel abed.
He is visiting home, as doth appear;
We will make his pleasure cost him dear."
And they fell on the hasty supper with zeal,
Close watched the while by Jennie McNeal.

4. For the gray-haired colonel they hovered near
Had been her true friend—kind and dear;
And oft, in her younger days, had he
Right proudly perched her upon his knee,
And told her stories, many a one
Concerning the French war lately done;
And oft together the two friends were,
And many the arts he had taught to her;
She had hunted by his fatherly side;
He had shown her how to fence and ride;

And once had said, "The time may be
Your skill and courage may stand by me."
So sorrow for him she could but feel,
Brave, grateful-hearted Jennie McNeal.

5. With never a thought or a moment more,
Bareheaded she slipped from the cottage door:
Ran out where the horses were left to feed,
Unhitched and mounted the captain's steed,
And down the hilly and rock-strewn way
She urged the fiery horse of gray.
Around her slender and cloakless form
Pattered and moaned the ceaseless storm;
Secure and tight, a gloveless hand
Grasped the reins with stern command;
And full and black her long hair streamed,
Whenever the ragged lightning gleamed,
And on she rushed for the colonel's weal,
Brave, lioness-hearted Jennie McNeal.

6. Hark! from the hills a moment mute,
Came a clatter of hoofs in hot pursuit;
And a cry from the foremost trooper said,
"Halt! or your blood be on your head!"
She heeded it not, and not in vain
She lashed the horse with the bridle-rein
So into the night the gray horse strode;
His shoes heaved fire from the rocky road;
And the high-born courage, that never dies,
Flashed from his rider's coal-black eyes.
The pebbles flew from the fearful race;
The rain-drops splashed on her glowing face.
"On, on, brave beast!" with loud appeal
Cried eager, resolute Jennie McNeal.

7. "Halt!" once more came the voice of dread,
   "Halt! or your blood be on your head!"
   Then, no one answering to the calls,
   Shed after her a volley of balls;
   They passed her in her rapid flight,
   They screamed to her left, they screamed to her right;
   But rushing still o'er the slippery track,
   She sent no token of answer back;
   Except a silvery laughter-peal,
   Brave, merry-hearted Jennie McNeal.

8. So on she rushed, at her own good will,
   Through wood and valley, o'er plain and hill;
   The gray horse did his duty well,
   Till all at once he stumbled and fell,
   Himself escaping the nets of harm,
   But flinging the girl with a broken arm.
   Still undismayed by the numbing pain,
   She clung to the horse's bridle-rein,
   And gently bidding him to stand,
   Petted him with her able hand;
   Then sprang again to the saddle-bow,
   And shouted, "One more trial now!"
   As if ashamed of the heedless fall,
   He gathered his strength once more for all,
   And, galloping down a hillside steep,
   Gained on the troopers at every leap;
   No more the high-bred steed did reel,
   But ran his best for Jennie McNeal.

9. They were a furlong behind or more,
   When the girl burst through the colonel's door,
   Her poor arm helpless hanging with pain,
   And she all drabbled and drenched with rain.

But her cheeks as red as firebrands are,
And her eyes as bright as a blazing star,
And shouted: "Quick! be quick, be quick, I say!
They come! they come! Away! away!"
Then sank on the rude white floor of deal,
Poor, brave, exhausted Jennie McNeal.

10. The startled colonel sprung and pressed
The wife and children to his breast,
And turned away from his fireside bright,
And glided into the stormy night;
Then soon and safely made his way
To where the patriot army lay;
But first he bent, in the dim firelight,
And kissed the forehead broad and white,
And blessed the girl who had ridden so well
To keep him out of a prison cell.

11. The girl roused up at the martial din,
Just as the troopers came rushing in,
And laughed, e'en in the midst of a moan,
Saying, "Good sirs, your bird has flown.
'Tis I who have scared him from his nest,
So deal with me now as you think best."
But the grand young captain bowed, and said—
"Never you hold a moment's dread;
Of womanhood I must crown you queen;
So brave a girl I have never seen.
Wear this gold ring as your valor's due;
And when peace comes, I will come for you."
But Jennie's face an arch smile wore,
As she said, "There's a lad in Putnam's corps
Who told me the same, long time ago;
You two would never agree, I know.

I promised my love to be true as steel,"
Said good, sure-hearted Jennie McNeal.

WILL CARLETON.

Who was Paul Revere (1)? What did he do for his country? What can you tell about Sheridan's ride (1)? By whom were poems written descriptive of their glorious deeds? Who was Putnam (11)? Point out the figures of speech used in the poem, as, "a gun that hung on the kitchen wall *looked solemnly quick* to heed her call" (2).

## LESSON XII.

1. çhĭv′ạl rŏụs; *a.* noble in bearing and spirit.
2. çhăm′ ois (*shăm′ mÿ*); *n.* a species of antelope.
5. do māĭn′; *n.* territory.
5. wāstẹs; *n.* wild, uncultivated country.
7. ex ŭlt′ing; *a.* joyous.
7. gā′ blẹ rōōf; *n.* a sloping roof which forms a triangle at each end.
7. ăl′ pĕn stŏẹk; *n.* a long staff, pointed with iron, used in traveling among the Alps.
8. pro jĕct′ ing; *a.* extending beyond.

### The Power of the Blessed Sacrament. Part I.

1. Maximilian I., Emperor of Germany, sometimes called the "Last Knight" for his chivalrous character, was in his youth remarkable for his high courage and love of adventure, which at times led him to feats of rash daring. Among the many lands over which he ruled, none was so dear to him as the mountainous Tyrol: partly from the simple and loving loyalty of the hardy race of shepherds and mountaineers who dwelt there, partly also because hunting among the Tyrolese Alps was one of his pleasures.

2. On Easter Monday, in the year 1493, the young Emperor, who was staying in the neighborhood of Innsbruck, rose before dawn for a day's chamois-hunting. He took with him a few courtiers and some experienced hunters. At sunrise they were already high up on the mountain pastures, which are the favorite haunts of the chamois;

the valleys beneath them were still covered by a sea of white mist, while the golden rays of morning shone from an unclouded sky on the snowy peaks and ridges above them.

3. Maximilian fixed a longing gaze on the rocky summits, which stood out clear and sharp against the blue heavens. He felt the power of the fresh mountain air and the sublime scenery, and it filled him with a spirit of daring. "I wish," said he, "that I could gain some spot to-day where the foot of man has never trod before, and where no man would dare follow; a spot amid the homes of the chamois and eagle; where the busy hum of men would be lost to my ear, and all the crowded earth would lie beneath my feet; where even the thunder-clouds would mutter far below me, while I stood in eternal sunshine! That would be a fit spot for the throne of an emperor!"

4. The courtiers replied that his majesty had but to wish and it would be fulfilled—to such a renowned hunter and intrepid mountaineer what could be impossible? At this moment, one of the huntsmen gave notice that he had sighted some chamois; the whole party, guided by him, cautiously approached a rocky point, behind which the animals were grazing. On this point of rock stood a single chamois, its graceful head raised as if on the watch.

5. Long before they were within range, they heard it utter the peculiar piping cry by which the chamois gives notice of danger to its fellows, and then off it bounded with flying leaps toward the rocky solitude above. Maximilian, on its track, had soon distanced his attendants. To be a good chamois hunter, a firm foot and a steady head are required, for these beautiful little animals lead their pursuer into their own peculiar domain, the rocky wastes just

below the regions of perpetual snow, and there they **climb** and spring with wonderful agility, and if they cannot **escape**, it is said that they will leap over a precipice and be **dashed** to pieces rather than fall into the power of man.

6. Maximilian had all the qualities necessary for this adventurous chase, and was generally most successful in it. Now he reached the brink of a chasm, which the chamois had passed; black yawned the abyss at his feet, while beyond, the rocks rose steep and forbidding, with but one little spot where a man could find footing. One moment he paused, then with a light spring gained the other side, while a shout, half of admiration, half of terror, burst from his astonished suite.

7. "That was a royal leap! Who follows?" cried Maximilian, with an exulting laugh. Then he sped onward, intensely enjoying the excitement of the chase. For a moment he lost the chamois from view, then it appeared again, its form standing out against the sky, on one of those rocky ridges that have been compared to the backbone of a fish, but are perhaps more like the upper edge of a steep gable roof. To gain this ridge it was needful to climb an almost perpendicular precipice; but Maximilian, nothing daunted, followed on, driving small iron holdfasts into the rock in places where he could gain no footing, and holding on by the hook at the upper end of his iron-pointed alpenstock.

8. At last he seized a projecting piece of rock with his hand, hoping to swing himself up by it, but the stone did not bear his weight, it loosened and fell, and the Emperor fell with it.

Give synonyms for *feats* (1); *dawn* (2); *intrepid* (4); *cautiously* (4); *grazing* (4); *bounded* (5); *agility* (5); *chasm* (6).

Be careful to give the proper pronunciation to *chivalrous*; *mountainous* (not mountain*ious*); *haunts*; *chasm*; *daunted*.

## LESSON XIII.

1. erĕv'Içę; n. a narrow opening caused by a split or crack.
2. lĕdgę; n. a shelf of rocks.
3. seâl' ing; v. climbing.
4. må nȩū' vẽr; n. trick; plan.
6. eŏm pås'sion åtę; a. sympathizing; kind.
7. suïtę (swēt); n. the attendants of a distinguished personage.
8. sŭs pĕnsę'; n. uncertainty; indecision.
9. lăm' ĕn tå'tion; n. expression of sorrow.

### The Power of the Blessed Sacrament. Part II.

1. Breathless and stunned, it was some minutes before the Emperor recovered consciousness after the fall. When he came to himself, he found that he had received no injury, except a few bruises, and his first thought was that he was most lucky to have escaped so well. Then he began to look about him. He had fallen into a sort of crevice, or hollow in the rocks; on one side rose above him a high wall which it was impossible to scale; on the other the rocks were hardly higher than his head, so that he had no difficulty in getting out of the hollow.

2. "Lucky again," thought Maximilian; but as he emerged from the crevice and rose to his feet, he remained motionless in awe-struck consternation. He stood on a narrow ledge, hardly wide enough for two men abreast, and beneath him, sheer down to a depth of many hundred feet, sank a perpendicular wall of rock. He knew the place; it was called St. Martin's Wall, from the neighboring chapel of St. Martin; and the valley below it, which was now concealed from his view by white rolling vapors, was the valley of Zierlein.

3. Above him rose the "wall," so straight and smooth that it was utterly hopeless to think of scaling it. The only spot within sight, where a man could find footing, was the

narrow shelf on which he stood. The ledge itself extended but a few feet on either side, and ceased abruptly. In vain Max gazed around for some means of escape. No hand's breadth was there to which to cling; no hold for foot or hand of the most expert climber—beneath, a sea of cloud; above, a sea of air.

4. Suddenly he was startled by a whir and a rush of great wings in his face;—it was a mountain eagle which had swooped past him, and the wind of whose flight was so strong that it had nearly thrown him off his balance. He recollected to have heard that these eagles try to drive any large prey, too heavy to be seized in their talons, to the edge of a precipice, so that, by suddenly whirling round, they may dash it over the brink; and that they had tried this maneuver more than once on hunters whom they found in critical and helpless positions.

5. Then his wish of the morning occurred to him. How literally and exactly it had been fulfilled! And how little could the Emperor exult in his lofty and airy throne! He merely felt with a shudder his own exceeding littleness in the face of the great realities of Nature and Nature's God.

6. Beneath, in the valley of Zierlein, a shepherd was watching his flocks. As the sun rose higher and drew off the mists which clung around the foot of St. Martin's Wall, he noticed a dark speck moving on the face of the rock. He observed it narrowly. "It is a man!" he cried; "what witchcraft has brought him there?" And he ran to tell the wonder to the inhabitants of the valley. Soon a little crowd was collected and stood gazing up at St. Martin's Wall. "God be with him!" was the compassionate exclamation of all. "He can never leave that spot alive—he must perish miserably of hunger!"

7. Just then a party of horsemen galloped along the

valley, and rode up to the crowd, which was increasing every moment. It was the Emperor's suite, who, giving up all hope of following his perilous course, had gone back to where they had left their horses in the morning, and ridden around, hoping to meet their master on the other side of the mountain. "Has the Emperor passed this way?" one of them called out. "He climbed up so far among the rocks that we lost sight of him." The shepherd cast a terrified look at the wall, and, pointing upward, said: "That must be he up yonder. God have mercy upon him!"

8. The Emperor's attendants gazed at the figure and at one another in horror. One of them had a speaking-trumpet such as mountaineers sometimes use for shouting among the hills. He raised it to his mouth, and cried at the pitch of his voice: "If it be the Emperor who stands there, we pray him to cast down a stone." There was a breathless hush of suspense now among the crowd, and down came the stone, crashing into the roof of a cottage at the foot of the rock.

9. A loud cry of lamentation broke from the people and was echoed on every side among the mountains. For the young Emperor was loved for the winning charm of his manner, and for his frank and kindly ways.

10. The sound reached Max's ears, and looking down, he could see the crowd of people, appearing from the giddy height like an army of ants—a black patch on the bright green of the valley. The sound and sight raised his hopes; he had completely given up all thought of delivering himself by his own exertions, but he still thought help from others might be possible. And now that his situation was discovered, the people he knew would do whatever lay in the power of man for his deliverance. So he kept up his

courage and waited patiently and hopefully. It was hard to believe that he, standing there in the bright sunshine, full of youthful health and strength, was a dying man, and never would leave that spot alive.

11. Higher and higher rose the sun. It was midday now, and the reflected heat from the rocky wall was well-nigh too great to bear. The stones beneath his feet became hot as a furnace, and the sunbeams smote fiercely on his head. Exhausted by hunger and thirst, by heat and weariness, he sank down on the scorching rock. The furious headache and dizziness which came over him made him think that he was about to become insensible. He longed for some certainty as to his fate before consciousness should forsake him, and, following a sudden thought, he drew from his pocket a small parchment book, tore out a blank leaf and wrote on it with a pencil, then tied the parchment to a stone with some gold ribbon he happened to have with him, and let the stone fall down into the valley as he had the first.

12. What he had written was the question whether any human help was possible. He waited long and patiently for the answer; but no sound reached his ear except the hoarse cry of the eagle. A second and a third time he repeated the message, lest the first should not have been observed—still there was silence, though the crowd in the valley had been increasing all day; and now a vast assembly—the inhabitants of Zierlein and all the district round—had gathered at the foot of the fatal throne which the Emperor had desired for himself.

Give synonyms for *emerged* (2); *abruptly* (3); *expert* (3); *talons* (4); *literally* (5); *exclamation* (6); *terrified* (7).

## LESSON XIV.

3. bōạst' fụl ness; *n.* bragging.
3. pĕn' ạl tỹ; *n.* punishment for an offense.
3. ĕn dūrẹ'; *v.* to suffer firmly.
3. fạl' tẽrẹd; *v.* trembled.
4. pär täk' ẽr; *n.* a sharer.
6. mōōd; *n.* state of mind.
6. vĭṣ' ion; *n.* a supernatural sight.
8. chĭŋk; *n.* an opening of greater length than breadth.
8. Ōrẹṣ; *n.* metals not freed from earth and other substances.

### The Power of the Blessed Sacrament. Part III.

1. Terrible indeed—who can tell how terrible?—were those hours of suspense to Max. Many deep and heart-searching thoughts visited him—thoughts of remorse for many sins, of self-reproach for great responsibilities unfulfilled. The day wore on; the sun was fast sinking toward the West, and Max could no longer resist the conviction that there was no help possible, that for him all hope was over. It seemed, as soon as he had faced this certainty, that a calm resignation, a high courage and resolve, took possession of his soul. If he was to die, he would die as became a king and a Christian—if this world were vanishing from him, he would lay firm hold of the next.

2. Again he tore a leaf from his book, and wrote on it. There was no more gold ribbon to bind it to the stone, so he took the chain of the Order of the Golden Fleece—what value had it for a dying man?—and from that high and airy grave he threw down the stone among the living. It was found, like the others before it. None had answered those, because no one was willing to be a messenger of death to the much-loved Emperor. The man who found the stone read the letter aloud to the assembled crowd, for the Emperor's message was addressed to all Tyrol.

3. And this was the message: "O Tyrol, my last warm

thanks to thee for thy love which has so long been faithful to me. In my pride and boastfulness I tempted God, and my life is now the penalty. I know that no help is possible. God's will be done—His will is just and right. Yet one thing, good friends, you can do for me, and I will be thankful to you even in death. Send a messenger to Zierlein immediately for the Blessed Sacrament, for which my soul thirsts. And when the priest has come, let it be announced to me by a shot, and let another shot tell me when I am to receive the blessing. And when I pray, unite your prayers with mine to the great Helper in time of need, that He may strengthen me to endure the pains of a lingering death. Farewell, my Tyrol. MAX." The reader's voice often faltered as he read this letter amid the cries and sobs of the multitude.

4. Off sped the messenger to Zierlein, and in all haste came the priest. Max heard the shot, and, looking down, could see the priest standing with uplifted hands holding the ostensorium. He threw himself on his knees, in all penitence and submission, praying that he might be a spiritual partaker of Christ, though he could not in reality receive the bread of salvation. Then the second shot rang on the air, and through the speaking-trumpet came the words of the blessing:

5. "May God's blessing be upon thee in thy great need—the blessing of the Father, the Son, and the Holy Ghost, whom heaven and earth praise forever." The Emperor felt a deep peace filling his heart as the words of the blessing were wafted to his ears. By this time the sun had sunk behind the mountain range beyond the valley of Zierlein; but a rosy flush still lingered on the snowy summits, and the western sky glowed in crimson and gold. Beneath, in the deep purple shade of the valley, the people all knelt

THE EMPEROR MAXIMILIAN ON THE MOUNTAIN.

and the Emperor could hear the faint murmur which told him that they were praying for him. Touched by their sympathy, he continued kneeling in prayer for the welfare of his subjects.

6. It was quite dark now, and one by one the stars came forth on the deep blue sky, till at last all the heavenly host stood in glittering array. The sublime peace of those silent eternal fires stole into Max's heart and drew his thoughts and desires heavenward to eternal Love and eternal Rest. So he knelt rapt in prayer and in lofty and holy thought. Suddenly a bright gleam flashed on his eyes, and a figure in a dazzle of light stood before him. No wonder that in his present mood, his spirits raised above earthly things, this vision should seem to him more than human.

7. "Lord Emperor," it spoke, "follow me quickly; the way is far and the torch is burning out." Hardly knowing whether he was still in the world of mortals or not, Max asked, "Who art thou?"—"A messenger sent to save the Emperor." Max rose; as he gazed it seemed to him that the vision assumed the form of a barefooted peasant youth, holding a torch in his hand. "How didst thou find thy way to the cliff?" asked the Emperor.—"I know the mountains well, and every path in them."—"Has Heaven sent thee to me?" asked Max, still feeling as if he were in a dream-world.—"Truly it is God's will to deliver thee by my hand," was the simple answer.

8. The youth now turned and slid down into the hollow out of which Max had climbed that morning, then glided through a crevice in the rock behind, which the Emperor had failed to detect. Stooping low, he with difficulty squeezed through the narrow chink, and saw the torch flickering below him, down a steep, rugged fissure which

led into the heart of the rock. Leaping and sliding he followed on, and the torch moved rapidly before him, its red light gleaming on metallic ores, and glittering on rock crystals.

9. Sometimes a low thundering sound was heard as of underground waterfalls; sometimes water dripping from the rocky roof made the torch hiss and sputter. Downward they went, miles and miles downward, till at last the ravine opened into a long, low, nearly flat-bottomed cavern, at the end of which torch and bearer vanished. But at the place where the youth had disappeared there was a glimmer of pale light. Max groped his way to it, and drew a long breath as he found himself again in the open air, with the silent stars above him and the soft grass beneath his feet.

10. He soon perceived that he was in the valley of Zierlein, and afar off he heard the confused noise of an assembled multitude. He followed the sound, but was forced to rest more than once from extreme weakness and weariness, before he reached the foot of St. Martin's Wall, and saw priest and people still kneeling in prayer for him. Deeply moved, he stepped into the midst of them and cried: "Praise the Lord with me, my people. He has delivered me."

11. The Emperor was never able to discover who had been the instrument of his wondrous rescue. A report soon spread among the people that an angel had saved him. When this rumor reached the Emperor's ears, he said: "Yes, truly, it was an angel, my guardian angel, who has many a time come to my help—he is called in German 'The People's Loyal Love.'"

Rev. Michael Müller, C.SS.R.

The Order of the Golden Fleece is the royal Order of Spain, instituted by Philip II. of Spain.

Tell briefly in your own language the story of these three Lessons.

Who is the chief personage described? What was he sometimes called? In what century did he live? Where is the scene laid which is described in the lessons? What do the lessons teach us?

## LESSON XV.

3. tĭĕr; *n.* row.
4. ŭn rŭf' flĕd; *a.* calm; quiet.
5. prow; *n.* the fore part of a ship.
8. gōa̤l; *n.* the end which a person tries to reach.
12. mā' nĭ ăc; *n.* a madman; a crazy person.
16. frīskĕd; *v.* leaped in play and gayety.
18. crouch' ing; *v.* lying close to the ground.

### Pancratius.

1. A hush lay on the multitudes. Softly and low
   Died out the echoes of that mighty roar,
   Which rose triumphant but a space ago,
   As the strong wrestler, pale as Alpine snow,
   Reeled in his agony, and stirred no more.

2. They bore him forth, and in his robe of pride
   The Roman courtier turned with smiling face
   To woo the fair girl resting at his side,
   Who, in her beauty, calm and starry-eyed,
   Could view such struggles with a careless grace.

3. But hark! Along the smiling, sparkling tier
   A murmur stole—the smile gave place to frown,
   And every eager eye grew cold and clear
   When, light and graceful as a mountain deer,
   A Christian martyr sprung to win his crown!

4. It was a youth—a slight yet manly form—
   Who, with an eye like some unruffled lake
   And virgin cheek with rosy blushes warm,
   Seemed all too tender for the cruel storm
   Whose giant force must either bend or break.

5. And yet there was a calm upon the brow,
   And in those thoughtful eyes a holy peace
  As though the youthful martyr stood e'en now
  In triumph on a noble vessel's prow,
   Whose port was nigh, whose labors soon should cease.

6. Slowly he turned, and o'er the swaying tide
   Of jeweled forms his gentle glance was flung
  Till many a Roman maiden turned aside,
  Lest some might note the grief she could not hide
   At thought of death to one so fair and young.

7. But pity, like the trembling moonbeam shed
   Athwart the dark waves of a stormy sea,
  O'er those untutored hearts, by passion led,
  Gleamed but a fitful space, then meekly fled,
   As things of light from darkness ever flee.

8. And he, Pancratius, in his joyous race
   Was nearing fast the long-desirèd goal,
  Ere age had dashed the beauty from that face
  Whose shrine should be in time the fitting place
   To nerve the fainting faith or sinking soul!

9. He stood unmoved, e'en as the warrior stands
   Who neither courts nor shuns the coming fight;
  But even as he clasped his slender hands,
  A door swung grating, and across the sands
   A lion stalked in majesty of might.

10. There was no fury in its stately tread,
    No bloody thirst which hastens to destroy,

But calm in power it raised its noble head,
And, with a kingly glory round it shed,
   Moved onward to that slender, graceful boy.

11. Nearer it came; upon the martyr's cheek
    The hot breath of the forest-monarch burned,
Till once—but once—that brave young heart grew weak,
When lo! with startled look, all mild and meek,
    Back to its den the moaning lion turned!

12. Then rose that mighty multitude, and loud
    Upswelled a shout of mingled joy and rage,
As some their gladly tearful faces bowed,
While others stood apart and, stormy-browed,
    Chafed like the maniac in his iron cage.

13. But o'er that tide of sound which rudely gushed
    Till Tiber all her slumbering echoes woke,
A clear young voice rang out, the din was hushed,
And while his brow, uplifted, brightly blushed,
    With gentle grace the young Pancratius spoke:

14. "Patience, sweet friends," he cried, "bear yet awhile,
    For see, yon panther thirsts for liberty.
'Twas he that freed my father from his toil;
Oh, may he not"—and here a glorious smile
    Parted his bright lips—"set Pancratius free?"

15. He paused—and men gazed wonder-stricken how
    Such thirst could be for that which mortals dread;
Yet, with a gloomy satisfaction on each brow,
The fatal sign was made, and, cageless now,
    A panther bounded forth with noiseless tread.

16. Joyous in liberty, it frisked and played,
    And turned its shining neck in conscious pride;
    Now in the yielding sand its form was laid;
    Anon, with cat-like glee, low murmurs made,
    And shook the dusk sand from its glittering hide.

17. At length it rose—its keen quick glance had caught
    The youthful martyr, as he stood apart,
    With all a mother's tender lips had taught
    And all a Saviour's tender love had wrought,
    In that dread moment stealing o'er his heart.

18. Earnest the Christian prayed, and, breathless, men
    Beheld the look that crouching panther wore;
    There was a pause—the echoes slept again—
    And then—oh, just and righteous Father! then
    One bound—one stroke—*Pancratius dies no more!*
                                    ELEANOR C. DONNELLY.

**Eleanor C. Donnelly** was born in Philadelphia in 1848. She is the author of many short stories, but is best known as a writer of religious poetry.

**Pancratius,** or St. Pancras as he is called in English, suffered martyrdom when only fourteen years old, during the reign of the emperor Diocletian. The story of his martyrdom is beautifully told in Cardinal Wiseman's "Fabiola."

**Explain** the expressions: "robe of pride" (2); "starry-eyed" (2); "the swaying tide of jeweled forms" (6); "that tide of sound which rudely gushed till Tiber all her slumbering echoes woke" (13); "yon panther thirsts for liberty" (14); "the echoes slept again" (18); "Pancratius dies no more" (18).

---

The blood of the martyrs is the seed of the Church.

A more glorious victory cannot be gained over another than this, that when the injury began on his part, the kindness should begin on ours.

## LESSON XVI.

1. re sôûrç'ĕṣ; *n.* the ability to supply necessary wants.
2. free' bōōt ẽrs; *n.* robbers.
4. hăv' ẽr săċk; *n.* a bag in which a soldier carries his food.
4. eóm' påsṣ; *n.* a magnetic needle arranged so as to determine the direction of the north and other cardinal points.
6. ŏb lĭv' ĭ ọŭs; *a.* forgetful.
6. răċk; *n.* destruction.
7. lŏḁth; *a.* unwilling.
9. pŭn' ġent; *a.* sharp; piercing.
11. pro bŏs' çĭs; *n.* a snout.
13. de plĕt' ed; *v.* emptied.
14. ȧ' pĕx; *n.* the point of anything.
16. ăn tĕn' næ; *n.* feelers of an insect.
16. eóm plā' çent; *a.* gratified; accompanied with pleasure.

### Hunting the Honey-bee.

1. It is not every novice that can find a bee-tree. The sportsman may track his game to its retreat by the aid of his dog, but in hunting the honey-bee one must be his own dog, and track his game through an element in which it leaves no trail. It is a task for a sharp, quick eye, and may test the resources of the best woodcraft.

2. One looks upon the woods with a new interest when he suspects they hold a colony of bees. What a pleasing secret it is: a tree with a heart of comb-honey; secret chambers where lies hidden the wealth of ten thousand little freebooters, great nuggets and wedges of precious ore gathered with risk and labor from every field and wood about.

3. But if you would know the delights of bee-hunting and how many sweets such a trip yields besides honey, come with me some bright, warm, late September or early October day.

4. So, with haversacks filled with grapes and peaches and apples and a bottle of milk,—for we shall not be home to dinner,—and armed with a compass, a hatchet, a pail, and a box with a piece of comb-honey neatly fitted into it,

we sally forth. After a refreshing walk of a couple of miles we reach a point where we will make our first trial —a high stone wall that runs parallel with a wooded ridge, and separated from it by a broad field.

5. There are bees at work there on that goldenrod, and it requires but little maneuvering to sweep one into our box. Almost any other creature rudely and suddenly arrested in its career and clapped into a cage in this way would show great confusion and alarm. The bee is alarmed for a moment, but the bee has a passion stronger than its love of life or fear of death, namely, desire for honey, not simply to eat, but to carry home as booty. "Such rage of honey in their bosoms beats," says Virgil. It is quick to catch the scent of honey in the box, and as quick to fall to filling itself.

6. We now set the box down upon the wall, and gently remove the cover. The bee is head and shoulders in one of the half-filled cells, and is oblivious to everything else about it. Come rack, come ruin, it will die at work. We step back a few paces, and sit down upon the ground so as to bring the box against the blue sky as a background.

7. In two or three minutes the bee is seen rising slowly and heavily from the box. It seems loath to leave so much honey behind, and it marks the place well. It mounts aloft in a rapidly increasing spiral, surveying the near and minute objects first, then the larger and more distant, till having circled above the spot five or six times, and taken all its bearings, it darts away for home. It is a good eye that holds fast to the bee till it is fairly off. Sometimes one's head will swim following it, and often one's eyes are "put out" by the sun.

8. This bee gradually drifts down the hill, then strikes off toward a farm-house half a mile away where I know

bees are kept. Then we try another, and another; and the third bee, much to our satisfaction, goes straight toward the woods. We can see the brown speck against the darker background for many yards.

9. Our bees are all soon back, and more with them, for we have touched the box here and there with the cork of a bottle of anise-oil, and this fragrant and pungent oil will attract bees half a mile or more. When no flowers can be found, this is the quickest way to obtain a bee.

10. It is a singular fact that when the bee first finds the hunter's box its first feeling is one of anger. But its avarice soon gets the better of its indignation, and it seems to say, "Well, I had better take possession of this and carry it home." So it settles down and fills itself.

11. It does not entirely cool off and get soberly to work till it has made two or three trips home with its booty. When other bees come, even if all from the same swarm, they quarrel and dispute over the box. A bee will usually make three or four trips from the hunter's box before it brings back a companion. I suspect the bee does not tell its fellows what it has found, but that they smell out the secret: it doubtless bears some evidence with it upon its feet or proboscis that it has been upon honeycomb and not upon flowers, and its companions take the hint and follow.

12. No doubt there are plenty of gossips about a hive that note and tell everything. "Oh, did you see that? Peggy Mel came in a few moments ago in great haste, and one of the up-stairs packers says she was loaded down with apple-blossom honey, which she deposited, and then rushed off again like mad. Apple-blossom honey in October! Fee, fi, fo, fum! Let's after!"

13. In about half an hour we have three well-defined

lines of bees established,—two to farm-houses and one to the woods, and our box is being rapidly depleted of its honey. About every fourth bee goes to the woods. The woods are rough and dense and the hills steep, and we do not like to follow the line of bees until we have tried at least to settle the problem as to the distance they go into the woods,—whether the tree is on this side of the ridge, or in the depth of the forest on the other side. So we shut up the box when it is full of bees, and carry it about three hundred yards along the wall.

14. Other bees have followed our scent, and it is not many minutes before a second line to the woods is established. This is called *cross-lining* the bees. The new line makes a sharp angle with the other line, and we know at once that the tree is only a few rods into the woods. The two lines we have established form two sides of a triangle of which the wall is the base; at the apex of the triangle, or where the two lines meet in the woods, we are sure to find the tree. We quickly follow up these lines, and where they cross each other on the side of the hill we scan every tree closely.

15. But not a bee is seen or heard; we do not seem as near the tree as we were in the fields; yet if some divinity would only whisper the fact to us we are within a few rods of the coveted prize, which is not in one of the large hemlocks or oaks that absorb our attention, but in an old stump not six feet high, and which we have seen and passed several times without giving it a thought.

16. After much searching, and after the mystery seems rather to deepen than to clear up, we chance to pause beside this old stump. A bee comes out of a small opening like that made by ants in decayed wood, rubs its eyes and examines its *antennæ*, as bees always do before leaving

their hive, then takes flight. At the same instant several bees come by us loaded with *our* honey, and settle home with that peculiar, low, complacent buzz of the well-filled insect. Here, then, is our prize, in a decayed stump of a hemlock-tree. We could tear it open with our hands, and a bear would find it an easy prize, and a rich one too, for we take from it fifty pounds of excellent honey.

JOHN BURROUGHS.

**John Burroughs** was born at Roxbury, N. Y., April 3, 1837. His writings show a lively poetic fancy, an intimate acquaintance with nature, and all the charms of a polished literary style.

**Virgil** (5), *Pub'lius Virgil'ius*, born about the year 70 B.C., was a Roman poet, famous as the author of the Æneid.

In paragraph 12 the gossips are supposed to be talking about a particular bee, here mentioned as *Peggy Mel*, a fanciful name which the author has coined from the Latin word *mel*, signifying *honey*.

## LESSON XVII.

3. wīnd'ĭng-shēet; *n.* a sheet in which a corpse is wrapped.
5. văn; *n.* the front of an army.
6. bāy; *n.* the state of facing an enemy when escape is impossible.
7. fĕll; *a.* cruel.
7. wāxĕd; *v.* increased.
8. pĕstĕ; *interj.* a French exclamation expressing indignation or anger.
9. rĕf' lū ĕnt; *a.* returning; flowing back.
12. strĭp' lĭng; *n.* a youth just passing from boyhood to manhood.

### Jacques Dufour.

1. Strolling in the cool of evening, drinking in the balmy air,
   I met a strange wayfaring man bowed down with grief and care.
   Eighty years had left their footprints on his gaunt and ashen cheek,
   And his hands were gray and shrunken, and his voice was thin and weak;

But his eyes, while he was speaking, kindled with a
 misty glow
'Mid their whitened brows and lashes, like a crater in
 the snow.
And this aged Frenchman told me (his name was
 Jacques Dufour)
The story of the faded shred of ribbon that he wore:

2. Just a scrap of scarlet ribbon pinned upon his shrunken
 breast,
But to him more rich and beautiful than rubies of the
 East.
'Twas in eighteen-twelve he won it, in that terrible
 campaign
When the French invaded Russia, but invaded her in
 vain;

3. And the starved and freezing Frenchmen had begun
 that sad retreat
Through the snow that proved for most of them both
 grave and winding-sheet.
There had been a bloody skirmish 'twixt the rear-
 guard and the foe,
And among the sorely wounded, whom the chance of
 fight laid low,
Was a gallant Polish Colonel, Marshal Davoust's favor-
 ite aide,
And the Marshal, kneeling o'er him, turned about, and
 sharply said:
"Halt, Company of Grenadiers, and see this wounded
 Pole!
He loves the French; he hates the Russ with all his
 fiery soul:

4. Will you let him fall a prisoner to his bloody-minded foe?"
And the Company of Grenadiers cried out as one man, *No!*
"Then lift him," said the Marshal. "You soldiers must have learned
That our wagons we've abandoned, and our baggage has been burned:

5. Make a litter—you must bear him; I trust him to your love;
He will burden, will impede you, but I know that you will prove
That you do your duty ever, and will guard this wounded man
As you guard your sacred colors when they lead the battle's van."
So they made the hasty litter, and the wounded man they bore
(Of the youngest and the cheeriest was Sergeant Jacques Dufour).
And day by day they fought their way, through deserts bleak and wild,
Guarding the crippled Colonel, as a woman guards her child.

6. But the work of love delayed them, and they slowly fell behind,
Yet not one of all that Company of Grenadiers repined.
Still they fought the cold and Cossacks; still they held their rugged way,
Falling back, but never fleeing: retreating, yet at bay.

7. But the foe was fell and agile, and the cold it waxed amain,
And so one by one they perished—some were frozen, some were slain,
Till the nineteenth day of marching came, and there were only five
Of that Company of Grenadiers who still remained alive.
Then spoke the wounded Colonel: "O my comrades, it is vain:
I can surely never live to see my native land again;
You are squandering your lives for naught, lives it were sweet to save
For France and future glory; so leave me, comrades brave."

8. "*Peste!*" said Jacques Dufour, "my Colonel, we take leave to answer *Nay*.
We have orders to deliver you at Wilna—we obey!"
So they lift again the litter, and they struggle on their way
Till the western clouds are lighted with the gleams of dying day:

9. And as they watch the glory, against those golden skies
The towers and walls of Wilna in welcome outline rise!
But too great the stress of feeling for those overburdened men:
Too swift the refluent flood of hope that swelled their hearts again:
Far too weak their feeble bodies for this beatific sight:
Two fell dying on the left hand, two fell dying on the right;

And, as faded in the frozen air their last convulsive moan,
Lo! of all that noble Company, Dufour was left alone!

10. Did he falter? No! He lifted in his arms the wounded man,
And with wild and desperate shouting towards the nearest outpost ran;
And the pickets came with succor, and the sun had just gone down
When they bore the Sergeant and his charge in safety to the town.

11. Then Dufour sent up a message to headquarters, quaint and short,
That "the Company of Grenadiers desired to report."
"Granted," said the bluff old Marshal, "let them do it here and now."
And Jacques Dufour came marching in and made his stiffest bow.
"Where is the wounded Colonel?" "Safe in the hospital,
Where you ordered us to place him, Monsieur le Maréchal."
"Where is the Company? They too have come in safety all?"
"The Company is present, Monsieur le Maréchal."

12. "Where is the Company, I repeat, the *Company?*" once more.
"The Company is *present*," said Sergeant Jacques Dufour.
"But your comrades—there were ninety or a hundred men, you know."

"Ah, mon Maréchal, my comrades lie buried in the snow!"

Then up rose the stout old Marshal, with his eyes brimful of tears,

Dashed aside the barriers of rank, the cold reserve of years:

Caught the stripling to his bosom, gave him a reverent kiss,

And the ribbon which Dufour has worn from that far day to this. WILLIAM W. HOWE.

**Explain** the expressions: "cool of evening" (1); "drinking in the balmy air" (1); "Eighty years had left their *footprints*" (1); "kindled with *a misty glow* . . . like a crater in the snow" (1); "the Russ" (3); "As they watch the glory, against those golden skies" (9); "too swift the refluent flood of hope that swelled their hearts again" (9); "dashed aside the barriers of rank, the cold reserve of years" (12).

The expression "Monsieur le Maréchal," though it literally means *Mister the Marshal*, really means *Marshal*, just as we say *General* in addressing an officer of that rank.

## LESSON XVIII.

2. ŏs tĕn sō' rĭęs; *n.* remonstrances; the vessels in which the Blessed Sacrament is placed when held up for the adoration of the faithful.
3. ăs çĕt' ĭc; *a.* severely religious.
5. gôr' ġęǫŭs; *a.* showy; magnificent.
5. ᴄrўpt; *n.* a vault under a church, used for burial purposes.
6. re tā' blę; *n.* an altar-screen.
7. bá ṣĭl' ĭ ᴄá; *n.* cathedral.
7. sĕlf-ăb' ne gā' tion; *n.* self-denial.
7. pä' tĭ o; *n.* a Spanish word meaning *court-yard*.

### The Cathedral of Seville and the Tomb of St. Ferdinand.

1. To understand the Cathedral at Seville, you must know it; you must feel it; you must live in it; you must

see it at the moment of the setting sun, when the light streams in golden showers through those wonderful painted glass windows (those masterpieces of Arnold of Flanders), jeweling the curling smoke of the incense still hanging around the choir; or else go there in the dim twilight, when the aisles seem to lengthen out into infinite space, and the only bright spot is from the ever-burning silver lamps which hang before the tabernacle.

2. One of our party, certainly not given to admiration of either churches or Catholicity, exclaimed on leaving it: "It is a place where I could not help saying my prayers." . . . Among the treasures is the cross made from the gold which Christopher Columbus brought home from America and presented to the king; the keys of the town given up to Ferdinand by the Moorish king at the conquest of Seville; two beautiful ostensories of the fifteenth century, covered with precious stones and magnificent pearls; beautiful reliquaries presented by different Popes; finely illuminated missals in admirable preservation; an exquisitely carved ivory crucifix; wonderful vestments, heavy with embroidery and seed-pearls; the crown of King Ferdinand; and last, not least, a magnificent tabernacle, altar-front, angels, and candlesticks, all in solid silver, beautiful in workmanship and design, used for Corpus Christi and other solemn feasts of the Blessed Sacrament.

3. The Royal Chapel contains the body of Ferdinand, the pious conqueror of Seville, which town, as well as Cordova, he rescued from the hands of the Moors after it had been in their possession 524 years. This pious King, son of Alfonso, King of Leon, bore witness by his conduct to the truth of his words on going into battle: "Thou, O Lord, who searchest the hearts of men, knowest that I desire but Thy glory and not mine!" To his saint-like

mother, Berangera, he owed all the good and holy impressions of his life. He helped to build the Cathedral of Toledo, of which he laid the first stone, and, in the midst of the splendors of the court, led a most ascetic and penitential life.

4. Seville surrendered to him in 1249, after a siege of sixteen months, on which occasion the Moorish general exclaimed that "only a saint, who, by his justice and piety, had won Heaven over to his interest, could have taken so strong a city with so small an army." By the Archbishop's permission, the body of the saint was exposed for our travelers. It is in a magnificent silver shrine; and the features still retain a remarkable resemblance to his portraits. His banner, crown, and sword were likewise shown to them, and the little ivory Virgin which he always fastened to the front of his saddle when going to battle.

5. The cedar coffin still remains in which his body rested previous to its removal to this more gorgeous shrine. On the three days in the year when his body is exposed, the troops all attend Mass, and lower their arms and colors to the great Christian conqueror. A little staircase at the back of the tomb brings you down into a tiny crypt, where, arranged on shelves, are the coffins of the beautiful Maria Padilla, of Pedro the Cruel, and of their two sons; latterly those of the children of the Duke and Duchess de Montpensier have been added.

6. Over the altar of the chapel above hangs a very curious wooden statue of the Virgin, given to St. Ferdinand by the good King Louis of France. King Ferdinand adorned it with the crown of emeralds and stomacher of diamonds belonging to his mother, on condition that they should never be removed from the image. The organs are among the wonders of this Cathedral, with their thou-

sands of pipes, placed horizontally in a fan-like shape. The retable at the back of the high altar is a marvel of wood-carving; and the hundreds of lamps which burn before the different shrines are all of pure and massive silver. One is tempted to ask: "Was it by men and women like ourselves that cathedrals such as this were planned and built and furnished?"

7. The Chapter who undertook it are said to have deprived themselves even of the necessaries of life to erect a basilica worthy of the name; and in this spirit of voluntary poverty and self-abnegation was it begun and completed. At the west end lies Fernando, son of the great Christopher Columbus, who himself died at Valladolid, and is said to rest in Havana. Passing at last under the Moorish arch toward the northeast end of the Cathedral, our travelers found themselves in a beautiful cloistered "patio" full of orange-trees in full blossom, with a magnificent fountain in the centre. In one corner is the old stone pulpit from which St. Vincent Ferrer, Venerable John of Avila, and other saints preached to the people; an inscription records the fact. LADY HERBERT.

Seville (1), Cordova (3), Toledo (3), and Valladolid (7) are cities of Spain.

The "Chapter" referred to in paragraph 7 was a body of Religious.

Explain the expression "jeweling the curling smoke" (1).

---

"To thine own self be true;
And it must follow, as the night the day,
Thou canst not then be false to any man."
SHAKESPEARE.

"Blessed are those who die for God,
And earn the martyr's crown of light;
Yet he who lives for God may be
A greater conqueror in His sight."
ADELAIDE A. PROCTER.

## LESSON XIX.

1. e nū' mer āt&d ; *v.* mentioned specially.
4. spăṣmṣ ; *n.* sudden, violent pains.
5. a bĕt' ted ; *v.* assisted.
7. a mēn' i tlĕṣ ; *n.* pleasant, agreeable qualities.
7. săt' ir ĭst ; *n.* one who writes keenly and severely in rebuke of wrongs.
10. ăd' vẽrsḙ ; *a.* unfortunate.
13. ġĕn' ius ; *n.* great natural gifts.
15. fĭt' fu̧l ; *a.* irregular.

### Thomas Hood.

1. Let us be grateful to those beneficent authors who in their works have taught us to be cheerful—men who have written "Pickwick Papers," and "Punch Papers," and "Sparrowgrass Papers," and all other kinds of papers, to make us laugh and be happy together. "To everything there is a season," says the best of books; and I am very glad "a time to laugh" is especially enumerated among those seasons.

2. But there is a kind of humor abroad in the world which is to be avoided everywhere. Indelicacy is never funny. Vulgarity is always out of place. The man who implants in my memory a coarse story or a broad jest does me an injury for life and is forever odious in my recollection. I thank no one for trying to make me laugh at the expense of decency.

3. Who would not like to go out of the world as Hood did, feeling sure that he had never given pain to any one's sense of refinement, but that he had added smiles, not tears, to human life?

4. Thomas Hood's unsullied pages are as nutritious and comforting as they are amusing. When you have a rebellious tooth, or a wicked headache, or an extra screw of rheumatism, or a stab in the back by a false friend, over-

haul your "Tom Hood," and, my word for it, you will feel better for the operation. One day I heard this order given from a sick-bed: "Bring me a bowl of gruel and the second volume of 'Hood's Own';" and it sounded most sensible and encouraging. I once asked a friend who had long and dangerous illnesses what he took when the spasms were severest; and he replied, "'Pickwick Papers' and 'Pagsley Papers' mixed."

5. Blessings, I say, on all who have contributed to the harmless laughter and simple amusement of mankind; who have aided and abetted in the cause of human love and charity,—the "week-day preachers," as Thackeray calls them, who have done what they could to help a universal good-will to man.

6. How to make people happier is one of the noblest employments of man or woman kind; how to be generous and forgiving to human frailty; how to be helpful to the poor; how to encourage the weak and suffering; how to be neighborly and considerate toward young persons, and very tenderly disposed toward the feelings of little children, who have a difficult time of it, poor things! for lack of sympathy, and are shoveled off to bed at eight o'clock, while everybody else is having a good time down-stairs.

7. Now, all these amenities of life Tom Hood came on a special mission to teach us in his cheerful pages. He was a wit, a humorist, a satirist, but never a buffoon. Great artists in fun, like Shakespeare, and Dickens, and Hood, are always masters of the revels, but are never mastered by them.

8. Ill health followed poor Hood through his whole career. Longfellow, who called to see him one day in 1843, with Dickens, described the poet to me as a small, thin man, looking very pale and worn, not saying much

himself, but listening to Dickens with evident affection and interest. A perfectly-well day Hood never experienced for twenty-five years; but his good spirits never deserted him, and his most humorous productions were composed when disease was preying most severely upon him. When the doctor told him that many of his pains came from the fact that, anatomically, his heart was placed lower down than is usual, he replied: "The more need for me to keep it up, then."

9. One day he said to his wife, "Never let us meet trouble half-way, but let him have the whole walk for his pains."

10. His energy and good spirits triumphed always over all oppositions to health and personal comfort. His famous poem of "Miss Killmansegg" was written under the most adverse circumstances, when he was suffering from weakness occasioned by loss of blood, and when he was kept alive only by the doctor's utmost skill.

11. In one of his prefaces, written after a long and severe illness, Hood tells his readers: "As to my health, which is the weather of the body, it hails, it rains, it blows, it snows, at present; but it may clear up by and by. Things may take a turn, as the pig said on the spit." His fortitude and fun under trouble never deserted him. He never repined or uttered a complaint.

12. When they were getting up a subscription in London for his monument, some of the most distinguished names in England were prominent on the list; but to my thinking, those small sums that came up from the working-people of Manchester and Bristol and Preston far outweighed the piles of guineas poured out by the great ones.

13. Some of those little packages that were sent in from the working districts were marked, "From a few

poor needle-women"; "From seven dressmakers"; "From twelve poor men in the coal-mines." The rich gave of their abundance, to honor the wit, the Englishmen of genius, the great author; but the poor women of Britain remembered who it was that sung the "Song of the Shirt" and "The Bridge of Sighs," and, down there in their dark dens of sorrow and poverty, they resolved to send up their mite, though coined out of heart's blood, for the good man's monument.

14. They had heard all about their dying friend, who had been pleading their cause through so many years. They knew that he had been sending out of his sick-chamber lessons of charity and forbearance: reminding Wealth of Want, Feasting of Fasting, and Society of Solitude and Despair.

15. Hood's breath of life—so fitful for years—went out at last without a struggle or a sigh. The month of May was always an eventful month to him. He was born in May, married in May, and was laid to rest under the pink and white blossoms of May.
JAMES T. FIELDS.

**Thomas Hood** was born in London, England, in 1798 and died May 3, 1845. He holds a high place both as a humorist and as a serious poet. His "Miss Killmansegg" (10) is one of the wittiest and most humorous poems in English, while his "Song of the Shirt" and "The Bridge of Sighs" (13) are among the most perfect poems of their kind we have.

**William Makepeace Thackeray** (5), born 1811, died 1863, was a writer of both prose and verse. He will be best remembered by his novels; from one of these, "The Newcomes," an extract will be found toward the end of this volume.

**Charles Dickens** (7), born 1812, died 1870, was one of the greatest novelists and humorists that England has produced. He occupies a field that no other writer has cultivated. His good characters, however, are only humanly good; their goodness does not spring from a moral or religious motive. *The Dublin Review* says of him: "He was certainly a moral writer and lauded the household virtues; but there is a higher aspect of morality, one in which Catholic readers are bound to regard every book which professes to deal with the condition of man; and so regarded, Mr. Dickens's works are false as any of those of the undisguised materialistic writers of the day."

**William Shakespeare** (7), the greatest of dramatic poets, was born in England in 1564 and died April 23, 1616. His genius was something wonderful. There is scarcely a subject of which he has not made some mention. "He was the man," says Dryden, "who of all modern and perhaps ancient poets had the largest and most comprehensive soul. All the images of nature were present to him, and when he describes anything, you more than see it—you feel it too."

**Henry W. Longfellow** (8) was born at Portland, Me., in 1807 and died in 1882. His poetry is remarkable for its simplicity, refinement, and grace. He is undoubtedly the most popular of American poets.

**Explain** the expressions "stab in the back" (4); "coined out of heart's blood" (13). What is meant by "the best of books," referred to in paragraph 1?

## LESSON XX.

1. scōpe; *n.* extent.
2. shōal; *n.* great multitude, said especially of fish.
3. scŏff'ing ly; *adv.* with contempt.
4. strănd; *n.* the sea-shore.
4. clēave; *v.* to divide by force.
4. phŏs' phor-līght' ed; *a.* lighted up by the phosphorous in the sea-water.
5. ŏff'ing; *n.* that part of the sea where there is deep water.
6. sough'ing (sŭf' ing); *a.* sighing.

### The Fishermen of Wexford.

1. There is an old tradition sacred held in Wexford town,
    That says: "Upon St. Martin's Eve no net shall be let down;
    No fisherman of Wexford shall, upon that holy day,
    Set sail or cast a line within the scope of Wexford Bay."

The tongue that framed the order, or the time, no one
  could tell;
And no one ever questioned, but the people kept it well.
And never in man's memory was fisher known to leave
The little town of Wexford on the good St. Martin's Eve.

2. Alas! alas for Wexford! once upon that holy day
  Came a wondrous shoal of herring to the waters of the
    Bay.
The fishers and their families stood out upon the beach,
And all day watched with wistful eyes the wealth they
    might not reach.
Such shoal was never seen before, and keen regrets
    went round—
Alas! alas for Wexford! Hark! what is that grating
    sound?
The boats' keels on the shingle! Mothers! wives! ye
    well may grieve,—
The fishermen of Wexford mean to sail on Martin's Eve!

3. "Oh, stay ye!" cried the women wild. "Stay!" cried
    the men white-haired;
"And dare ye not to do this thing your fathers never
    dared.
No man can thrive who tempts the Lord!" "Away!"
    they cried: "the Lord
Ne'er sent a shoal of fish but as a fisherman's reward."
And scoffingly they said, "To-night our nets shall
    sweep the Bay,
And take the Saint who guards it, should he come
    across our way!"
The keels have touched the water, and the crews are
    in each boat;
And on St. Martin's Eve the Wexford fishers are afloat!

4. The moon is shining coldly on the sea and on the land,
　On dark faces in the fishing-fleet and pale ones on the strand,
　As seaward go the daring boats, and heavenward the cries
　Of kneeling wives and mothers with uplifted hands and eyes.
　"Oh Holy Virgin! be their guard!" the weeping women cried;
　The old men, sad and silent, watched the boats cleave through the tide,
　As past the farthest headland, past the lighthouse, in a line
　The fishing-fleet went seaward through the phosphor-lighted brine.

5. Oh, pray, ye wives and mothers! All your prayers they sorely need
　To save them from the wrath they've roused by their rebellious greed.
　Oh! white-haired men and little babes, and weeping sweethearts, pray
　To God to spare the fishermen to-night in Wexford Bay!

6. The boats have reached good offing, and, as out the nets are thrown,
　The hearts ashore are chilled to hear the soughing sea-wind's moan:
　Like to a human heart that loved, and hoped for some return,
　To find at last but hatred. so the sea-wind seemed to mourn.

But ah! the Wexford fishermen! their nets did scarcely sink
One inch below the foam, when, lo! the daring boatmen shrink
With sudden awe and whitened lips and glaring eyes agape,
For breast-high, threatening, from the sea uprose a Human Shape!

7. Beyond them,—in the moonlight,—hand upraised and awful mien,
Waving back and pointing landward, breast-high in the sea 'twas seen.
Thrice it waved and thrice it pointed,—then, with clenchéd hand upraised,
The awful shape went down before the fishers as they gazed!
Gleaming whitely through the water, fathoms deep they saw its frown,—
They saw its white hand clenched above it,—sinking slowly down!
And then there was a rushing 'neath the boats, and every soul
Was thrilled with greed; they knew it was the seaward-going shoal!

3. Defying the dread warning, every face was sternly set,
And wildly did they ply the oar, and wildly haul the net.
But two boats' crews obeyed the sign,—God-fearing men were they,—
They cut their lines and left their nets, and homeward sped away;
But darkly rising sternward did God's wrath in tempest sweep,

And they, of all the fishermen, that night escaped the deep.

Oh, wives and mothers, sweethearts, sires! well might ye mourn next day;

For seventy fishers' corpses strewed the shores of Wexford Bay!

JOHN BOYLE O'REILLY.

**John Boyle O'Reilly** was born in Ireland in 1844 and died in Boston August 10, 1890. He was a writer of very vigorous prose and of some remarkably sweet poetry. For twenty years prior to his death he was the editor of the Boston *Pilot*. He was a strict Catholic, a brilliant speaker, a man whose heart beat in sympathy with the helpless and friendless of every creed and clime.

Wexford (1) is a seaboard town in Ireland.

**Explain** the expression: "seventy fishers' corpses strewed the shores of Wexford Bay" (8).

## LESSON XXI.

2. çĭr′ cŭit; *n.* round-about journey.
2. en sconçe′; *v.* hide securely.
2. çĭr′ cum-spĕc′ tion; *n.* caution.
3. frāys; *n.* combats.
3. rĕc on noi′ ter; *v.* examine.
5. trĕnch′ er; *n.* a large wooden plate.
5. thrĭft; *n.* economy.
7. ôrd′ nançe; *n.* cannon and other heavy instruments of war.
8. wạr′ rant; *v.* declare with assurance.
8. fee′ sĭm′ plĕ; *n.* an absolute right forever; a fee without conditions.

### A Military Stratagem. Part I.

1. On the morning that succeeded the night in which Horse Shoe Robinson arrived at Musgrove's, the stout and honest sergeant might have been seen, about eight o'clock, leaving the main road from Ninety Six at the point where that leading to David Ramsay's separated from it, and cautiously urging his way into the deep forest by the more private path into which he had entered.

2. The knowledge that Innis was encamped along the Ennoree, within a short distance of the mill, had compelled him to make an extensive circuit to reach Ramsay's dwelling, whither he was now bent; and he had experienced considerable delay in his morning journey, by finding himself frequently in the neighborhood of small foraging-parties of Tories, whose motions he was obliged to watch for fear of an encounter. He had once already been compelled to use his horse's heels in what he called "fair flight," and once to ensconce himself a full half-hour under cover of the thicket afforded him by a swamp. He now, therefore, according to his own phrase, "dived into the little road that scrambled down through the woods toward Ramsay's, with all his eyes about him, looking out as sharply as a fox on a foggy morning," and, with this circumspection, he was not long in arriving within view of Ramsay's house.

3. Like a practiced soldier, whom frequent frays have taught wisdom, he resolved to reconnoiter before he advanced upon a post that might be in possession of an enemy. He therefore dismounted, fastened his horse in a fence-corner, where a field of corn concealed it from notice, and then stealthily crept forward until he came immediately behind one of the out-houses.

4. The barking of a house-dog brought out a negro boy, to whom Robinson instantly addressed the query:

"Is your master at home?"

"No, sir. He's got his horse, and gone off more than an hour ago."

"Where is your mistress?"

"Shelling beans, sir."

"I didn't ask you," said the sergeant, "what she is doing, but where she is."

"In course, she is in the house, sir," replied the negro, with a grin.

"Any strangers there?"

"There was plenty of 'em a little while ago, but they've been gone a good bit."

5. Robinson, having thus satisfied himself as to the safety of his visit, directed the boy to take his horse and lead him up to the door. He then entered the dwelling.

"Mistress Ramsay," said he, walking up to the dame, who was occupied at a table, with a large trencher before her, in which she was plying that household thrift which the negro described, "luck to you, ma'am, and all your house!"

6. "Good lack, Mr. Horse Shoe Robinson!" exclaimed the matron, offering the sergeant her hand. "What has brought you here? What news? Who are with you? For patience' sake, tell me!"

"I am alone," said Robinson, "and a little wet," he added as he took off his hat and shook the water from it; "it has just begun to rain, and it looks as if it was going to give us enough of it. Where's Davy?"

"He's gone over to the meeting-house on Ennoree, hoping to hear something of the army at Camden. Perhaps you can tell us the news from that quarter?"

7. "Faith, that's a mistake, Mistress Ramsay. At this present speaking I command the flying artillery. We have but one man in the corps—and that's myself; and all the guns we have is this piece of ordnance that hangs in this old belt by my side" (pointing to his sword), "and that I captured from the enemy at Blackstock's. I was hoping I might find John Ramsay at home: I have need of him as a recruit."

8. "Ah, Mr. Robinson, John has a heavy life of it over

there with Sumter. I haven't the heart to complain, as long as John's service is of any use, but it does seem like needless tempting of the mercies of Providence. We thought that he might have been here to-day; yet I am glad he didn't come—for he would have been certain to get into trouble. Who should come in this morning, just after my husband had cleverly got away on his horse, but a young ensign that belongs to Ninety Six, and four great Scotchmen with him, all in red coats; they had been out thieving, I warrant, and were now going home again. Here they were, swaggering all about my house, and calling for this and calling for that, as if they owned the fee-simple of everything on the plantation. And it made my blood rise, Mr. Horse Shoe, to see them run out in the yard and catch up my chickens and ducks and kill as many as they could string about them, and I not daring to say a word: though I did give them a piece of my mind, too."

9. "Who is at home with you?" inquired the sergeant.

"Nobody but my youngest boy, Andrew," answered the dame.

"What arms have you in the house?"

"We have a rifle, and a horseman's pistol that belongs to John. They must call for drink, too, and turn my house, of a Sunday morning, into a tavern—"

"They took the route toward Ninety Six, you said, Mistress Ramsay?"

"Yes, they went straight forward upon the road. But, look you, Mr. Horse Shoe, you're not thinking of going after them?"

"Isn't there an old field, about a mile from this, on that road?" inquired the sergeant, still intent upon his own thoughts.

"There is," replied the dame, "with the old school-house upon it."

"A lop-sided, rickety log-cabin in the middle of the field. Am I right, good woman?"

"Yes."

"And nobody lives in it? It has no door to it?"

"There ha'n't been anybody in it these seven years."

10. "I know the place very well," said the sergeant, thoughtfully; "there is woods just on this side of it."

"That's true," replied the dame. "But what is it you are thinking about, Mr. Robinson?"

"How long before this rain began was it that they quitted this house?"

"Not above fifteen minutes."

"Mistress Ramsay, bring me the rifle and pistol, both— and the powder-horn and bullets."

"As you say, Mr. Horse Shoe," answered the dame, as she turned round to leave the room; "but I am sure I can't suspicion what you mean to do."

HORSE SHOE ROBINSON (1) is the hero of a story of that name. The scene is laid in the South during the Revolutionary War, and the language of the characters is somewhat different from that of the present day.—NINETY SIX (1) is a village in Abbeville, South Carolina.—ENNOREE (2) is a river in South Carolina.—"In course" (4) is an illiterate way of saying "of course."—CAMDEN (6) is the county-seat of Kershaw County, South Carolina.—"This piece of ordnance" (7) is a humorous way of referring to the sword, which is *not* a piece of ordnance.—SUMTER (8) is General Thomas Sumter, a hero of the Revolutionary War.

Explain the expressions: "plying that household thrift" (5); "There ha'n't been anybody" (9).

---

". . . When a great man dies,
  For years beyond our ken,
    The light he leaves behind him lies
      Upon the paths of men." LONGFELLOW.

## LESSON XXII.

1. rīfẹ; *a.* abounding.
2. scrŭm' magẹ; *n.* a corruption of *skirmish*, that is, a fight.
6. tĭẹk' lish; *a.* difficult.
8. quạr' ter; *n.* merciful treatment.
10. fŏr lŏrn'-hōpẹ; *n.* men appointed to lead an assault.
11. tăr' rĭẹd; *v.* waited.
12. lĕv' ĕl; *n.* line of direction of the aim.
12. mŭs' tĕr-rōll; *n.* list of men.

### A Military Stratagem. Part II.

1. In a few moments the woman returned with the weapons, and gave them to the sergeant.

"Where is Andy?" asked Horse Shoe.

The hostess went to the door and called her son, and almost immediately afterward a sturdy boy, of about twelve or fourteen years of age, entered the apartment, his clothes dripping with rain. He modestly and shyly seated himself on a chair near the door, with his soaked hat flapping down over a face full of freckles, and not less rife with the expression of an open, dauntless hardihood of character.

2. "How would you like a scrummage, Andy, with them Scotchmen that stole your mother's chickens this morning?" asked Horse Shoe.

"I'm agreed," replied the boy, "if you will tell me what to do."

"You are not going to take the boy out on any of your desperate projects, Mr. Horse Shoe?" said the mother, with the tears starting instantly into her eyes. "You wouldn't take such a child as that into danger?"

"Bless your soul, Mistress Ramsay, there is not the least danger about it! It's a thing that is either done at a blow, or not done—and there's an end of it. I want the lad only to bring home the prisoners for me, after I have taken them."

3. "Ah, Mr. Robinson, I have one son already in these wars—God protect him!—and you men don't know how a mother's heart yearns for her children in these times. I cannot give another," she added, as she threw her arms over the shoulders of the youth and drew him to her bosom.

"Oh, it isn't anything," said Andrew, in a sprightly tone. "It's only snapping of a pistol, mother. Pooh! If I'm not afraid, you oughtn't to be."

4. "I give you my honor, Mistress Ramsay," said Robinson, "that I will bring or send your son safe back in one hour; and that he sha'n't be put in any sort of danger whatsoever: come, that's a good woman!"

"You are not deceiving me, Mr. Robinson?" asked the matron, wiping away a tear. "You wouldn't mock the sufferings of a weak woman in such a thing as this?"

"On the honesty of a soldier, ma'am," replied Horse Shoe, "the lad shall be in no danger, as I said before—whatsoever."

"Then I will say no more," answered the mother. "But, Andy, my child, be sure to let Mr. Robinson keep before you."

5. Horse Shoe now loaded the firearms, and, having slung the pouch across his body, he put the pistol into the hands of the boy; then, shouldering his rifle, he and his young ally left the room.

"Now, Andy, my lad," said Horse Shoe, after he had mounted his horse, "you must get up behind me. Turn the lock of your pistol down," he continued, as the boy sprung upon the horse's back, "and cover it with the flap of your jacket, to keep the rain off. It won't do to hang fire at such a time as this."

The lad did as he was directed, and Horse Shoe, having secured his rifle in the same way, put his horse to a gallop and took the road in the direction that had been pursued by the soldiers.

6. As soon as our adventurers had gained a wood, at the distance of about half a mile, the sergeant relaxed his speed and advanced at a pace a little above a walk.

"Andy," he said, "we have rather a ticklish sort of a job before us; so I must give you your lesson, which you will understand better by knowing something of my plan. As soon as your mother told me that these thieving villains had left her house about fifteen minutes before the rain came on, and that they had gone along upon this road, I remembered the old field up here and the little log-hut in the middle of it; and it was natural to suppose that they had just got about near that hut when this rain came up; and then it was the most supposable case in the world that they would naturally go into it, as the driest place they could find. So now you see it's my calculation that the whole batch is there at this very point of time. We will go slowly along until we get to the other end of this wood, in sight of the old field; and then, if there is no one on the lookout, we will open our first trench; you know what that means, Andy?"

"It means, I suppose, that we'll go right at them," replied Andrew.

7. "Exactly," said the sergeant. "But listen to me. Just at the edge of the woods you will have to get down and put yourself behind a tree. I'll ride forward, as if I had a whole troop at my heels; and if I catch them, as I expect, they will have a little fire kindled, and, as likely as not, they'll be cooking some of your mother's fowls."

8. "Yes, I understand," said the boy, eagerly.

"No, you don't," replied Horse Shoe; "but you will

when you hear what I am going to say. If I get at them unawares they'll be very apt to think they are surrounded, and will bellow like fine fellows for quarter. And thereupon, Andy, I'll cry out, 'Stand fast!' as if I were speaking to my own men, and when you hear that, you must come up at once, because it will be a signal to you that the enemy has surrendered. Then it will be your business to run into the house and bring out the muskets as quick as a rat runs through a kitchen; and when you have done that—why, all's done. But if you should hear any popping of fire-arms—that is, more than one shot, which I may chance to let off—do you take that for a bad sign, and get away as fast as you can heel it. You comprehend?"

9. "Oh, yes," replied the lad, "and I'll do what you want—and more too, maybe, Mr. Robinson."

"*Captain* Robinson, remember, Andy: you must call me *captain* in the hearing of these Scotchmen."

"I'll not forget that, neither," answered Andrew.

10. By the time that these instructions were fully impressed upon the boy, our adventurous forlorn-hope, as it may fitly be called, had arrived at the place which Horse Shoe had designated for the commencement of active operations. They had a clear view of the old field, and it afforded them a strong assurance that the enemy was exactly where they wished him to be when they discovered smoke arising from the chimney of the hovel.

11. Andrew was soon posted behind a tree, and Robinson only tarried a moment to make the boy repeat the signals agreed on, in order to ascertain that he had them correctly in his memory. Being satisfied from this experiment that the intelligence of his young companion might be depended upon, he galloped across the intervening

space, and in a few seconds abruptly reined up his steed in the very doorway of the hut. The party within was gathered around a fire at the farther end; and in the corner near the door were four muskets thrown together against the wall. To spring from his saddle and thrust himself one pace inside of the door was a movement which the sergeant executed in an instant, shouting at the same time:

"Halt! File off right and left to both sides of the house, and wait orders. I demand the surrender of all here," he said, as he planted himself between the party and their weapons. "I will shoot down the first man who moves a foot."

12. "Leap to your arms!" cried the young officer who commanded the little party inside of the house. "Why do you stand?"

"I don't want to do you or your men any harm, young man," said Robinson, as he brought his rifle to a level, "but I will not leave one of you to be put upon a muster-roll if you raise a hand at this moment!"

The instructions to Andy to turn the lock of his pistol down and cover it with the flap of his jacket to keep the rain off, were for the reason that below the lock in the old-fashioned pistols there was a pan in which powder was placed, and if this powder was wet the pistol would not go off. The percussion-cartridge used to-day is a great improvement on the "flint-lock" pistol of former days.

**Explain the expressions:** "active operations" (10) ; "reined up his steed" (11) ; "planted himself" (11).

---

Laziness grows on people: it begins in cobwebs and ends in iron chains.

Nothing is denied to well-directed labor: nothing is ever to be attained without it.

Character is like stock in trade: the more of it a man possesses, the greater his facilities for making additions to it.

## LESSON XXIII.

1. străt'a ġem; *n.* a trick or artifice in war for deceiving an enemy.
2. dough'ty; *a.* brave; terrible to foes.
3. ŏp' pŏr tūne'; *a.* timely.
4. fŏr' ag ing; *a.* in search of provisions.
5. lăm' bent; *a.* gliding over; meaning, in this case, just seen for an instant.
6. sŭm' mā ry; *a.* quickly executed.
9. aux il' ia ry; *n.* helper.
10. pĕr' tur bā' tion; *n.* agitated state.

**A Military Stratagem. Part III.**

1. Both parties now stood for a brief space eying each other, in a fearful suspense, during which there was an expression of doubt and irresolution visible on the countenances of the soldiers as they surveyed the broad proportions and met the stern glance of the sergeant; while the delay also began to raise an apprehension in the mind of Robinson that his stratagem would be discovered.

2. "Shall I let loose upon them, captain?" said Andrew Ramsay, now appearing, most unexpectedly to Robinson, at the door of the hut. "Come on, boys!" he shouted, as he turned his face towards the field.

"Keep them outside of the door. Stand fast!" cried the doughty sergeant, with admirable promptitude, in the new and sudden posture of his affairs caused by this opportune appearance of the boy. "Sir, you see that it's not worth while fighting five to one; so take my advice, and surrender to the Continental Congress and this scrap of its army which I command."

3. During this appeal the sergeant was ably seconded by the lad outside, who was calling out first on one name and then on another, as if in the presence of a troop. The officer within, believing the forbearance of Robinson to be real, at length said:

"Lower your rifle, sir. In the presence of a superior force, taken by surprise and without arms, it is my duty to save bloodshed. With the promise of fair usage and the rights of prisoners of war, I surrender this little foraging party under my command."

4. "I'll make the terms agreeable," replied the sergeant. "Never doubt me, sir. Right-hand file, advance, and receive the arms of the prisoners!"

"I'm here, captain," said Andrew, in a conceited tone, as if it were an occasion of merriment; and the lad quickly entered the house and secured the weapons, retreating with them some paces from the door.

5. "Now, sir," said Horse Shoe to the ensign, "your sword, and whatever else you may have about you of the ammunitions of war!"

The officer delivered up his sword and a pair of pocket-pistols.

As Horse Shoe received these tokens of victory, he asked, with a lambent smile and what he intended to be an elegant and condescending composure, "Your name, sir, if I may take the freedom?"

"Ensign St. Jermyn, of his Majesty's Seventy-first Regiment of Light Infantry."

6. "Ensign, your servant," added Horse Shoe, still preserving this unusual exhibition of politeness. "You have defended your post like an old soldier, although you haven't much beard on your chin; but seeing you have given up, you shall be treated like a man who has done his duty. You will walk out now, and form yourselves in line at the door. I'll engage my men shall do you no harm."

7. When the little squad of prisoners submitted to this command, and came to the door, they were stricken with

equal astonishment and mortification to find, in place of the detachment of cavalry which they expected to see, nothing but a man, a boy, and a horse. Their first emotions were expressed in curses, which were even succeeded by laughter from one or two of the number. There seemed to be a disposition, on the part of some, to resist the authority that now controlled them; and sundry glances were exchanged which indicated a purpose to turn upon their captors. The sergeant no sooner perceived this than he halted, raised his rifle to his breast, and at the same instant gave Andrew Ramsay an order to retire a few paces and to fire one of the captured pieces at the first man who opened his lips.

8. "By my hand," he said, "if I find any trouble in taking you, all five, safe away from this house, I will thin your numbers with your own muskets! And that's as good as if I had sworn to it."

"You have my word, sir," said the ensign. "Lead on."

"By your leave, my pretty gentleman, you will lead, and I'll follow," replied Horse Shoe. "It may be a new piece of drill to you, but the custom is to give the prisoners the post of honor."

9. Finding the conqueror determined to execute summary martial law upon the first who should mutiny, the prisoners submitted, and marched in double file from the hut back toward Ramsay's—Horse Shoe and his gallant young auxiliary, Andrew, bringing up the rear. In this order victors and vanquished returned to David Ramsay's.

10. "Well, I have brought you your ducks and chickens back, mistress," said the sergeant, as he halted the prisoners at the door, "and, what's more, I have brought home a young soldier that's worth his weight in gold."

"Heaven bless my child! my brave boy!" cried the mother, seizing the lad in her arms, unheeding anything else in the present perturbation of her feelings. "I feared ill would come of it; but Heaven has preserved him. Did he behave handsomely, Mr. Robinson? But I am sure he did."

11. "A little more venturesome, ma'am, than I wanted him to be," replied Horse Shoe. "But he did excellent service. These are his prisoners, Mistress Ramsay; I should never have taken them if it hadn't been for Andy. Show me another boy in America that's made more prisoners than there were men to fight them with, that's all!"

JOHN P. KENNEDY.

John P. Kennedy was born in Baltimore, Md., in 1795 and died in 1870. He was the author of several popular stories, the best known being "Horse Shoe Robinson" and "Swallow Barn." He also wrote a "Life of William Wirt." He was for a time a member of Congress from his native state, and served as Secretary of the Navy under President Fillmore.

**Explain** the expressions "broad proportions" (1); "by my hand" (8).

Tell what the "Continental Congress" (2) was.

Give synonyms for "merriment" (4); "engage" (6); "squad" (7); "mutiny" (9).

---

Let your words be few, especially when your superiors or strangers are present, lest you betray your own weakness and rob yourself of the opportunity which you might otherwise have had to gain knowledge, wisdom, and experience, by hearing those whom you silence by your idle talking.

Consider before you speak, especially when the business is of moment; weigh the sense of what you mean to utter, and the expressions you intend to use, that they may be significant, pertinent, and inoffensive. Inconsiderate persons do not think till they speak; or they speak and then think.

## LESSON XXIV.

1. dō′ ñà (dō′ nyà); *n.* lady; a title of respect used in Spain with the Christian name of a lady.
2. pōr′ tàls; *n.* gates.
2. bǎsk′ ing; *v.* lying in warmth.
3. gall; *n.* a bitter liquid.
6. dōle; *n.* alms; that which is given in charity.

### Charity.

[Suggested by Doré's "Spanish Beggars."]

1. Doña Inez was a lady
Very rich and fair to see,
And her heart was like a lily
In its holy purity.
Through the widest street in Cadiz
Doña Inez rode one day,
Clad in costly silk and laces,
'Mid a group of friends as gay.

2. Near the portals of a convent—
From the Moors just lately won—
Sat a crowd of dark-skinned beggars
Basking in the pleasant sun ;
One an old man—he a Christian,
Blind to all the outward light—
Told his black beads, praying softly
For all poor souls still in night.

3. "I am but a Moorish beggar,"
Said a woman with a child ;
"I am but a Moorish beggar,
And the Moors are fierce and wild.
*You* may *talk* of Christian goodness—
Christian Faith and Charity,

CHARITY.

But *I'll* never be a Christian
Till some proof of these I see.
Christians are as proud and haughty
As the proudest Moor of all;
And they hate the men that hate them
With a hate like bitter gall."

4. "You judge rashly, O my sister,
In the words you speak to me."
"I would be a Christian, blind man:
Show me Christian charity!

5. "Lo! here comes proud Doña Inez,
Very rich and fair to see;
I am but a Moorish beggar,
Will the lady come to me?
No! she will not, for she hateth
All the children of the Moor.
If she come, I tell you, blind man,
I will kneel, and Christ adore!"

6. Passing was the Lady Inez,
When the dark group met her eye,
And she leant from out her litter
Smiling on them tenderly.
"They are poor, they are God's children,"
Said a voice within her soul,
And she lightly from her litter
Stepped to give the beggars dole.

7. Sneered and laughed, and, laughing, wondered
All the other ladies gay;
And the Lady Inez knew not
She had saved a soul that day.

MAURICE F. EGAN.

Cadiz is a town in the province of Seville, Spain. Tell the story of the poem in your own language.

**Maurice Francis Egan** was born in Philadelphia, May 24, 1853. Since leaving college he has been by turns college professor, law student, journalist, and editor, and at the present writing is Professor of English Literature in the University of Notre Dame. He is a successful writer of that difficult form of verse, the sonnet, and the author of many popular tales; in the latter he has succeeded in faithfully depicting life among "Irish-Americans."

## LESSON XXV.

1. măg' nātes; *n.* persons of rank.
1. rĕt' i nūe; *n.* followers; attendants.
2. jăun' tỹ; *a.* showy.
4. ex pănse'; *n.* wide extent of space.
9. bûrn' ishęd; *a.* made bright; polished.
9. văl' ançes; *n.* hanging draperies, especially the curtains which hang around a bedstead from the bed to the floor.
12. for măl' i tīes; *n.* usual rules of proceeding.
14. răm' pärt; *n.* wall.
14. so nō' rọus; *a.* loud-sounding.

### The Search for Livingstone.

1. On the second day after Stanley's arrival at the capital of Unyanyembe, the Arab magnates of Tabora came to congratulate him. Tabora is the principal Arab settlement in Central Africa, with a population of about five thousand. The Arabs were fine, handsome men, mostly from Oman, and each had a large retinue of servants with him.

2. After having exchanged the usual stock of congratulations, Stanley accepted an invitation to return the visit at Tabora, and three days afterward, accompanied by eighteen bravely dressed soldiers, he was presented to a group of stately Arabs in long white dresses and jaunty caps of snowy white, and introduced to the hospitalities of Tabora.

3. On the 20th of September the American flag was again hoisted, and the caravan, consisting of fifty-four per-

sons, started along the southern route toward Ujiji and Livingstone. It moved forward through forests of immense extent, that stretched in grand waves beyond the range of vision;—among ridges, forest-clad, rising gently one above another, until they receded through a leafy ocean into the purple blue distance, where was only a dim outline of a hill far away.

4. Stanley next passed through a grand and noble expanse of grass-land,—which was one of the finest scenes he had witnessed since leaving the coast. Great herds of buffalo, zebra, giraffe, and antelope course through the plain, and the expedition indulged in a day or two of hunting. While crossing a river at this point, Stanley narrowly escaped being devoured by a crocodile, but cared little for the danger, led on, as he was, by the excitement of stalking wild boars and shooting buffalo cows.

5. Now from time to time Stanley heard, from passing savages, occasional rumors of the presence of white men at various points. This encouraged him to believe that Livingstone was not far off, and gave him the necessary boldness to traverse the great wilderness beyond Marara, the crossing of which he was warned would occupy nine days. The negroes became exceedingly pleased at the prospect of their journey's end. They therefore boldly turned their faces north and marched for the Malagarazi, a large river flowing from the east to Lake Tanganyika.

6. On the 1st of November they arrived at the long-looked-for river, and, after crossing the ferry, they met a caravan coming from the interior, and were told that a white man had just arrived at Ujiji.

"A white man?" cried Stanley.

"Yes, an old white man, with white hair on his face, and he was sick."

"Where did he come from?"

"From a very far country indeed."

"Where was he—staying at Ujiji?"

"Yes."

"And was he ever at Ujiji before?"

"Yes; he went away a long time ago."

"Hurrah!" said Stanley; "this must be Livingstone."

7. He determined to hasten forward at all hazards. The caravan arrived on the 8th of November at the Rugufu River, at which point they could distinctly hear the thunders from the mysterious torrents which rolled into the hollow recesses of Kabogo Mountain on the farther side of Lake Tanganyika. This noise gave Stanley the heartiest joy, because he knew that he was only forty-six miles from Ujiji and possibly Livingstone.

8. About midday on the 9th of November they reached a beautiful series of valleys, where wild fruit-trees grew and rare flowers blossomed. On this day they caught sight of the hills from which Lake Tanganyika could be seen. Stanley ordered his boy, Selim, to brush up his tattered traveling suits, that he might make as good an appearance as possible.

9. On the two hundred and thirty-sixth day from Bagamoyo, and the fifty-first day from Unyanyembe, they saw Lake Tanganyika spread out before them, and around it the great, blue-black mountains of Ugoma and Ukaramba. It was an immense, broad sheet—a burnished bed of silver—a lucid canopy of blue above, lofty mountains for its valances and palm forests for its fringes. Descending the western slope of the mountain, the port of Ujiji lay below, embowered in palms.

10. "Unfurl your flags and load your guns!" cried Stanley.

"Yes, yes!" eagerly responded the men.

"One, two, three!" and a volley from fifty muskets woke up the peaceful village below. The American flag was raised aloft once more; the men stepped out bravely as the crowds of villagers came flocking around them.

Suddenly Stanley heard a voice on his right say in English, "Good-morning, sir." A black man dressed in a long, white shirt announced himself as "Susi," the servant of Dr. Livingstone.

"What! Is Dr. Livingstone here?"

"Yes, sir."

"In the village?"

"Yes, sir."

"Are you sure?"

"Sure, sure, sir. Why, I left him just now."

11. Then another servant introduced himself; the crowds flocked around anew; and finally, at the head of his caravan, Stanley found himself before a semicircle of Arab magnates, in front of whom stood an old white man with a gray beard.

12. As Stanley advanced toward him, he noticed that he was pale, looked wearied, had on his head a bluish cap with a faded gold band around it, a red-sleeved waistcoat, and a pair of gray tweed trousers. He walked to him, took off his hat, and said, "Dr. Livingstone, I presume."

"Yes," said he, with a smile, lifting his cap slightly.

Then they clasped hands, and after the necessary formalities with the Arab magnates, Stanley explained himself and his mission.

13. It was a great day for the old explorer. There were letters from his children. "Ah!" he said patiently, "I have waited years for letters." And you may picture for yourselves that strangely met pair, seated in the ex-

plorer's house, Livingstone hearing for the first time of the great changes in Europe.

14. They sat long together, with their faces turned eastward, noting the dark shadows creeping up above the groves of palms beyond the village and the rampart of mountains; listening to the sonorous thunder of the surf of Tanganyika, and to the dreamy chorus which the night-insects sang.

15. Mr. Stanley remained four months in the company of Dr. Livingstone, during which time an intimate and rich friendship grew up between the two men. From November 10, 1871, until March 14, 1872, they were together daily. Dr. Livingstone had been in Africa since March, 1866. He left Zanzibar in April of that year for the interior, with thirty men, and worked studiously at his high mission of correcting the errors of former travelers until early in 1869, when he arrived at Ujiji and took a brief rest.

16. He had been deserted in the most cowardly manner by the majority of his followers, and was much of the time in want. At the end of June, 1869, he went on to a lake into which the Lualaba ran, and then was compelled to return the weary distance of seven hundred miles to Ujiji. The magnificent result of his labors, both in the interest of science and humanity, are now known to all the world.

17. Livingstone returned with Stanley to Unyanyembe, and on the 14th of March the two men parted, not without tears. It was not until sunset on the 6th of May that the worn and fatigued Stanley re-entered Bagamoyo. The next morning he crossed to Zanzibar, and thence as soon as possible departed for Europe with his precious freight—the Livingstone journals and letters, and his own rich experience.     EDWARD KING.

Henry M. Stanley (1) is a native of Wales and was born in the year 1840. His name, originally, was John Rowlands, but he was adopted when a lad by a merchant named Stanley, who gave him the name by which he has become famous. He is one of the most daring and best known of African explorers. In 1871 he was sent to Africa by the *New York Herald* to find Dr. Livingstone, and was successful in his search, as we have learned from the lesson.

David Livingstone (5), African traveler and Protestant missionary, was born in Scotland in the year 1813, and died in Africa in 1873. When only twenty-seven years old he was sent to Africa by the London Missionary Society. The rest of his life, with the exception of a little over a year, was spent in exploring that country, and the importance of his discoveries can hardly be overestimated. Dr. Livingstone published several books containing accounts of his travels.

## LESSON XXVI.

1. per sist' ed ; *v.* persevered; stood firm.
2. col' league ; *n.* associate; helper.
2. pro scrib ed'; *a.* doomed to destruction.

2. pre des' tined ; *a.* decided beforehand.
3. plight' ing ; *n.* pledging.
5. e rad' i cat ed ; *v.* rooted out.
5. im mū' ni ties ; *n.* privileges.

### Supposed Speech of John Adams.

1. Sink or swim, live or die, survive or perish, I give my hand and my heart to this vote. It is true, indeed, that in the beginning we aimed not at independence. But

"There's a divinity that shapes our ends."

The injustice of England has driven us to arms; and, blinded to her own interest, she has obstinately persisted, till independence is now within our grasp. We have but to reach forth to it, and it is ours. Why, then, should we defer the Declaration?

2. Is any man so weak as now to hope for a reconciliation with England which shall leave either safety to

the country and its liberties, or security to his own life and his own honor? Are not you, sir, who sit in that chair; is not he, our venerable colleague near you—are you not both already the proscribed and predestined objects of punishment and of vengeance? Cut off from all hope of royal clemency, what are you, what can you be, while the power of England remains, but *outlaws?*

3. If we postpone independence, do we mean to carry on or to give up the war? Do we mean to submit, and consent that we shall be ground to powder, and our country and its rights trodden down in the dust? I *know* we do not mean to submit. We NEVER *shall submit!* Do we intend to violate that most solemn obligation ever entered into by men, that plighting, before God, of our sacred honor to Washington, when, putting him forth to incur the dangers of war as well as the political hazards of the times, we promised to adhere to him in every extremity with our fortunes and our lives? I know there is not a man here who would not rather see a general conflagration sweep over the land, or an earthquake sink it, than one jot or tittle of that plighted faith fall to the ground. For myself, having twelve months ago, in this place, moved you that George Washington be appointed commander of the forces raised, or to be raised, for the defense of American liberty, may my right hand forget her cunning, and my tongue cleave to the roof of my mouth, if I hesitate or waver in the support I give him.

4. The war, then, must go on. We must fight it through. And, if the war must go on, why put off the Declaration of Independence? That measure will strengthen us. It will give us character abroad. Nations will then treat with us, which they never can do while we acknowledge ourselves subjects in arms against our sovereign. Nay, I

maintain that England herself will sooner treat for peace with us on the footing of independence than consent, by repealing her acts, to acknowledge that her whole conduct toward us has been a course of injustice and oppression. Her pride will be less wounded by submitting to that course of things which now predestinates our independence than by yielding the points in controversy to her rebellious subjects. The former, she would regard as the result of fortune; the latter, she would feel as her own deep disgrace. Why, then, do we not change this from a civil to a national war? And, since we must fight it through, why not put ourselves in a state to enjoy all the benefits of victory, if we gain the victory?

5. If we fail, it can be no worse for us. But we shall not fail. The cause will raise up armies; the cause will create navies. The people—the people, if we are true to them, will carry us, and will carry themselves, gloriously through this struggle. I care not how fickle other people have been found. I know the people of these colonies; and I know that resistance to British aggression is deep and settled in their hearts and cannot be eradicated. Sir, the Declaration of Independence will inspire the people with increased courage. Instead of a long and bloody war for the restoration of privileges, for redress of grievances, for chartered immunities, held under a British king, set before them the glorious object of entire independence, and it will breathe into them anew the spirit of life.

6. Read this Declaration at the head of the army: every sword will be drawn, and the solemn vow uttered to maintain it or perish on the bed of honor. Publish it from the pulpit: religion will approve it, and the love of religious liberty will cling around it, resolved to stand with it or fall with it. Send it to the public halls; proclaim it

there. Let *them* see it who saw their brothers and their sons fall on the field of Bunker Hill and in the streets of Lexington and Concord, and the very walls will cry out in its support.

7. Sir, I know the uncertainty of human affairs, but I see—I see clearly through this day's business. You and I, indeed, may rue it. We may not live to see the time this Declaration shall be made good. We may die; die colonists; die slaves; die, it may be ignominiously, and on the scaffold. Be it so: be it so. If it be the pleasure of Heaven that my country shall require the poor offering of my life, the victim shall be ready at the appointed hour of sacrifice, come when that hour may. But while I do live, let me have a country, or at least the *hope* of a country, and that a FREE *country*.

8. But whatever may be our fate, be assured—be assured that this Declaration will stand. It may cost treasure and it may cost blood; but it will stand, and it will richly compensate for both. Through the thick gloom of the present I see the brightness of the future as the sun in heaven. We shall make this a glorious, an immortal day. When we are in our graves, our children will honor it. They will celebrate it with thanksgiving, with festivity, with bonfires and illuminations. On its annual return they will shed tears—copious, gushing tears; not of subjection and slavery, not of agony and distress, but of exultation, of gratitude, and of joy.

9. Sir, before God, I believe the hour is come. My judgment approves the measure, and my whole heart is in it. All that I have, and all that I am, and all that I hope in this life, I am now ready here to stake upon it; and I leave off as I began, that live or die, survive or perish, I am for the Declaration. It is my living sentiment, and, by

the blessing of God, it shall be my dying sentiment: independence *now*, and INDEPENDENCE FOREVER.

DANIEL WEBSTER.

**Daniel Webster**, one of America's greatest orators, was born in Salisbury, New Hampshire, in January, 1782, and died in October, 1852. His life was devoted, with but slight interruption, to the practice of law, in which his great talent shone pre-eminent, and to the service of his country. Besides many years passed, with high renown, as Representative and Senator to Congress from Massachusetts, he was twice called to the Cabinet as Secretary of State. In reputation he stands peerless in history as the Constitutional Lawyer and Orator of America.

Our Lesson is taken from a speech upon the life and character of John Adams, delivered by Webster. He imagines that some one has opposed the Declaration of Independence while its adoption was being urged in the Continental Congress, and makes Adams, who was the ardent champion of the measure, answer the objections.

"There's a divinity that shapes our ends" (1) is a quotation from Shakespeare's play of "Hamlet." "You, sir," (2) refers to John Hancock, President of the Continental Congress; and "venerable colleague," (2) to Samuel Adams.

LESSON XXVII.

1. găl' ley; n. a vessel with one deck, often rowed by slaves or prisoners.
4. fŭr' rōwed; a. cut into grooves by a plough.
5. be sŏught'; v. begged.
5. quâffed (kwäft); v. drank.
6. cŏt' ter; n. one who lives in a cottage.
6. de fault'; n. failure.
7. prŏf' fered; a. offered.
9. hīed; v. hastened.

**The Galley Slave.**

1. There lived in France, in days not long now dead,
 A farmer's sons, twin brothers, like in face;
And one was taken in the other's stead
 For a small theft, and sentenced in disgrace
To serve for years a hated galley slave—
Yet said no word, his prized good name to save.

2. Trusting remoter days would be more blessed,
      He set his will to wear the verdict out,
   And knew most men are prisoners at best
      Who some strong habit ever drag about,
   Like chain and ball; then meekly prayed that he
   Rather the prisoner he was should be.

3. But best resolves are of such feeble thread,
      They may be broken in temptation's hands.
   After long toil the guiltless prisoner said:
      Why should I thus, and feel life's precious sands
   The narrow of my glass, the present, run,
   For a poor crime that I have never done?

4. Such questions are like cups, and hold reply;
      For when the chance swung wide the prisoner fled,
   And gained the country road, and hastened by
      Brown furrowed fields and skipping brooklets, fed
   By shepherd clouds, and felt 'neath sapful trees
   The soft hand of the mesmerizing breeze.

5. Then, all that long day having eaten naught,
      He at a cottage stopped, and of the wife
   A brimming bowl of fragrant milk besought.
      She gave it him; but as he quaffed the life,
   Down her kind face he saw a single tear
   Pursue its wet and sorrowful career.

6. Within the cot he now beheld a man
      And maiden, also weeping. "Speak," said he,
   "And tell me of your grief; for if I can,
      I will disroot the sad, tear-fruited tree."
   The cotter answered: "In default of rent,
   We shall to-morrow from this roof be sent."

7. Then said the galley slave: "Whoso returns
   A prisoner escaped may feel the spur
To a right action, and deserves and earns
   Proffered reward. I am a prisoner!
Bind these my arms, and drive me back my way,
That your reward the price of home may pay."

8. Against his wish the cotter gave consent,
   And at the prison-gate received his fee,
Though some made it a thing for wonderment
   That one so sickly and infirm as he,
When stronger would have dared not to attack,
Could capture this bold youth and bring him back.

9. Straightway the cotter to the mayor hied,
   And told him all the story; and that lord
Was much affected, dropping gold beside
   The pursed sufficient silver of reward;
Then wrote his letter in authority,
Asking to set the noble prisoner free.

10. There is no nobler, better life on earth
    Than that of conscious, meek self-sacrifice.
Such life Our Saviour, in His lowly birth
    And holy work, made His sublime disguise—
Teaching this truth, still rarely understood:
'Tis sweet to suffer for another's good.

HENRY ABBEY.

**Explain** the expressions: "one was taken in the other's stead" (1); "Why should I thus" (3); "I will disroot the sad, tear-fruited tree" (6).

Paraphrase the second and the fourth stanza.

What does this poem teach us?

## LESSON XXVIII.

1. mī′ ero scōpe; *a.* an instrument for examining objects which are too small to be seen by the naked eye.
3. toil′ sŏme; *a.* laborious.
4. gär′ nered; *v.* gathered for preservation.
5. be lēa′ guered; *a.* surrounded by an army.
6. ĭn′ do lençe; *n.* laziness.

### On Learning by Heart.

1. Till he has fairly tried it, I suspect a reader does not know how much he would gain from committing to memory passages of real excellence, precisely because he does not know how much he overlooks when merely reading. Learn one true poem by heart, and see if you do not find it so. Beauty after beauty will reveal itself, in chosen phrase, or happy music, or noble suggestion, otherwise undreamed of. It is like looking at one of Nature's wonders through a microscope.

2. Again: how much in such a poem that you really did feel admirable and lovely on a first reading passes away if you do not give it a further and much better reading!—passes away utterly, like a sweet sound, or an image on the lake, which the first breath of wind dispels. If you could only fix that image, as the photographers do theirs, so beautifully, so perfectly! And you can do so! Learn it by heart, and it is yours forever!

3. It is not difficult or toilsome to learn that which pleases us; and the labor, once given, is forgotten, while the result remains. Poems, and noble extracts, whether of verse or of prose, once so reduced into possession and rendered truly our own, may be to us a daily pleasure;— better far than a whole library *unused*. They may come to us in our dull moments, to refresh us as with spring flowers; in our selfish musings, to win us by pure delight

from the tyranny of foolish castle-building, self-gratulations, and mean anxieties. They may be with us in the workshop, in the crowded street, by the fireside; sometimes, perhaps, on pleasant hillsides, or by sounding shores;—noble friends and companions—our own! never intrusive, ever at hand, coming at our call!

4. Shakespeare, Milton, Wordsworth, Tennyson,—the words of such men do not stale upon us, they do not grow old or cold. Further: though you are young now, some day you may be old. Some day you may reach that time when a man lives in great part *for* memory and *by* memory. I can imagine a chance renewal, a chance visitation, of the words long remembered, long garnered in the heart, and I think I see a gleam of rare joy in the eyes of the old man.

5. For those, in particular, whose leisure time is short, and precious as scant rations to beleaguered men, I believe there could not be a better expenditure of time than deliberately giving an occasional hour—it requires no more —to committing to memory chosen passages from great authors. If the mind were thus daily nourished with a few choice words of the best English poets and writers; if the habit of learning by heart were to become so general that, as a matter of course, any person presuming to be educated might be expected to be equipped with a few good pieces,—I believe that it would lead, much more than the mere sound of it suggests, to the diffusion of the best kind of literature, and to the right appreciation of it; and that men would not long rest satisfied with knowing a few stock pieces.

6. Learning by heart is a good thing, and it is neglected among us. Why is it neglected? Partly because of our indolence; but partly, I believe, because we do not

sufficiently consider that it *is* a good thing, and needs to be taken in hand. We need to be reminded of it. I here remind you. Like a town-crier, ringing my bell, I would say to you, "Oyez, oyez! Lost, stolen, or strayed, a good ancient practice—the good ancient practice of learning by heart. Every finder shall be handsomely rewarded."

7. If you ask, "What shall I learn?" the answer is, Do as you do with tunes—begin with what you sincerely like best, what you would most wish to remember, what you would most enjoy saying to yourself or repeating to another. You will soon find the list inexhaustible. Then "keeping up" is easy. Every one has a spare ten minutes: one of the problems of life is how to employ them usefully. You may well spend some in looking after and securing this good property you have won.

**John Milton** (4), England's greatest epic poet, was born in London in December, 1608, and died in November, 1674. His greatest poem is "Paradise Lost."

**William Wordsworth** (4), Poet Laureate of England, was born in 1770 and died in 1850. He holds a very high rank among the later English poets.

**Alfred Tennyson** (4) was born in England in 1809 and died in 1892. He succeeded Wordsworth as Poet Laureate. His verses are distinguished by their purity and felicity of diction. His "Idylls of the King" are his masterpieces, but he is best known to the general reader by his shorter poems.

"Town-crier" (6) is one who goes about the streets crying out for lost persons or things; the occupation is now almost done away with. "Oyez" (6) means "hear ye," and is generally pronounced *O yes*.

---

Count life a stage upon thy way,
And follow conscience, come what may ;
Alike with heaven and earth sincere,
With hand and brow and bosom clear;
" Fear God "—and know no other fear.

## LESSON XXIX.

1. mis quōte'; *v.* repeat incorrectly.
2. măt'in; *a.* used in the morning.
3. păn' de mō' ni ŭm; *n.* the great hall of the evil spirits; hence, a noisy place.
5. găm'ĭn; *n.* a neglected city child. (French.)
5. tĕn' or; *n.* the general direction of thought.
8. ve răn' dá; *n.* a kind of roofed gallery, platform, or projection beyond the outer wall of a house.
9. dŏg' ġed ness; *n.* obstinate resolution.
9. dĭs' con çĕrt' ed; *v.* thrown into confusion.
14. pro pĕn' sĭ tў; *n.* natural inclination.
15. grŭb; *n.* worm.

### A Ruffian in Feathers.

1. We all know Shakespeare's opinion of the "man that hath no music in himself," although we usually misquote it. If this be a fair judgment of the human race, how much more justly may it be said of the bird, to whom we look for the sweetest harmonies of nature!

2. I do not think his best friend will claim that the common house-sparrow has the soul of music in him; certainly not if he has ever been wakened in a glorious dawn by the indescribable jangle of harsh sounds which constitute this bird's only morning hymn, at the hour when every bird in the woods, from the noble singers of the thrush family down to the least chipping sparrow, is greeting the new day in his most musical fashion.

3. The matin song of the house-sparrow, in which he indulges unsparingly, being of similar quality, harmonizes perfectly with the jarring sounds of man's contriving: the clatter of iron-shod wheels over city pavements, the warwhoop of the ferocious milkman, the unearthly cries of the venders, and above all the junkman's pandemonium of "bells jangled out of tune." The harshest cries of our native birds, if not always musical in themselves, seem at

least to accord in some way with sounds of nature. The house-sparrow alone is entirely discordant—the one bird without a pleasing note, whose very love-song is an unmusical squeak. Nor is his appearance more interesting than his voice, and on looking into his manners and customs we discover most unlovely characteristics.

4. One of my windows looks into a large yard, with trees so thick that when the foliage is out I cannot see the street, from which the roar of vehicles alone reminds me that I am in the closely-built city. The birds are fond of this pleasant green nook, and here I have often studied their ways.

5. For cool impudence and offensive intrusion upon the rights of humanity about him this bird has no equal. He is a genuine *gamin*, and shows the effect of life in the streets even on a bird. One of the most familiar habits of this graceless bird is his delight in a mob. No sooner does anything occur to disturb the even tenor of sparrow life, whether a domestic skirmish, the first outing of a young family, or some danger to a nest, than a crowd collects, not only as interested spectators, but quite ready and willing to take a hand in any sport or crime that is going—not only a hand, but a voice as well. Loud cries always announce when a rabble is at work. Whether, as is declared by some observers, they drive away our native birds by this means I am not sure.

6. I have seen them annoy the cat-bird, the robin, and the Baltimore oriole, but in each case they were put to flight by the native bird; though no doubt the experience is sufficiently disagreeable to induce either of these birds to select a more retired neighborhood for nest-building. I once noticed the same tactics successfully applied to a cat which climbed up among the nests.

7. An amusing instance in which the birds were worsted took place under my eye last summer. Hearing the usual outcry one morning, I looked out, and saw a great crowd of sparrows perched on the branches of a tall maple-tree, shrieking at the top of their voices, craning their necks, and hopping ever nearer to one of the houses so kindly provided for their use, a single cottage, with room for but one couple, and quite high up in the tree.

8. The excitement centered around this house, and for a long time I could not see what was the disturbing cause. Close watching with a glass at length revealed a small reddish head, with very sharp eyes, occupying the doorway of the cottage, and after some time the owner of these features calmly stepped out on the veranda and showed himself—a small red squirrel, with a silver collar, which proclaimed him an escaped pet. He looked thin, with a tail almost as bare as a rat's. He had evidently not fared well in captivity, and I rejoiced in his freedom.

9. But the sparrow world had decided to eject him from the neighborhood, and faithfully, with true sparrow-doggedness, they worked at this problem. No sooner did he appear than they resumed their attack, flying around him, screaming, and making quick dashes at him. He was somewhat disconcerted, and ran up a long branch, followed by the whole gang, which grew more bold as he apparently retreated, dashing ever nearer as though to peck him, but never actually touching him. While he was running they were very bold, but the moment he sat up and faced them they drew off a little, though they never went quite away.

10. For several days not a movement of his escaped their notice. It was amusing to see how quickly the smallest stir on his part was announced to the world. "There

he is! He's coming out!" one could easily understand, and every sparrow within hearing responded by instantly deserting his business or pleasure, and adding his presence and cries to the mob.

11. But the squirrel, finding fruit-trees with green apples and pears, resolved to stay, and after a week or two they became so far accustomed to his presence as to be less alarmed, though they never lost interest in him. His eating especially seemed to divert and astonish them. I have seen fifty birds at once hovering around an evergreen-tree, too small to afford them perching-places, far enough from the enemy, while he gathered and nibbled the small cones. When he sat up on a branch, holding a green pear in his tiny paws, their amusement knew no bounds. They sat around at a safe distance, exchanging remarks in the amiable manner of some of the human race at the ways of a foreigner.

12. The squirrel had by this time resumed his wild instincts, cared nothing for them, and would even answer back with a sharp little cry. He had taken up his summer residence in the maple-tree cottage, and all through the fall, while pears hung on the trees of the neglected yard next ours, he lived in clover. His tail became bushy, his coat grew sleek, and he looked like a different animal. Still the sparrows attended his every movement, following him like a train of courtiers wherever he went, though they did not make quite so much noise about it as at first.

13. The household became as keenly interested as the birds in the doings of the pretty fellow. All through the winter he appeared on the mild days, running and bounding all over the tall maples. We saw him gather grass and carry it off in great bundles in his mouth to make a bed, and after an unusually cold season he spent part of two

days in removing his residence from an ornamental pile of stones in a neighbor's yard to warmer quarters he had discovered under the house. He had evidently collected a quantity of stores of some sort. No doubt as soon as spring opened he would vary his diet with fresh eggs, but as I left the vicinity I did not have opportunity to observe whether the sparrow family suffered from him.

14. Next to the sparrow's mobbing propensity is his impudence. Not only will he insist on sharing the food of chickens and domestic animals, but he is a common guest at the table of the great bald eagles in the parks, and does not disdain the crumbs that fall from the repast of the polar bear, one touch of whose paw would flatten him like a wafer.

15. Perhaps the most saucy thing reported of a sparrow was witnessed in Brooklyn by a well-known artist. He was watching a robin hard at work on the lawn, gathering food for his family, when he noticed a sparrow who also seemed interested in the operation. The sparrow looked on, evidently with growing excitement, while one bit after another was uncovered, till at last a particularly large and attractive grub was brought to light. This was too much for sparrow philosophy. He made one dash, snatched the tempting morsel from the very bill of the robin, and disappeared before the astounded bird recovered from his surprise.

With this unparalleled act of impertinence to a bird big enough to eat him, this true chronicle of the most unattractive fellow that wears feathers shall close.

OLIVE THORNE MILLER.

The "man that hath no music in himself" (1) is a quotation from Shakespeare's "Merchant of Venice," Act v. Scene 1. "Bells jangled out of tune" (3) is also from Shakespeare, see "Hamlet," Act iii. Scene 1.

Explain in your own words the expressions: "harmonizes perfectly with the jarring sounds of man's contriving" (8); "exchanging remarks in the amiable manner of some of the human race at the ways of a foreigner" (11).

What kind of a "glass" is meant in the expression "close watching with a glass" (8)?

## LESSON XXX.

2. blīthe; a. joyous.
4. ĕlf; n. an imaginary diminutive spirit, supposed to haunt wild places and take pleasure in mischievous tricks.
10. ġĕn' der; v. to cause.
10. păġ' eănt rȳ; n. show.
11. hănts; n. places which one frequently visits.
13. mo nĭ' tion; n. warning.

### The Yellow-hammer.

1. A yellow-hammer in the rain!
 And that on this Carinthian plain,
 So far, so far from home!
 It fills me with old childish years:
 And then these happy, happy tears,
 Do what I will they come!

2. Behold him now: he never stops,
 Among the pattering raindrops
 A blithe disturbance making,
 Beating forever on one key,
 Pleased with his own monotony,
 And his wet feathers shaking.

3. What tender memories are bound
 To this familiar hedge-row sound!
 The creature's homely glee
 Associates me with the hours
 When, so pure childhood willed, all showers
 Were sunshine showers to me.

4. Away he goes, and hammers still
   Without a rule but his free will,
   A little gaudy Elf!
   And there he is within the rain,
   And beats and beats his tune again,
   Quite happy in himself.

5. Within the heart of this great shower
   He sits, as in a secret bower,
   With curtains drawn about him:
   And, part in duty, part in mirth,
   He beats, as if upon the earth
   Rain could not fall without him.

6. Ah, homely bird! thou canst not know
   How far into my heart doth go
   That melancholy key,
   How from thy little straining throat
   Each separate, successive note
   Beats like a pulse in me.

7. Through blinding tears meek fancy weaves
   Far other fields, far other leaves,
   Than those by Drava's side;
   For now the looks of long-lost faces,
   And the calm features of old places,
   Like magic, round me glide.

8. Thou art a power of other days,
   A voice from old deserted ways
   Obscured by trackless flowers,
   An echo of the childish past,
   Thus touchingly and strangely cast
   Into these foreign bowers.

9. O it was right and well with me
   When I could love a single tree
   As a green sanctuary,
   When I could in the meadow lie
   And look into the silky sky
   For hours, and not be weary!

10. Now over sea and over earth
    I pass with hollow, heated mirth
    Which doth but gender sadness,
    And with uneasy heart I range
    Through all the pageantry of change
    To gather moods of gladness.

11. Time flies, and life; and many thought,
    Into unsunny currents wrought,
    Is in hoarse eddies wheeling:
    I am a man of growing wants,
    And I have many wayward haunts,
    Haunts both of thought and feeling.

12. When joys were simple, days were long,
    All woven into one bright throng,
    Like golden bees at play,
    One with another softly blending,
    As though they could not have an ending,
    And all were but one day.

13. I thank thee, gentle bird! for this;
    Thou hast awakened childish bliss,
    A sweet monition given;
    And willing tears for youthful sin
    Are fragrant rituals, that may win
    The old light back from Heaven.

14. And sure I am that summer day
   Ne'er shone on a more grand array
   Or gorgeous pomp of mountains;
   And o'er the plain in shining rings
   The Drave with blithest murmurings
   Comes from his Alpine fountains:

15. And seen through this bright, dazzling rain
   How fair is yon Carinthian plain,
   A richly wooded park,
   Where groups of birch with silver stems
   Rise up, like scepters of white gems,
   Among the fire-clumps dark.

16. Yet am I cast upon lost years;
   The Present is dissolved in tears;
   So is this bird empowered;
   An oracle upon the bough
   He sits, through him the Present now
   Is by the Past deflowered.

F. W. FABER.

**Rev. Frederick William Faber** was born in England in 1814 and died in 1863. He was a minister of the Church of England until his conversion to Catholicity in 1845. Two years later he was ordained a priest and entered the Congregation of the Oratory of St. Philip Neri. He was a poet of no mean ability and wrote exquisite prose.

The Yellow-hammer is a European bird, but the name is often applied in the United States to a species of woodpecker. The "Carinthian plain" (1 and 15) means a field in Carinthia, a duchy of Austria; the "Drave," poetically called "Drava" (7), is a river in Germany.

**Explain** the expressions: "an echo of the childish past" (8); "into unsunny currents wrought" (11).

Let the pupils, with the aid of the teacher, give in simple language the meaning of stanza 16.

## LESSON XXXI.

2. flŏŏd-tīde; *n.* the flowing in of the tide.
3. härd' tăck; *n.* bread made for long voyages.
3. cŭn' ners; *n.* small salt-water fish.
4. nōōn' ing; *n.* rest at noon.
5. cŭt'-wạ' ter; *n.* the fore part of a boat which projects beyond the bow and cuts the water.
9. lŭrks; *v.* lies hidden.

### The Cruise of the Dolphin. Part I.

1. It was a proud moment when I stood on the wharf, with my partners, inspecting the Dolphin, moored at the foot of a very slippery flight of steps. She was painted white, with a green stripe outside, and on the stern a yellow dolphin, with its scarlet mouth wide open, stared with a surprised expression at its own reflection in the water. The boat was a great bargain.

2. Not long after the purchase of the boat, we planned an excursion to Sandpeep Island, the last of the islands in the harbor. We proposed to start early in the morning, and return with the tide in the moonlight. We were up before sunrise the next morning, in order to take advantage of the flood-tide, which waits for no man. Our preparations for the cruise were made the previous evening.

3. In the way of eatables and drinkables, we had stored in the stern of the Dolphin a generous bag of hard-tack (for the chowder), a piece of pork to fry the cunners in, three gigantic apple-pies, half a dozen lemons, and a keg of spring-water,—the last-named article we slung over the side to keep it cool, as soon as we got under way.

4. The crockery, and the bricks for our camp-stove, we placed in the bow with the groceries, which included sugar, pepper, salt, and a bottle of pickles. Phil Adams

contributed to the outfit a small tent of unbleached cotton cloth, under which we intended to take our nooning.

5. We unshipped the mast, threw in an extra oar, and were ready to embark. How calm and lovely the river was! Not a ripple stirred on the glassy surface, broken only by the sharp cutwater of our tiny craft. The sun, as round and red as an August moon, was by this time peering above the water-line. The town had drifted behind us, and we were entering among the group of islands. Sometimes we could almost touch with our boat-hook the shelving banks on either side. As we neared the mouth of the harbor, a little breeze now and then wrinkled the blue water, shook the spangles from the foliage, and gently lifted the spiral mist-wreaths that still clung alongshore.

6. The measured dip of our oars and the drowsy twitterings of the birds seemed to mingle with, rather than break, the enchanted silence that reigned about us. The scent of the new clover comes back to me now, as I recall that delicious morning when we floated away in a fairy-boat down a river like a dream.

7. The sun was well up when the nose of the Dolphin nestled against the snow-white bosom of Sandpeep Island. This island was the last of the cluster, one side of it being washed by the sea. We landed on the river side, the sloping sands and quiet water affording us a good place to moor the boat.

8. It took us an hour or two to transport our stores to the spot selected for the encampment. Having pitched our tent, using the five oars to support the canvas, we got out our lines, and went down the rocks seaward to fish. It was early for cunners, but we were lucky enough to catch as nice a mess as ever you saw. A cod for the chowder

was not so easily secured. At last Binny Wallace hauled in a plump little fellow, crusted all over with flaky silver.

9. To skin the fish, build our fireplace, and cook the chowder kept us busy the next two hours. The fresh air and the exercise had given us the appetites of wolves, and we were about famished by the time the savory mixture was ready for our clam-shell saucers. How happy we were, we four, sitting cross-legged in the crisp salt grass, with the invigorating sea-breeze blowing gratefully through our hair! What a joyous thing was life, and how far off seemed death,—death, that lurks in all pleasant places, and was so near!

The *harbor* referred to in the Lesson (2) is that of Portsmouth, New Hampshire; the scene of the story is laid around that place.

## LESSON XXXII.

2. scŭd′ ded; *v.* passed over quickly.
2. ăd jọ̆ụrnĕd′; *v.* used here in the sense of *removed to*, although the proper meaning of the word is to *put off*.
4. ō′ ver sīg̱ht′; *n.* neglect.
4. pāint′ er; *n.* a rope at the bow of a boat.
8. scŭll; *n.* a short oar used at the stern of a boat.
14. săg̱g̱ĕd; *v.* settled down.
15. lee; *n.* that part toward which the wind blows.
15. lū′ mi nọ̆ŭs; *a.* bright; clear.
16. rōw′ lŏcks; *n.* arrangements for supporting oars in rowing.

### The Cruise of the Dolphin. Part II.

1. The wind had freshened by this, and we found it comfortable to put on the jackets which had been thrown aside in the heat of the day. We strolled along the beach, and gathered large quantities of the fairy-woven Iceland moss, which, at certain seasons, is washed to these shores; then we played at ducks and drakes; and then, the sun being sufficiently low, we went in bathing.

2. Before our bath was ended, a slight change had

come over the sky and sea; fleecy white clouds scudded here and there, and a muffled moan from the breakers caught our ears from time to time. While we were dressing, a few hurried drops of rain came lisping down, and we adjourned to the tent to await the passing of the squall.

3. "We're all right anyhow," said Phil Adams. "It won't be much of a blow, and we'll be as snug as a bug in a rug, here in the tent, particularly if we have that lemonade which some of you fellows were going to make."

4. By an oversight, the lemons had been left in the boat. Binny Wallace volunteered to go for them.

"Put an extra stone on the painter, Binny," said Adams, calling after him; "it would be awkward to have the Dolphin give us the slip, and return to port minus her passengers."

"That it would," answered Binny, scrambling down the rocks.

5. Sandpeep Island is diamond-shape,—one point running out into the sea, and the other looking towards the town. Our tent was on the river side. Though the Dolphin was also on the same side, it lay out of sight by the beach at the farther extremity of the island.

6. Binny Wallace had been absent five or six minutes, when we heard him calling our several names in tones that indicated distress or surprise, we could not tell which. Our first thought was, "The boat has broken adrift!"

7. We sprung to our feet, and hastened down to the beach. On turning the bluff which hid the mooring-place from our view, we found the conjecture correct. Not only was the Dolphin afloat, but poor little Binny Wallace was standing in the bow with his arms stretched helplessly toward us,—*drifting out to sea!*

8. " Head the boat in shore!" shouted Phil Adams.

Wallace ran to the tiller; but the slight cockleshell merely swung round, and drifted broadside on. Oh, if we had but left a single scull in the Dolphin!

9. " Can you swim it?" cried Adams desperately, using his hand as a speaking-trumpet, for the distance between the boat and the island widened momentarily.

10. Binny Wallace looked down at the sea, which was covered with white-caps, and made a despairing gesture. He knew, and we knew, that the stoutest swimmer could not live forty seconds in those angry waters.

11. A wild, insane light came into Phil Adams's eyes, as he stood knee-deep in the boiling surf, and for an instant I think he meditated plunging into the ocean after the receding boat.

12. The sky darkened, and an ugly look stole rapidly over the broken surface of the sea. Binny Wallace half rose from his seat in the stern, and waved his hand to us in token of farewell. In spite of the distance, increasing every instant, we could see his face plainly. The anxious expression it wore at first had passed. It was pale and meek now; and I love to think there was a kind of halo about it, like that which painters place around the forehead of a saint. So he drifted away.

13. The sky grew darker and darker. It was only by straining our eyes through the unnatural twilight that we could keep the Dolphin in sight. The figure of Binny Wallace was no longer visible, for the boat itself had dwindled to a mere dot on the black water. Finally it went out like a spark, and we saw it no more. Then we gazed at one another, and dared not speak.

14. Absorbed in following the course of the boat, we had scarcely noticed the huddled inky clouds that sagged

down all around us. From these threatening masses, seamed at intervals with pale lightning, there now burst a heavy peal of thunder that shook the ground under our feet.

15. It was impossible any longer to keep our footing on the beach. The wind and the breakers would have swept us into the ocean if we had not clung to one another. We crawled up the sands on our hand and knees, and pausing in the lee of the granite ledge to gain breath, returned to the camp. We fell to crying, the three of us, and cried I know not how long. The wind rose higher and higher, cutting long slits in the tent, through which the rain poured incessantly. To complete the sum of our miseries, the night was at hand. It came down suddenly, at last, like a curtain, shutting in Sandpeep Island from all the world.

16. What an endless night it was! I have known months that did not seem so long. Fred Langdon was the first to discover a filmy, luminous streak in the sky, the first glimmering of sunrise. "Look, it is nearly daybreak!" While we were following the direction of his finger, a sound of distant oars fell on our ears. Running down to the water's edge, we hailed the boats with all our might. The call was heard, for the oars rested a moment in the rowlocks, and then pulled in toward the island. It was two boats from the town.

17. Our story was soon told. A solemn silence fell upon the crowd of rough boatmen. The sea was still running too high for any small boat to venture out; so it was arranged that one boat should take us back to town, leaving the other, with a picked crew, to hug the island until daybreak, and then set forth in search of the Dolphin.

18. Poor little Binny Wallace! How strange it seemed, when I went to school again, to see that empty

seat in the fifth row! One day a folded sheet slipped from my algebra: it was the last note he ever wrote me. Poor little Binny Wallace! Always the same to me! The rest of us have grown up into hard, worldly men; but you are forever young, and gentle, and pure; a part of my own childhood that time cannot wither; always a little boy, always poor little Binny Wallace!

THOMAS BAILEY ALDRICH.

"Played at ducks and drakes" (1) means throwing flat stones on the surface of the water so that they will rebound repeatedly; "came lisping down" (2), that is, came down in few, scattered drops; "white-caps" (10) are waves crested with white foam; "to hug the island" (17) is to keep close to the island.

## LESSON XXXIII.

| | |
|---|---|
| 2. văs'sạl; *n.* slave; servant. | 5. sĕrf; *n.* slave. |
| 2. re tāin'er; *n.* servant. | 5. wạs'sạil; *n.* festivity. |
| 4. klŏs'ter; *n.* a German word meaning *cloister* or *monastery*. | 5. wāits; *n.* serenaders; musical watchmen. |

### The Norman Baron.

1. In his chamber, weak and dying,
    Was the Norman baron lying;
    Loud, without, the tempest thundered,
        And the castle-turret shook.

2. In this fight was Death the gainer,
    Spite of vassal and retainer,
    And the lands his sires had plundered,
        Written in the Doomsday Book.

3. By his bed a monk was seated,
    Who in humble voice repeated
    Many a prayer and pater-noster,
        From the missal on his knee;

THE NORMAN BARON.

4. And, amid the tempest pealing,
    Sounds of bells came faintly stealing,
    Bells that, from the neighboring kloster,
        Rang for the Nativity.

5. In the hall, the serf and vassal
    Held, that night, their Christmas wassail;
    Many a carol, old and saintly,
        Sang the minstrels and the waits;

6. And so loud these Saxon gleemen
    Sang to slaves the songs of freemen,
    That the storm was heard but faintly,
        Knocking at the castle-gates.

7. Till at length the lays they chanted
    Reached the chamber terror-haunted,
    Where the monk, with accents holy,
        Whispered at the baron's ear.

8. Tears upon his eyelids glistened,
    As he paused awhile and listened,
    And the dying baron slowly
        Turned his weary head to hear.

9. "Wassail for the kingly stranger
    Born and cradled in a manger!
    King, like David, priest, like Aaron,
        Christ is born to set us free!"

10. And the lightning showed the sainted
    Figures on the casement painted,
    And exclaimed the shuddering baron,
        "Miserere, Domine!"

11. In that hour of deep contrition
   He beheld, with clearer vision,
   Through all outward show and fashion,
      Justice, the Avenger, rise.

12. All the pomp of earth had vanished,
   Falsehood and deceit were banished,
   Reason spake more loud than passion,
      And the truth wore no disguise.

13. Every vassal of his banner,
   Every serf born to his manor,
   All those wronged and wretched creatures,
      By his hand were freed again.

14. And, as on the sacred missal
   He recorded their dismissal,
   Death relaxed his iron features,
      And the monk replied, "Amen!"

15. Many centuries have been numbered
   Since in death the baron slumbered
   By the convent's sculptured portal,
      Mingling with the common dust:

16. But the good deed, through the ages
   Living in historic pages,
   Brighter grows and gleams immortal,
      Unconsumed by moth or rust.

HENRY W. LONGFELLOW.

Arrange the construction of the first stanza in natural order. The "Doomsday Book" (2) was compiled by order of William the Conqueror, and contains a survey of all the lands in England, their value, ownership, etc. Let the pupils give in their own language the meaning of the fourth stanza. Point out an example of alliteration in the sixth stanza. What does the ninth stanza mean? Explain the last two stanzas.

## LESSON XXXIV.

2. me ri'noes; *n.* dresses made of wool.
3. chips; *n.* bonnets made of a fine straw.
3. minx'es; *n.* saucy girls.
6. pound; *n.* twenty shillings English money, equal in value to about $4.84.
7. can'ni bals; *n.* people who eat human flesh.

### Mrs. Caudle Wants Money for Clothes.

1. If there's anything in the world I hate—and you know it—it is asking you for money. I am sure, for myself, I'd rather go without a thing a thousand times—and I do, the more shame for you to let me! "What do I want now?" As if you didn't know! I'm sure, if I'd any money of my own, I'd never ask you for a farthing—never! It's painful to me, gracious knows! What do you say? "If it's painful, why so often do it?" I suppose you call that a joke—one of your club-jokes. As I say, I only wish I'd any money of my own. If there is anything that humbles a poor woman, it is coming to a man's pocket for every farthing. It's dreadful!

2. Now, Caudle, you hear me, for it isn't often I speak. Pray, do you know what month it is? And did you see how the children looked at church to-day?—like nobody else's children! "What was the matter with them?" O Caudle! how can you ask? Weren't they all in their thick merinoes and beaver bonnets?

3. What do you say? "What of it?" What! You'll tell me that you didn't see how the Briggs girls in their new chips turned their noses up at 'em? And you didn't see how the Browns looked at the Smiths, and then at our poor girls, as much as to say, "Poor creatures! what figures for the first of May!" "You didn't see it"? The more shame for you! I'm sure those Briggs girls—the

little minxes!—put me into such a pucker, I could have pulled their ears for 'em over the pew.

4. What do you say? "I ought to be ashamed to own it"? Now, Caudle, it's no use talking; those children shall not cross over the threshold next Sunday if they haven't things for the summer. Now mind—they sha'n't; and there's an end of it! "I'm always wanting money for clothes"? How can you say that? I'm sure there are no children in the world that cost their father so little; but that's it—the less a poor woman does upon, the less she may.

5. Now, Caudle, dear! What a man you are! I know you will give me the money, because, after all, I think you love your children, and like to see 'em well dressed. It's only natural that a father should. "How much money do I want?" Let me see, love. There's Caroline, and Jane, and Susan, and Mary Anne, and—What do you say? "I needn't count 'em! You know how many there are!" That's just the way you take me up!

6. "Well, how much money will it take?" Let me see—I'll tell you in a minute. You always love to see the dear things look like new pins. I know that, Caudle; and, though I say it—bless their little hearts!—they do credit to you, Caudle. "How much?" Now don't be in a hurry! Well, I think, with good pinching—and you know, Caudle, there's never a wife who can pinch closer than I can—I think, with pinching, I can do with twenty pounds.

7. What did you say? "Twenty fiddlesticks"? What! "You won't give half the money"! Very well, Mr. Caudle; I don't care. Let the children go in rags; let them stop from church, and grow up like heathens and cannibals; and then you'll save your money, and, I suppose, be satisfied.

8. What do you say? "Ten pounds enough"? Yes, just like you men; you think things cost nothing for women; but you don't care how much you lay out upon yourselves. "They only want frocks and bonnets"? How do you know what they want? How should a man know anything at all about it? And you won't give more than ten pounds? Very well. Then you may go shopping with it yourself, and see what *you'll* make of it! I'll have none of your ten pounds, I can tell you—no, sir!

9. No; you've no cause to say that. I don't want to dress the children up like countesses! You often throw that in my teeth, you do; but you know it's false, Caudle; you know it! I only wish to give 'em proper notions of themselves; and what, indeed, can the poor things think, when they see the Briggses, the Browns, and the Smiths —and their father don't make the money you do, Caudle —when they see them as fine as tulips? Why, they must think themselves nobody. However, the twenty pounds I *will* have, if I've any, or not a farthing.

10. No, sir—no! I don't want to dress up the children like peacocks and parrots! I only want to make 'em respectable. What do you say? "You'll give me fifteen pounds"? No, Caudle—no! Not a penny will I take under twenty. If I did, it would seem as if I wanted to waste your money; and I'm sure, when I come to think of it, twenty pounds will hardly do!

DOUGLAS WILLIAM JERROLD.

"Mrs. Caudle's Curtain Lectures," from which this Lesson is taken, first appeared in London *Punch*, an English humorous paper, and were very widely read. They are in a highly amusing style, and although but one person, Mrs. Caudle, speaks, we can infer from her questions and answers what Mr. Caudle says. The Lesson will prove an excellent drill in emphasis and inflection.

## LESSON XXXV.

1. In′ dĭ vĭd′ u al ĭşm ; *n.* that quality which distinguishes one person from another.
2. Ir′ re prĕss̨′ ĭ bĭl′ i tў ; *n.* the quality of not being subdued.
3. dĕs′ po tĭşm ; *n.* tyranny.
4. păs′ sĭvę ; *a.* not opposing.
4. ag grĕss̨′ ĭvę ; *a.* making the first attack.
4. In′ tu ĭ′ tion ; *n.* immediate knowledge, without reasoning.
5. hŏm′ aǵę ; *n.* respect; honor.
6. trĕnch′ ąnt ; *a.* severe; sharp-cutting.
7. crĭt′ ĭ çĭş ĭng ; *v.* passing judgment upon.
8. prĕl′ atę ; *n.* a clergyman having authority over the lower clergy.

### John Hughes, First Archbishop of New York.

1. Archbishop Hughes was a self-made man, one of a class for which our country is remarkable. Our institutions, which foster and develop individualism, putting no limit to the aspirations or the possibilities of natural ability or genius, are the nursing mother of men like Hughes,—men of grit, of courage, of talent, and of perseverance. He rose by sheer strength of character and natural genius from the lowest to the highest rank.

2. Everything was against him when he landed on our shores. His race and religion were despised. He had very little education, no money, and no powerful friends. He began as a day-laborer in the fields and on the roadside. Almost without friends he succeeded; he persisted. He had formed a purpose and he would realize it. He studied; he prayed. With God and manly courage he conquered every difficulty.

3. He had the faith, the valor, the irrepressibility, and the piety of the old Irish race. His piety led him into the sanctuary; but if he had not become a priest, there was material in him to make a great general, a great lawyer, a great politician, or a great statesman. If he had not be-

come a bishop, he would have ranked in another career with other distinguished men of his race, with General Sheridan, Marshal Nugent, Count Taafe, O'Connell, O'Donnell, or O'Conor. He was physically as brave and as daring as the gallant soldier who made the wonderful ride down the Shenandoah valley. Had he lived in the Middle Ages he would have probably been made Pope, and ranked with Gregory VII. or Alexander III.

4. He would never have yielded to the despotism of a king or to the violence of a mob. The mob might kill him, but he would die with his face to the foe. He would not have been merely passive in a fight; his courage was active and aggressive. If the "Know-Nothings" had dared to carry out their threats, the archbishop himself would have planned and led the defense of his people and of his Church. He would never be found in the rear of a battle. With what a soldier's eye he followed the fights of the Civil War, and with what Napoleonic intuition he saw the strong and the weak points of the campaigns of our generals!

5. He had the diplomatic talent of a Richelieu. Secretary Seward, who was himself a clever statesman, recognizing his power and influence, saw in Archbishop Hughes an equal, if not a superior, to himself in the art of governing men. No one did more than the first Catholic Archbishop of New York for our country in her hour of peril, by his influence both at home and abroad. Let us hope that some day our grateful citizens, remembering his patriotism and all his services to his country, will erect to his memory a statue to perpetuate his fame. It should be erected near that of his friends, the great secretary of state, Seward, and the great war-president, Lincoln. Less worthy citizens have received this homage after their death.

6. But whatever our citizens or the State may do to

keep his memory green, the Catholic Church in America, and especially in New York, will never forget his invaluable services. He found her on the ground, despised and dejected. He lifted her up and made her respectable. She was looked upon as the despised sect of foreign immigrants; he made her respected and feared. How he fought, and how he despised, and how he struck those who assailed her! He stood in front, like a giant, dealing death-blows to prejudice and bigotry. He exposed them to public contempt and ridicule by his trenchant logic, his cutting sarcasm, and his clear statement of the truth. He fought for God, his Church, and his country. If he did not succeed in everything, his failures were few. He failed to secure the blessings of religious education for the children of the public schools. But his arguments in this cause live after him, and have never been answered.

7. He was a man both feared and loved; but no one hated or could hate him. Even those who feared him admired him. He was so open, so just, so fair, so impartial, and so manly in his fight for what he thought right. I crossed the ocean with him in 1862. I was then a young priest, returning home from the Eternal City. He was coming back after his mission to Europe, where he had done so much to keep France and England from recognizing the Southern Confederacy. I remember how he used to stand in the evening in some sheltered spot, surrounded by a group of passengers anxious to catch a word from his lips. Every one listened to him as to a chief, a leader, an oracle. He stood among the passengers like one born to command. He seemed the owner of the vessel, and he looked as if he could command the very waves. I remember how he defended our national Government from some who were criticising it; how warmly he praised our

free institutions, showed the error of the Southern secession and the necessity of sticking to the Union. His voice was clear, his manner quiet, but his words were forcible and silenced the critic.

8. The free institutions of America were almost as dear to him as his Christian faith. Take him all in all he was not only the greatest prelate the Catholic Church in America has ever had, but he was as great and as good a citizen as ever deserved well of the American republic. Let her do him honor !
Rev. Henry A. Brann, D.D.

John Hughes, first Archbishop of New York, was born June 24, 1797, at Annaloghan, County Tyrone, Ireland, and died in January, 1864.

The " Know-Nothing " (4) was a secret political party, the object of which was not only to oppose Catholics in every way, but more especially to prevent them from holding public office. The " Know-Nothings " burned several Catholic churches, and caused many bloody riots. They threatened to burn and destroy the old St. Patrick's Cathedral, New York, but were deterred by the action of Archbishop Hughes.

Armand Jean Duplessis, Cardinal, Duke of Richelieu (5), was an eminent French statesman and for many years minister of state under Louis XIII. By a succession of vigorous and energetic measures Richelieu succeeded in breaking down the political power of the nobles, which till then had been absolute, and bringing France under the control of the King.

Who was Secretary Seward (5) ? Which is " the Eternal City " (7) ? What was " the Southern Confederacy " (7) ?

---

Better than gold is a peaceful home<br>
Where all the fireside characters come,<br>
The shrine of love, the heaven of life,<br>
Hallowed by mother, or sister, or wife.<br>
However humble the home may be,<br>
Or tried with sorrow by heaven's decree,<br>
The blessings that never were bought or sold,<br>
And center there, are better than gold.

## LESSON XXXVI.

2. dôr′ mẽr-wĭn′ dowṣ; *n.* windows placed on the inclined plane of the roof of a house.
2. kĭr′ tlĕs; *n.* gowns.
2. dĭs′ tạff; *n.* the staff for holding the bunch of flax, etc., from which the thread is drawn in spinning by hand.
5. stạl′worth; *a.* strong; bold; brave.
5. kĭnĕ; *n.* cows.
6. hy̆s′ sŏp; *n.* a plant having an aromatic smell and a pungent taste.
6. e thē′ re ạl; *a.* spirit-like.
8. wạĭns; *n.* wagons.

### Evangeline.

1. In the Acadian land, on the shores of the Basin of Minas
   Distant, secluded, still, the little village of Grand-Pré
   Lay, in the fruitful valley. Vast meadows stretched to the eastward,
   Giving the village its name, and pasture to flocks without number.
   Dikes, that the hands of the farmers had raised with labor incessant,
   Shut out the turbulent tides; but at stated seasons the flood-gates
   Opened, and welcomed the sea to wander at will o'er the meadows.
   West and south there were fields of flax, and orchards and corn-fields
   Spreading afar and unfenced o'er the plain; and away to the northward
   Blomidon rose, and the forests old, and aloft on the mountains
   Sea-fogs pitched their tents, and mists from the mighty Atlantic
   Looked on the happy valley, but ne'er from their station descended.

2. There, in the midst of its farms, reposed the Acadian
    village.
   Strongly built were the houses, with frames of oak and
    of hemlock,
   Such as the peasants of Normandy built in the reign of
    the Henries.
   Thatched were the roofs, with dormer-windows; and
    gables projecting
   Over the basement below, protected and shaded the
    doorway.
   There, in the tranquil evenings of summer, when
    brightly the sunset
   Lighted the village street, and gilded the vanes on the
    chimneys,
   Matrons and maidens sat in snow-white caps, and in
    kirtles
   Scarlet and blue and green, with distaffs spinning the
    golden
   Flax for the gossiping looms, whose noisy shuttles
    within doors
   Mingled their sound with the whir of the wheels and
    the songs of the maidens.

3. Solemnly down the street came the parish priest, and
    the children
   Paused in their play to kiss the hand he extended to
    bless them.
   Reverend walked he among them; and up rose ma-
    trons and maidens,
   Hailing his slow approach with words of affectionate
    welcome.
   Then came the laborers home from the field, and
    serenely the sun sank

Down to his rest, and twilight prevailed. Anon from the belfry
Softly the Angelus sounded, and over the roofs of the village
Columns of pale blue smoke, like clouds of incense ascending,
Rose from a hundred hearths, the homes of peace and contentment.

4. Thus dwelt together in love these simple Acadian farmers—
Dwelt in the love of God and of man. Alike were they free from
Fear, that reigns with the tyrant, and envy, the vice of republics.
Neither locks had they to their doors nor bars to their windows;
But their dwellings were open as day and the hearts of the owners;
There the richest was poor, and the poorest lived in abundance.

5. Somewhat apart from the village, and nearer the Basin of Minas,
Benedict Bellefontaine, the wealthiest farmer of Grand-Pré,
Dwelt on his goodly acres; and with him, directing his household,
Gentle Evangeline lived, his child, and the pride of the village.
Stalworth and stately in form was the man of seventy winters;
Hearty and hale was he, an oak that is covered with snow-flakes;

White as the snow were his locks, and his cheeks as
    brown as the oak-leaves.
Fair was she to behold, that maiden of seventeen sum-
    mers.
Black were her eyes as the berry that grows on the
    thorn by the wayside,
Black, yet how softly they gleamed, beneath the brown
    shade of her tresses!
Sweet was her breath as the breath of kine that feed in
    the meadows.

6. Fairer was she when, on Sunday morn, while the bell
    from its turret
    Sprinkled with holy sounds the air, as the priest with
        his hyssop
    Sprinkles the congregation, and scatters blessings upon
        them,
    Down the long street she passed, with her chaplet of
        beads and her missal,
    Wearing her Norman cap, and her kirtle of blue, and
        the ear-rings
    Brought in the olden time from France, and since, as an
        heirloom,
    Handed down from mother to child, through long gen-
        erations.
    But a celestial brightness—a more ethereal beauty—
    Shone on her face and encircled her form when, after
        confession,
    Homeward serenely she walked with God's benediction
        upon her.
    When she had passed, it seemed like the ceasing of ex
        quisite music.

7. Firmly builded with rafters of oak, the house of the farmer
　Stood on the side of a hill commanding the sea; and a shady
　Sycamore grew by the door, with a woodbine wreathing around it.
　Rudely carved was the porch, with seats beneath; and a foot-path
　Led through an orchard wide, and disappeared in the meadow.
　Under the sycamore-tree were hives overhung by a penthouse,
　Such as the traveler sees in regions remote by the roadside,
　Built o'er a box for the poor, or the blessed image of Mary.

8. Farther down, on the slope of the hill, was the well with its moss-grown
　Bucket, fastened with iron, and near it a trough for the horses.
　Shielding the house from storms, on the north, were the barns and the farm-yard;
　There stood the broad-wheeled wains and the antique plows and the harrows.
　Bursting with hay were the barns, themselves a village. In each one
　Far o'er the gable projected a roof of thatch; and a staircase,
　Under the sheltering eaves, led up to the odorous corn-loft.
　There, too, the dove-cot stood, with its meek and innocent inmates

Murmuring ever of love; while above in the variant breezes

Numberless noisy weathercocks rattled and sang of mutation.

Thus, at peace with God and the world, the farmer of Grand-Pré

Lived on his sunny farm, and Evangeline governed his household.
　　　　　　　　　　　　　　　HENRY W. LONGFELLOW.

The "Acadian land" (1) refers to Nova Scotia, which was originally known as Acadia. "The Basin of Minas" (1) is in the Bay of Fundy. "Grand-Pré" (1) means *Great Meadows*, hence the line "giving the village its name." Normandy (2) was formerly a province in the north of France, bordering on the English Channel.

## LESSON XXXVII.

1. ap prē' cĭ āte; *v.* estimate justly.
1. căl' a băsh eş; *n.* fruit of the calabash tree; when dried and cleaned they are used for cups, bottles, etc.
3. răt tăn'; *n.* the stem of a plant growing in India.
3. joists; *n.* small pieces of timber.
4. ē' las tĭç' ĭ tȳ; *n.* springiness.
8. gŭl' lĭeş; *n.* hollows worn in the earth by a current of water.
10. dī ăg' o năl; *a.* crossing at an angle.

### Bamboo. Part I.

1. During my many journeys in Borneo, and especially during my various residences among the Dyaks, I first came to appreciate the admirable qualities of the bamboo. In those parts of South America which I had previously visited, these gigantic grasses were comparatively scarce, and where found but little used, their place being taken, as to one class of uses, by the great variety of palms, and as to another, by calabashes and gourds. Almost all tropical countries produce bamboos, and wherever they are found in abundance the natives apply them to a variety of uses.

2. Their strength, lightness, smoothness, straightness, roundness, and hollowness, the facility and regularity with which they can be split, their many different sizes, the varying length of their joints, the ease with which they can be cut and with which holes can be made through them, their hardness outside, their freedom from any pronounced taste or smell, their great abundance, and the rapidity of their growth and increase, are all qualities which render them useful for a hundred different purposes, to serve which, other materials would require much more labor and preparation. The bamboo is one of the most wonderful as well as beautiful productions of the tropics, and one of nature's most valuable gifts to uncivilized man.

3. The Dyak houses are all raised on posts, and are often two or three hundred feet long and forty or fifty feet wide. The floor is always formed of strips, split from large bamboos, each nearly flat, and about three inches wide, and these are firmly tied down with rattan to the joists beneath. When well made, this is a delightful floor to walk upon barefooted, the rounded surfaces of the bamboo being very smooth and agreeable to the feet, while at the same time affording a firm hold.

4. But what is more important, they form, with a mat over them, an excellent bed, the elasticity of the bamboo and its rounded surface being far superior to a more rigid and a flatter floor. Here we at once find a use for bamboo which cannot be supplied so well by another material without a vast amount of labor. Palms and other substitutes require much cutting and smoothing, and are not equally good when finished.

5. When, however, a flat, close floor is required, excellent boards are made by splitting open large bamboos on one side only, and flattening them out so as to form thin

boards eighteen inches wide and six feet long, with which some Dyaks floor their houses. These, with constant rubbing of the feet and the smoke of years, become dark and polished, like walnut or old oak, so that their real material can hardly be recognized.

6. What labor is here saved to a savage, whose only tools are an ax and a knife, and who, if he wants boards, must hew them out of the solid trunk of a tree, and give days and weeks of labor to obtain a surface as smooth and beautiful as the bamboo thus treated affords him!

7. Again, if a temporary house is wanted, either by the native on his plantation or by the traveler in the forest, nothing is so convenient as the bamboo, with which a house can be constructed with a quarter of the labor and time required if other materials were used.

8. The Dyaks in the interior make paths for long distances, from village to village, and to their cultivated grounds, in the course of which they have to cross many gullies and ravines, and even rivers, or sometimes, to avoid a long circuit, to carry the path along the face of a precipice. In all these cases, the bridges they construct are of bamboo, and so admirably adapted is the material for this purpose, that it seems doubtful whether they would ever have attempted such works if they had not possessed it.

9. The Dyak bridge is simple but well designed. It consists merely of stout bamboos crossing each other at the roadway like the letter X, and rising a few feet above it. At the crossing they are firmly bound together, and to a large bamboo which lies upon them, and forms the only pathway, with a slender and often very shaky one to serve as a hand-rail.

10. When a river is to be crossed, an overhanging tree

is chosen, from which the bridge is partly suspended and partly supported by diagonal braces from the banks, so as to avoid placing posts in the stream itself, which would be liable to be carried away by floods.

11. In carrying a path along the face of the precipice, trees and roots are made use of for suspension; braces arise from suitable notches or crevices in the rocks; and if these are not sufficient, immense bamboos, fifty or sixty feet long, are fixed on the banks or on the branch of a tree below.

12. These bridges are traversed daily by men and women carrying heavy loads, so that any insecurity is soon discovered, and, as the materials are close at hand, immediately repaired.

13. When a path goes over very steep ground, and becomes slippery in very wet or very dry weather, the bamboo is used in another way. Pieces are cut about a yard long, and opposite notches being made at each end, holes are formed through which pegs are driven, and firm and convenient steps are thus constructed with the greatest ease and celerity. It is true that much of this will decay in one or two seasons; but it can be so quickly replaced as to make it more economical than using a harder and more durable wood.

Borneo (1) is an island in the Indian Archipelago. Next to Australia it is the largest island in the world.

The Dyaks (1) are the aboriginal inhabitants of the island of Borneo. They are well formed, yellowish in color, cruel, and wild; when once their favor is won they prove faithful friends.

Where do the bamboos grow? What qualities render them useful for a hundred different purposes? Tell how the Dyak houses are made. What sort of a bed does bamboo make? How are boards made when a flat, close floor is required? How is a Dyak bridge made?

## LESSON XXXVIII.

6. scrăm' blĕd; *v.* climbed with hands and feet.
7. prŏp' ẽr tĭĕs; *n.* the peculiar qualities of anything.
8. çȳ lĭn' drĭc ạl; *a.* having a roller-like form.
10. cŏn' ic ạl; *a.* having a circle for its base and its top ending in a point.
11. ăq' ue dŭcts; *n.* artificial channels for conveying water.
12. u tĕn' sĭls; *n.* that which is used; especially an instrument or vessel used in a kitchen, or in domestic and farming business.
13. ŏb lique' lȳ; *adv.* in a slanting manner.

### Bamboo. Part II.

1. One of the most striking uses to which bamboo is applied by the Dyaks is to assist them in climbing lofty trees. One day I was so fortunate as to shoot a small monkey, which fell dead, but caught in a fork of a tree and remained fixed. As I was very anxious to get it, I tried to persuade two young Dyaks who were with me to cut down the tree, which was tall, perfectly straight, and smooth-barked, and without a branch for fifty or sixty feet.

2. To my surprise they said they would prefer climbing up it, although it would be a good deal of trouble; but after a little talking together, they said they would try. They first went to a clump of bamboos that stood near, and cut down one of the largest stems. From this they chopped off a short piece, and splitting it, made a couple of stout pegs, about a foot long, and sharp at one end.

3. Then cutting a thick piece of wood for a mallet, they drove one of the pegs into the tree and hung their weight upon it. It held, and this seemed to satisfy them, for they immediately began making a quantity of pegs of the same kind, while I looked on with great interest, wondering how they could possibly ascend such a lofty tree by merely

driving pegs in it, the failure of any one of which at a good height would certainly cause their death.

4. When about two dozen pegs were made, one of them began cutting some very long and slender bamboo from another clump, and also prepared some cord from the bark of a small tree. They now drove in a peg very firmly at about three feet from the ground, and bringing one of the long bamboos, stood it upright, close to the tree, and bound it firmly to the first two pegs, by means of the bark cord and small notches near the head of each peg.

5. One of the Dyaks now stood on the first peg, and drove in a third, about level with his face, to which he tied the bamboo in the same way, and then mounted another step, standing on one foot, and holding by the bamboo at the peg immediately above him, while he drove in the next one. In this manner he ascended about twenty feet, when the upright bamboo becoming thin, another was handed up by his companion, and this was joined on by tying both bamboos to three or four of the pegs.

6. When this was also nearly ended, a third was added, and shortly after the lowest branches of the tree were reached, along which the young Dyak scrambled, and soon sent the monkey tumbling headlong down.

7. I was exceedingly struck by the ingenuity of this mode of climbing, and the admirable manner in which the peculiar properties of the bamboo were made available. The ladder itself was perfectly safe, since if any one peg were loose or faulty, and gave way, the strain would be thrown on several others above and below it. I now understood the use of the line of bamboo pegs sticking in trees, which I had often seen and wondered for what purpose they could have been put there.

8. This method of climbing is constantly used in order

to obtain wax, which is one of the most valuable products of the country. The honey-bee of Borneo very generally hangs its combs under the branches of the tappan, a tree which towers above all others in the forest, and whose smooth, cylindrical trunk often rises a hundred feet without a branch. The Dyaks climb these lofty trees at night, building up their bamboo ladder as they go, and bringing down gigantic honeycombs.

9. These furnish them with a delicious feast of honey and young bees, and also wax which they sell to traders and with its proceeds buy the much-coveted brass wire, ear-rings, and gold-edged handkerchiefs with which they love to decorate themselves. In ascending durion and other fruit trees, which branch at from thirty to fifty feet from the ground, I have seen them use the bamboo pegs only, without the upright bamboo which renders them so much more secure.

10. The outer rind of the bamboo, split and shaved thin, is the strongest material for baskets; hen-coops, bird-cages, and conical fish-traps are very quickly made from a single joint, by splitting the skin in narrow strips, which are left attached to one end, while rings of the same material, or rattan, are twisted in at regular distances.

11. Water is brought to the house by little aqueducts formed of large bamboos split in half and supported on crossed sticks of various heights to give it a regular fall. Thin long-jointed bamboos form the Dyak's only water vessels, and a dozen of them stand in the corner of every house. They are clean, light, and easily carried, and are in many ways superior to earthen vessels for the same purpose.

12. They also make excellent cooking utensils; vegetables can be boiled in them to perfection, and they are

often used when traveling. Salted fruit or fish, sugar, vinegar, and honey are preserved in them instead of in jars or bottles. In a small bamboo case, prettily carved and ornamented, the Dyak carries his materials for betel chewing, and his little long-bladed knife has a bamboo sheath.

13. His favorite pipe is a large hubble-bubble, which he will construct in a few minutes, by inserting a small piece of bamboo obliquely, about six inches from the bottom, into a large cylinder containing water. Through this the smoke passes to a long, slender bamboo tube.

14. There are many other small matters for which bamboo is daily used, but enough has now been mentioned to show its value. In other parts of the archipelago I have myself seen it applied to many new uses, and it is probable that my limited means of observation did not make me acquainted with one half the ways in which it is serviceable to the Dyaks. A. R. WALLACE.

Betel (12) is a narcotic stimulant, much used in the East. It consists of a leaf of a certain kind of pepper, plucked green, spread over with moistened quick-lime, and wrapped around a few scrapings of the betel-nut. This is chewed by men and women in the East Indies, from morning to night.

Hubble-bubble (13) is a tobacco-pipe arranged with a lower vessel or jar containing water. Through this the smoke passes and is cooled. The bubbling noise caused by the passage of the smoke gives the pipe its name.

Tell how the Dyak climbs lofty trees. What valuable product of the country is obtained by climbing the trees? Where does the honey-bee of Borneo generally hang its combs? How high does the tappan tree grow? What does the native buy with the proceeds of the wax? How does he ascend the durion and other fruit trees? What does the Dyak make of bamboo? How is water brought to the Dyak's house? What other utensils are made of bamboo? Which is the favorite pipe of the Dyak? How does he make it?

## LESSON XXXIX.

1. yōre; *adv.* in old time.
2. ĕn shroud'; *v.* cover, as with a shroud.
2. wān' ing; *v.* failing.
3. sheen; *n.* brightness.
3. ĕm blā' zŏnĕd; *v.* adorned; decorated.
5. pĭn' ions; *n.* wings.

### Erin's Flag.

1. Unroll Erin's flag! fling its folds to the breeze!
Let it float o'er the land, let it flash o'er the seas!
Lift it out of the dust—let it wave as of yore,
When its chiefs with their clans stood around it and swore
That never! no, never! while God gave them life,
And they had an arm and a sword for the strife,
That never! no, never! that banner should yield
As long as the heart of a Celt was its shield;
While the hand of a Celt had a weapon to wield,
And his last drop of blood was unshed on the field.

2. Lift it up! wave it high! 'tis as bright as of old!
Not a stain on its green nor a blot on its gold,
Though the woes and the wrongs of three hundred long years
Have drenched Erin's Sunburst with blood and with tears!
Though the clouds of oppression enshroud it in gloom,
And around it the thunders of Tyranny boom.
Look aloft! look aloft! lo! the cloud's drifting by,
There's a gleam through the gloom, there's a light in the sky,
'Tis the Sunburst resplendent—far-flashing on high!
Erin's dark night is waning; her day-dawn is nigh!

3. Lift it up! lift it up! the old banner of green!
   The blood of its sons has but brightened its sheen;
   What though the tyrant has trampled it down,
   Are its folds not emblazoned with deeds of renown?
   What though for ages it droops in the dust,
   Shall it droop thus forever? No! no! God is just!
   Take it up! take it up! from the tyrant's foul tread
   Let him tear the Green Flag—we will snatch its last shred,
   And beneath it we'll bleed as our forefathers bled,
   And we'll vow by the dust in the graves of our dead,

4. And we'll swear by the blood which the Briton has shed,
   And we'll vow by the wrecks which through Erin he spread,
   And we'll swear by the thousands who, famished, unfed,
   Died down in the ditches, wild-howling for bread,
   And we'll vow by our heroes whose spirits have fled,
   And we'll swear by the bones in each coffinless bed,
   That we'll battle the Briton through danger and dread!
   That we'll cling to the cause which we glory to wed,
   Till the gleam of our steel and the shock of our lead
   Shall prove to our foe that we meant what we said—
   That we'll lift up the green, and we'll tear down the red!

5. Lift up the Green Flag! oh! it wants to go home,
   Full long has its lot been to wander and roam,
   It has followed the fate of its sons o'er the world,
   But its folds, like their hopes, are not faded nor furled,
   Like a weary-winged bird, to the East and the West
   It has flitted and fled—but it never shall rest,

Till, pluming its pinions, it sweeps o'er the main,
And speeds to the shores of its old home again,
When its fetterless folds o'er each mountain and plain
Shall wave with a glory that never shall wane.

6. Take it up! take it up! bear it back from afar!
That Banner must blaze 'mid the lightnings of war;
Lay your hands on its folds, lift your gaze to the sky,
And swear that you'll bear it triumphant or die,
And shout to the clans scattered over the earth
To join in the march to the land of their birth;
And wherever the Exiles, 'neath heaven's broad dome,
Have been fated to suffer, to sorrow and roam,
They'll bound on the sea, and away o'er the foam
They'll sail to the music of " Home, Sweet Home!"

REV. ABRAM J. RYAN.

**Rev. Abram Joseph Ryan,** known as the "Poet-priest of the South," was the writer of many graceful and vigorous verses, and also won distinction as an orator, a lecturer, and an essayist. The exact date and place of his birth are uncertain, though it is believed he was born in this country about the year 1836. During the Civil War he was a chaplain in the Southern army. Afterward he was stationed in various places until 1870, when he was appointed pastor of St. Mary's Church, Mobile, which position he occupied for nearly thirteen years. His remaining years were devoted to literary labors. He died April 23, 1886.

"Erin's Sunburst" (2) is the Irish emblem, so called because it represents the rising sun. When was it that "thousands who, famished, unfed, died down in the ditches, wild-howling for bread" (4)? Give a synonym for "pluming its pinions" (5). Who are the "Exiles" (6)?

Let the pupils give the sense of the second stanza in their own language, changing the wording as much as possible.

## LESSON XL.

1. hăg' gard ; *a.* having the look of being wasted by want.
2. hŭm' mŏċks ; *n.* piles of ice.
3. ŭn' ŏn cŭm' bēr̃ed ; *v.* free from burdens.
4. pĕrm' mĭ căn ; *n.* meat dried in the sun.
7. flōe ; *n.* a large surface of ice floating in the ocean.
7. cāċhe ; *n.* a hiding-place or hole in the ground.
8. căus' tic ; *n.* a substance which, when applied to the flesh, will burn.

### Lost on the Floes. Part I.

1. We were only waiting for intelligence that our advance party had deposited its provisions in safety to begin our transit of the bay. We were at work cheerfully, sewing away at the skins of some moccasins by the blaze of our lamps, when, toward midnight, we heard the noise of steps above, and the next minute Sontag, Ohlsen, and Petersen came down into the cabin. Their manner startled me even more than their unexpected appearance on board. They were swollen and haggard, and hardly able to speak.

2. Their story was a fearful one. They had left their companions in the ice, risking their own lives to bring us the news: Brooks, Baker, Wilson, and Pierre were all lying frozen and disabled. Where? They could not tell: somewhere in among the hummocks to the north and east; it was drifting heavily round them when they parted. Irish Tom had stayed by to feed and care for the others; but the chances were sorely against them. It was in vain to question them further. They had evidently traveled a great distance, for they were sinking with fatigue and hunger, and could hardly be rallied enough to tell us the direction in which they had come.

3. My first impulse was to move on the instant with an unencumbered party: a rescue to be effective, or even

hopeful, could not be too prompt. What pressed on my mind most was, where the sufferers were to be looked for among the drifts. Ohlsen seemed to have his faculties rather more at command than his associates, and I thought that he might assist us as a guide; but he was sinking with exhaustion, and if he went with us we must carry him.

4. There was not a moment to lose. While some were still busy with the newcomers and getting ready a hasty meal, others were rigging out the Little Willie with a buffalo cover, a small tent, and a package of pemmican; and as soon as we could hurry through our arrangements, Ohlsen was strapped on in a fur bag, his legs wrapped in dogskins and eider-down, and we were off upon the ice. Our party consisted of nine men and myself. We carried only the clothes on our backs. The thermometer stood at —46 degrees, seventy-eight degrees below the freezing-point.

5. A well-known peculiar tower of ice, called by the men the "Pinnacly Berg," served as our first landmark; other icebergs of colossal size, which stretched in long, beaded lines across the bay, helped to guide us afterward; and it was not until we had traveled for sixteen hours that we began to lose our way.

6. We knew that our lost companions must be somewhere in the area before us, within a radius of forty miles. Mr. Ohlsen, who had been for fifty hours without rest, fell asleep as soon as we began to move, and awoke now with unequivocal signs of mental disturbance. It became evident that he had lost the bearing of the icebergs, which in form and color endlessly repeated themselves; and the uniformity of the vast field of snow utterly forbade the hope of local landmarks.

7. Pushing ahead of the party, and clambering over

some rugged ice piles, I came to a long, level floe, which I thought might probably have attracted the eyes of weary men in circumstances like our own. It was a light conjecture; but it was enough to turn the scale, for there was no other to balance it. I gave orders to abandon the sledge and disperse in search of foot-marks. We raised our tent, placed our pemmican in cache, except a small allowance for each man to carry on his person; and poor Ohlsen, now just able to keep his legs, was liberated from his bag.

8. The thermometer had fallen by this time to $-49$ degrees, and the wind was setting in sharply from the northwest. It was out of the question to halt: it required brisk exercise to keep us from freezing. I could not even melt ice for water; and, at these temperatures, any resort to snow for the purpose of allaying thirst was followed by bloody lips and tongue: it burned like caustic.

9. It was indispensable, then, that we should move on, looking out for traces as we went. Yet when the men were ordered to spread themselves, so as to multiply the chances, though they all obeyed heartily, some painful impress of solitary danger, or perhaps it may have been the varying configuration of the ice-field, kept them closing up continually into a single group.

10. The strange manner in which some of us were affected I now attribute as much to shattered nerves as to the direct influence of the cold. Men like McGary and Bonsall, who had stood out our severest marches, were seized with trembling-fits and short breath, and, in spite of all my efforts to keep up an example of sound bearing, I fainted twice on the snow.

11. We had been nearly eighteen hours out without water or food, when a new hope cheered us. I think it was Hans, our Esquimau hunter, who thought he saw a

broad sledge-track. The drift had nearly effaced it, and we were some of us doubtful at first whether it was not one of those accidental rifts which the gales make in the surface snow.

12. But as we traced it on to the deep snow among the hummocks, we were led to footsteps; and following these with religious care, we at last came in sight of a small American flag fluttering from a hummock. It was the camp of our disabled comrades; we reached it after an unbroken march of twenty-one hours.

13. The little tent was nearly covered. I was not among the first to come up; but, when I reached the tent curtain, the men were standing in silent file on each side of it. With more kindness and delicacy of feeling than is often supposed to belong to sailors, but which is almost characteristic, they intimated their wish that I should go in alone. As I crawled in, and, coming upon the darkness, heard before me the burst of welcome gladness that came from the four poor fellows stretched on their backs, and then for the first time the cheer outside, my weakness and my gratitude together almost overcame me. "They had expected me: they were sure I would come!"

Explain the expressions: "could hardly be rallied enough" (2); "icebergs of colossal size" (5); "it was a light conjecture" (7); "with religious care" (12).

The "Little Willie" (4) was the name given to a sledge. An "Esquimau" (11) is an Indian of any of the tribes inhabiting Arctic America or Greenland.

---

Howe'er it be, it seems to me
'Tis only noble to be good:
Kind hearts are more than coronets,
And simple faith than Norman blood.

TENNYSON.

## LESSON XLI.

4. ĕs sĕn' tial ; *a.* highly important.
5. stăy ; *v.* to hold.
6. su pẽr' flu ŏus ; *a.* more than is sufficient; unnecessary.
7. prē' mo nī' tion ; *n.* a previous warning.
8. le thär' ġie ; *a.* strangely inclined to sleep.
9. ar tīc' ṳ lāte ; *v.* to utter any words.

### Lost on the Floes. Part II.

1. We were now fifteen souls ; the thermometer 75 degrees below the freezing-point, and our sole accommodation a tent barely able to contain eight persons ; more than half our party were obliged to keep from freezing by walking outside while the others slept. We could not halt long. Each of us took a turn of two hours' sleep ; and then we prepared for our homeward march.

2. We took with us nothing but the tent, furs to protect the rescued party, and food for a journey of fifty hours. Everything else was abandoned. Two large buffalo-bags, each made of four skins, were doubled up, so as to form a sort of sack, lined on each side by fur, closed at the bottom but open at the top. This was laid on the sledge ; the tent, smoothly folded, serving as a floor.

3. The sick, with their limbs sewed up carefully in reindeer-skins, were placed upon the bed of buffalo-robes, in a half-reclining posture ; other skins and blanket-bags were thrown above them ; and the whole litter was lashed together so as to allow but a single opening opposite the mouth for breathing.

4. This necessary work cost us a great deal of time and effort ; but it was essential to the lives of the sufferers. It took us no less than four hours to strip and refresh them, and then to embale them in the manner I have described.

Few of us escaped without frost-bitten fingers; the thermometer was 55 degrees below zero, and a slight wind added to the severity of the cold.

5. It was completed at last, however; all hands stood round; and, after repeating a short prayer, we set out on our retreat. It was fortunate indeed that we were not inexperienced in sledging over the ice. A great part of our track lay among a succession of hummocks; some of them extending in long lines, fifteen and twenty feet high, and so uniformly steep that we had to turn them by a considerable deviation from our direct course; others that we forced our way through, far above our heads in height, lying in parallel ridges, with the space between too narrow for the sledge to be lowered into it safely, and yet not wide enough for the runners to cross without the aid of ropes to stay them.

6. These spaces too were generally choked with light snow, hiding the openings between the ice fragments. They were fearful traps to disengage a limb from, for every man knew that a fracture or a sprain even would cost him his life. Besides all this, the sledge was top-heavy with its load: the maimed men could not bear to be lashed down tight enough to secure them against falling off. Notwithstanding our caution in rejecting every superfluous burden, the weight, including bags and tent, was eleven hundred pounds.

7. And yet our march for the first six hours was very cheering. We made, by vigorous pulls and lifts, nearly a mile an hour, and reached the new floes before we were absolutely weary. Our sledge sustained the trial admirably. Ohlsen, restored by hope, walked steadily at the leading belt of the sledge-lines; and I began to feel certain of reaching our half-way station of the day before, where we had left our tent. But we were still nine miles from it,

when, almost without premonition, we all became aware of an alarming failure of our energies.

8. I was of course familiar with the benumbed and almost lethargic sensation of extreme cold; but I had treated the sleepy comfort of freezing as something like the embellishment of romance. I had evidence now to the contrary.

9. Bonsall and Morton, two of our stoutest men, came to me, begging permission to sleep: "They were not cold: the wind did not enter them now: a little sleep was all they wanted!" Presently Hans was found nearly stiff under a drift; and Thomas, bolt upright, had his eyes closed, and could hardly articulate.

10. At last John Blake threw himself on the snow, and refused to rise. They did not complain of feeling cold: but it was in vain that I wrestled, boxed, ran, argued, jeered, or reprimanded; an immediate halt could not be avoided.

11. We pitched our tent with much difficulty. Our hands were too powerless to strike a fire; we were obliged to do without water or food. Even the spirits (whisky) had frozen at the men's feet, under all the coverings. We put Bonsall, Ohlsen, Thomas, and Hans, with the other sick men, well inside the tent, and crowded in as many others as we could. Then leaving the party with Mr. McGary, with orders to come on after four hours' rest, I pushed ahead with William Godfrey, who volunteered to be my companion.

**Explain** the expressions: "fifteen souls" (1); "the embellishment of romance" (8), "jeered or reprimanded" (10).

---

Eight hours to work, to soothing slumber seven,
Nine to the world allot, and *all* to heaven.

## LESSON XLII.

1. ăp′ pre hĕn′ sion ; *n.* idea.
2. jŭmp′ ẽr ; *n.* a fur under-jacket.
9. e mẽr′ ġen çў ; *n.* any event which calls for an immediate remedy.
10. de lĩr′ĭ ǫŭs ; *a.* wandering in mind.
13. strȧ bĭṣ′ mŭs ; *n.* squinting.
13. ăm′ pu tā′ tion ; *n.* the cutting off.

### Lost on the Floes. Part III.

1. My aim was to reach the half-way tent, and thaw some ice and pemmican before the others arrived. The floe was of level ice, and the walking excellent. I cannot tell how long it took us to make the nine miles; for we were in a strange sort of stupor, and had little apprehension of time. It was probably about four hours.

2. We kept ourselves awake by imposing on each other a continued articulation of words. I recall these hours as among the most wretched I have ever gone through ; we were neither of us in our right senses, and retained a very confused recollection of what preceded our arrival at the tent. We both of us, however, remember a bear that walked leisurely before us and tore up, as he went, a jumper that Mr. McGary had carelessly thrown off the day before. He tore it into shreds and rolled it into a ball, but never offered to interfere with our progress. I remember this, and with it a confused sentiment that our tent and buffalo-robes might probably share the same fate.

3. Godfrey had a better eye than myself; and, looking some miles ahead, he could see that our tent was undergoing the same unceremonious treatment. I thought I saw it too, but we were so drunken with cold that we strode on steadily, and, for aught I know, without quickening our pace.

4. Probably our approach saved the contents of the

tent; for when we reached it the tent was uninjured, though the bear had overturned it, tossing the buffalo-robes and pemmican into the snow; we missed only a couple of blanket-bags. What we recollect, however, and perhaps all we recollect, is that we had great difficulty in raising it.

5. We crawled into our reindeer sleeping-bags without speaking, and for the next three hours slept on in a dreamy but intense slumber. When I awoke, my long beard was a mass of ice, frozen fast to the buffalo-skin; Godfrey had to cut me out with his jackknife. Four days after our escape, I found my woolen comfortable with a goodly share of my beard still adhering to it.

6. We were able to melt water and get some soup cooked before the rest of our party arrived; it took them but five hours to walk the nine miles. They were doing well, and, considering the circumstances, were in wonderful spirits. The day was windless, with a clear sun. All enjoyed the refreshment we had got ready; the crippled were repacked in their robes; and we sped briskly toward the hummock-ridges which lay between us and the "Pinnacly Berg."

7. The hummocks we had now to meet came properly under the designation of squeezed ice. It required desperate efforts to work our way over the surface floes,— literally desperate, for our strength failed us anew, and we began to lose our self-control. We could not abstain any longer from eating snow; our mouths swelled, and some of us became speechless. Happily the day was warmed by a clear sunshine, and the thermometer rose to − 4 degrees in the shade; otherwise we must have frozen.

8. Our halts multiplied, and we fell half-sleeping on the snow. I could not prevent it. Strange to say, it refreshed us. I ventured upon the experiment myself, mak-

ing Riley wake me at the end of three minutes; and I felt so much benefited by it that I timed the men in the same way. They sat on the runners of the sledge, fell asleep instantly, and were forced to wakefulness when their three minutes were out.

9. By eight in the evening we emerged from the floes. The sight of the "Pinnacly Berg" revived us. Brandy, an invaluable resource in emergency, had already been served out in tablespoonful doses. We now took a longer rest, and a last but stouter dram, and reached the brig at 1 P.M., we believe without a halt.

10. I say *we believe;* and here perhaps is the most decided proof of our sufferings; we were quite delirious, and had ceased to entertain a sane apprehension of the circumstances about us. We moved on like men in a dream. Our foot-marks, seen afterward, showed that we had steered a bee-line for the brig. It must have been by a sort of instinct, for it left no impress on the memory.

11. Bonsall was sent staggering ahead, and reached the brig God knows how, for he had fallen repeatedly at the track lines; but he delivered with accuracy the messages I had sent by him to Dr. Hayes. I thought myself the soundest of all, and can recall the muttering delirium of my comrades when we got back into the cabin of our brig. Yet I have been told since of some speeches and some orders too of mine, which I should have remembered for their absurdity if my mind had retained its balance.

12. Petersen and Whipple came out to meet us about two miles from the brig. They brought my dog team, with the restoratives I had sent for by Bonsall. I do not remember their coming. Dr. Hayes entered with judicious energy upon the treatment our condition called for, administering morphine freely, after the usual frictions.

13. He reported none of our brain-symptoms as serious, referring them properly to the class of those indications of exhausted power which yield to generous diet and rest. Mr. Ohlsen suffered some time from strabismus and blindness; two others underwent amputation of parts of the foot, without unpleasant consequences; and two died in spite of all our efforts.

14. This rescue party had been out for seventy-two hours. We had halted in all eight hours, half of our number sleeping at a time. We traveled between eighty and ninety miles, most of the way dragging a heavy sledge. The mean temperature of the whole time, including the warmest hours of three days, was at −41 degrees. We had no water except at our two halts, and were at no time able to intermit vigorous exercise without freezing.

ELISHA KENT KANE.

**Elisha Kent Kane, M.D.**, was born in Philadelphia, February 3, 1820. He entered the University of Virginia, afterward studied medicine, and entered the navy as a surgeon. He visited many parts of the world and served in the Mexican War. In 1850 he began his career of Arctic discovery. In 1853 he commanded a second Arctic expedition, in which he gained important results. On his return home he was honored in many ways for his discoveries. His health failing, he went to Havana, where he died February 16, 1857, leaving a name distinguished as an explorer, an author, and a naturalist.

**Isaac Israel Hayes** (11), who was surgeon of Dr. Kane's Arctic expedition, was born in 1832 and died December 27, 1881. In 1860 he again visited the Arctic regions in command of an expedition, and in 1869 explored the southern coasts of Greenland. He was the author of several books recounting his adventures and discoveries in the frozen North.

**Explain** the expressions: "had little appreciation of time" (1) "unceremonious treatment" (3); "our halts multiplied" (8); "we had steered a bee-line" (10).

## LESSON XLIII.

1. mē' te ŏr; *n.* a bright body hovering in the air.
2. erī'sĭs; *n.* turning-point.
3. rĕc' re ănt; *a.* cowardly.
4. rīve; *v.* to rend asunder by force.
8. lăb' ă rŭm; *n.* a standard or flag.

### The American Flag.

1. They say I do not love thee,
    Flag of my native land,
   Whose meteor-folds above me
    To the free breeze expand;
   Thy broad stripes proudly streaming,
   And thy stars so brightly gleaming.

2. They say I would forsake thee,
    Should some dark crisis lower;
   That, recreant, I should make thee
    Crouch to a foreign power;
   Seduced by license ample,
   On thee, blest flag, to trample.

3. False are the words they utter,
    Ungenerous their brand,
   And rash the oaths they mutter,
    Flag of my native land;
   While still, in hope, above me
   Thou wavest—and I love thee!

4. They say that bolts of thunder,
    Hurled by the Pontiff's hand,
   May rive and bring thee under,
    Flag of my native land,
   And with one blow dissever
   My heart from thee forever.

5. God's is my love's first duty,
   To whose eternal Name
  Be praise for all thy beauty,
   Thy grandeur, and thy fame;
  But ever have I reckoned
  Thine, native flag, its second.

6. Woe to the foe or stranger
   Whose sacrilegious hand
  Would touch thee, or endanger,
   Flag of my native land!
  Though some would fain discard me,
  Mine should be raised to guard thee.

7. Then wave, thou first of banners,
   And in thy genial shade
  Let creeds, opinions, manners,
   In love and peace be laid;
  And there, all discord ended,
  Our hearts and souls be blended.

8. Stream on, stream on before us,
   Thou labarum of light,
  While in one general chorus
   Our vows to thee we plight;
  Unfaithful to thee?—Never!
  My country's flag forever!
  
  REV. CHARLES CONSTANTINE PISE, D.D.

Rev. Charles Constantine Pise, D.D., was born at Annapolis, Md., November 22, 1801. As a young man he joined the Society of Jesus, and went to Rome to pursue his theological studies, but his father dying, he returned home. In 1825 he was ordained priest, and was appointed as an assistant at the Cathedral, Baltimore. He was, later, sent to St. Matthew's Church, Washington, and while there was elected chaplain to the United States Senate, the only

Catholic priest, we believe, on whom that position was ever bestowed. At the time of his death, which occurred May 26, 1858, he was pastor of St. Charles Borromeo's Church, Brooklyn, N. Y. Dr. Pise was a graceful, prolific writer, the author of many books, a fine linguist, a man of elegant, polished manners.

## LESSON XLIV.

2. dr̄ŏm′e da rў; *n.* a species of camel.
3. im pĕt′u ǫŭs; *a.* passionate.
6. in stĭnċt′ ĭvḙ lў; *adv.* by natural impulse.
8. sten tō′ ri ąn; *a.* extremely loud.
11. ĕx′ e ḉrā′ tions; *n.* curses.
13. prox ĭm′ i tў; *n.* nearness.
14. dis ċŏm′ fit ed; *v.* defeated; overpowered.
16. in ḉĕn′ di a rў; *n.* a person who maliciously sets fire to a building.

### The Escape of Harvey Birch.

1. The gathering mists of evening had begun to darken the valley, as the detachment of Lawton made its reappearance at its southern extremity. The march of the troops was slow, and their line extended, for the benefit of ease in their progress. In the front rode the Captain, side by side with his senior subaltern, apparently engaged in close conference, while the rear was brought up by a young cornet, humming an air, and thinking of the sweets of a straw bed after the fatigues of a hard day's duty.

2. Stretching forward his body in the direction he was gazing, as if to aid him in distinguishing objects through the darkness, the Captain asked, "What animal is moving through the field on our right?"

"'Tis a man," said Mason, looking intently at the suspicious object.

"By his hump 'tis a dromedary," added the Captain, eying it keenly. Wheeling his horse suddenly from the highway, he exclaimed: "Harvey Birch, the peddler-spy! —take him, dead or alive!"

3. Mason and a few of the leading dragoons only understood the sudden cry, but it was heard throughout the line. A dozen of the men, with the Lieutenant at their head, followed the impetuous Lawton, and their speed threatened the pursued with a sudden termination of the race.

4. Birch prudently kept his position on the rock until evening had begun to shroud the surrounding objects in darkness. From this height he had seen all the events of the day as they occurred. He had watched, with a beating heart, the departure of the troops under Dunwoodie, and with difficulty had curbed his impatience until the obscurity of night should render his moving free from danger.

5. He had not, however, completed a fourth of his way to his own residence, when his quick ear distinguished the tread of the approaching horse. Trusting to the increasing darkness, he determined to persevere. By crouching and moving quickly along the surface of the ground, he hoped yet to escape unnoticed. Captain Lawton was too much engrossed in conversation to suffer his eyes to indulge in their usual wandering; and the peddler, perceiving by the voices that the enemy he most feared had passed, yielded to his impatience, and stood erect, in order to make greater progress. The moment his body arose above the shadow of the ground it was seen, and the chase commenced.

6. For a single instant Birch was helpless, his blood curdling in his veins at the imminence of the danger, and his legs refusing their natural, and what was now so necessary, office. But it was for a moment only. Casting his pack where he stood, and instinctively tightening the belt he wore, the peddler betook himself to flight. He new that by bringing himself in a line with his pursuers

and the wood, his form would be lost to sight. This he soon effected, and he was straining every nerve to gain the wood itself, when several horsemen rode by him but a short distance on his left, and cut him off from this place of refuge.

7. The peddler threw himself on the ground as they came near him, and was in this manner passed unseen. But delay now became too dangerous for him to remain in that position. He accordingly arose, and, still keeping in the shadow of the wood, along the skirts of which he heard voices crying to each other to be watchful, he ran with incredible speed in a parallel line, but in an opposite direction, to the march of the dragoons.

8. The confusion of the chase had been heard by the whole of the men, though none distinctly understood the order of Lawton but those who followed. The remainder were lost in doubt as to the duty that was required of them; and the aforesaid cornet was making eager inquiries of the trooper near him on the subject, when a man, at a short distance in his rear, crossed the road at a single bound. At the same instant, the stentorian voice of Captain Lawton rang through the valley shouting—"Harvey Birch!—take him, dead or alive!"

9. Fifty pistols lighted the scene instantly, and the bullets whistled in every direction round the head of the devoted peddler. A feeling of despair seized his heart, and he exclaimed bitterly—"Hunted like a beast of the forest!"

10. He felt life and its accompaniments to be a burden, and was about to yield himself to his enemies. Nature, however, prevailed; he feared that if taken he would not be honored with the forms of a trial, but that most probably the morning sun would witness his ignominious execution; for he had already been condemned to death, and

only escaped that fate by stratagem. These considerations, with the approaching footsteps of his pursuers, roused him to new exertions; and he fled again before them.

11. A fragment of a wall, that had withstood the ravages made by war in the adjoining fences of wood, fortunately crossed his path. He hardly had time to throw his exhausted limbs over this barrier, before twenty of his enemies reached its opposite side. Their horses refused to take the leap in the dark, and amid the confusion of the rearing chargers and the execrations of their riders, Birch was enabled to gain a sight of the base of the hill on whose summit was a place of perfect security against the approach of any foe.

12. The heart of the peddler now beat high with hope, when the voice of Captain Lawton again rang in his ears, shouting to his men to give him room. The order was obeyed, and the fearless trooper rode at the wall at the top of his horse's speed, plunged the rowels in his charger, and flew over the obstacle like lightning, and in safety. The triumphant hurrahs of the men, and the thundering tread of the horse, too plainly assured the peddler of the emergency of his danger. He was nearly exhausted, and his fate no longer seemed doubtful.

13. "Stop, or die!" was uttered above his head, in fearful proximity to his ears.

Harvey stole a glance over his shoulder, and saw, within a bound of him, the man he most dreaded. By the light of the stars he beheld the uplifted arm and the threatening saber. Fear, exhaustion, and despair seized on his heart, and the intended victim suddenly fell at the feet of the dragoon. The horse of Lawton struck the prostrate peddler, and both steed and rider came violently to the earth.

14. As quick as thought Birch was on his feet again,

HARVEY BIRCH SPARES CAPTAIN LAWTON'S LIFE.

and with the sword of the discomfited dragoon in his hand. Vengeance seems but too natural to human passions. There are few who have not felt the seductive pleasure of making our injuries recoil on their authors; and yet there are some who know how much sweeter it is to return good for evil. All the wrongs of the peddler shone on his brain with a dazzling brightness. For a moment the demon within him prevailed, and Birch brandished the powerful weapon in the air; in the next, it fell harmless on the reviving but helpless trooper; and the peddler vanished up the side of the friendly rock.

15. "Help Captain Lawton there!" cried Mason, as he rode up, followed by a dozen of his men; "and some of you dismount with me, and search these rocks; the villain lies here concealed."

"Hold!" roared the discomfited Captain, raising himself with difficulty to his feet; "if one of you dismounts, he dies; Tom, my good fellow, you will help me to straddle Roanoke again."

16. The astonished subaltern complied in silence, while the wondering dragoons remained as fixed in their saddles as if they composed part of the animals they rode.

"You are much hurt, I fear," said Mason, with something of condolence in his manner, as they re-entered the highway.

"Something so, I do believe," replied the Captain, catching his breath, and speaking with difficulty; "I wish our bone-setter was at hand to examine into the state of my ribs."

"Captain Lawton," said the orderly of his troop, riding to the side of his commanding officer, "we are now passing the house of the peddler spy; is it your pleasure that we burn it?"

"No!" roared the Captain, in a voice that startled the disappointed Sergeant; "are you an incendiary? would you burn the house in cold blood? Let a spark approach it, and the hand that carries it will never light another."

"There is life in the Captain, notwithstanding his tumble," exclaimed the sleepy cornet in the rear, as he was nodding on his horse. —JAMES FENIMORE COOPER.

James Fenimore Cooper was born at Burlington, N. J., September 15, 1789. As a lad he studied for three years at Yale College, and then entered the navy, but resigned at the time of his marriage in 1811. He settled at Mamaroneck, Westchester County, N. Y., and in that neighborhood is laid the scene of "The Spy," the story from which our Lesson is taken. Harvey Birch, a peddler and the hero of the tale, is a spy in the service of Washington, but so well is this secret guarded that the truth is not revealed until after his death. In the meanwhile he is hated and hunted by both Americans and British. The story bristles with adventure, is written in graphic style, and perhaps more than any other of his many books made Cooper's reputation. Cooper died September 14, 1851.

Give synonyms for "detachment" (1); "conference" (1); "termination" (3); "shroud" (4); "obscurity" (4); "engrossed" (5); "incredible" (7); "ravages" (11); "complied" (16).

## LESSON XLV.

2. ma tūre'; *a.* perfect.
2. be nĭg'nĭ tў; *n.* goodness.
6. mĕl'low ing; *v.* softening.
9. trăn'quil; *a.* peaceful.

### The Last of the Signers.

1. Come to the window, old man! Come, and look your last upon this beautiful earth! The day is dying—the year is dying—you are dying; so light, and leaf, and life mingle in one common death, as they shall mingle in one resurrection.

2. Clad in a dark morning gown, that revealed the outline of his tall form, now bent with age—once so beautiful

in its erect manhood, rises a man from his chair, which is covered with pillows, and totters to the window, spreading forth his thin, white hands. Did you ever see an old man's face that combines all the sweetness of childhood with the vigor of mature intellect? Snow-white hair, in waving flakes, around a high and open brow; eyes that gleam with clear light, a mouth moulded in an expression of benignity almost divine!

3. It is the fourteenth of November, 1832; the hour is sunset, and the man, Charles Carroll, of Carrollton, THE LAST OF THE SIGNERS. Ninety-five years of age, a weak and trembling old man, he has summoned all his strength, and gone along the carpeted chamber to the window, his dark gown contrasting with the purple curtains.

4. He is the last! Of the noble fifty-six who in the Revolution stood forth undismayed by the ax or gibbet—their mission, the freedom of an age, the salvation of a country—he alone remains! One by one, the pillars have crumbled from the roof of the temple, and now the last—a trembling column—glows in the sunlight, as it is about to fall.

5. But for the pillar that crumbles there is no hope that it shall ever tower aloft in its pride again, while for this old man, about to sink into the night of the grave, there is a glorious hope. His memory will live. His soul will live, not only in the presence of its God, but on the tongues and in the hearts of millions. The band in which he counts one can never be forgotten.

6. The last! As the venerable man stands before us, the declining day imparts a warm flush to his face, and surrounds his brow with a halo of light. His lips move without a sound: he is recalling the scenes of the Declaration—he is murmuring the names of his brothers in the

good work. All gone but he! Upon the woods dyed with the rainbow of the closing year, upon the stream darkened by masses of shadow, upon the home peeping out from among the leaves, falls mellowing the last light of the declining day.

7. He will never see the sun rise again! He feels that the silver cord is slowly, gently loosening; he knows the golden bowl is crumbling at the fountain's brink. But death comes on him as a sleep, as a pleasant dream, as a kiss from beloved lips! He feels that the land of his birth has become a mighty people, and thanks God that he was permitted to behold its blossoms of hope ripen into full life.

8. In the recesses near the window, you behold an altar of prayer; above it, glowing in the fading light, the image of Jesus seems smiling, even in agony, around that death-chamber. The old man turns aside from the window. Tottering on, he kneels beside the altar, his long dark robe drooping over the floor. He reaches forth his white hands—he raises his eyes to the face of the Crucified.

9. There, in the sanctity of an old man's last prayer, we will leave him. There where, amid the deepening shadows, glows the image of the Saviour; there where the light falls over the mild face, the wavy hair and tranquil eyes of the aged patriarch. The smile of the Saviour was upon that perilous day, the 4th of July, 1776; and now that its promise has brightened into fruition, He seems to—He does smile on it again—even as His sculptured image meets the dying gaze of Charles Carroll, of Carrollton, THE LAST OF THE SIGNERS. GEO. LIPPARD.

Charles Carroll, of Carrollton, the last of the signers of the Declaration of Independence, was born in 1737 and died November 14, 1832. He was an ardent patriot, a devout Catholic. "I have lived," he said, "to my ninety-sixth year. I have enjoyed continued health. I have been blessed with great wealth, prosperity, and most of the good things which the world could bestow—public approbation, esteem, applause—but that upon which I now look back with the greatest satisfaction to myself is that I have practiced the duties of religion."

What is the meaning of the expression "by the ax or gibbet"? (4).

The sentence "the silver cord is slowly, gently loosening; he knows the golden bowl is crumbling at the fountain's brink" (7) is a paraphrase of the verse from Ecclesiastes, xii. 6: "Before the silver cord be broken, and the golden fillet shrink back, and the pitcher be crushed at the fountain."

## LESSON XLVI.

1. lŭng' ing; *v.* thrusting.
1. grŭm' mēr; *a.* more rumbling.
2. hŏr' Ĭ zŏn' tạl; *a.* on a level.
3. mē' tēr; *n.* a regular succession of sounds.

### The Old Continentals.

1. In their ragged regimentals
   Stood the old Continentals,
      Yielding not
   When the Grenadiers were lunging,
   And like hail fell the plunging
      Cannon-shot:
      When the files
      Of the Isles,
From the smoky night encampment, bore the banner of the rampant
      Unicorn,
And grummer, grummer, grummer rolled the roll of the drummer,
      Through the morn!

2. But with eyes to the front all,
   And with guns horizontal,

Stood our sires;
And the balls whistled deadly,
And in streams flashing redly
   Blazed the fires;
   As the roar
   On the shore
Swept the strong battle-breakers o'er the green-sodded acres
   Of the plain;
And louder, louder, louder cracked the black gunpowder.
   Cracking amain!

3. Now like smiths at their forges
Worked the red St. George's
   Cannoneers;
And the "villainous saltpeter"
Rang a fierce, discordant meter
   Round their ears;
   As the swift
   Storm-drift,
With hot sweeping anger came the Horse-guards' clangor
   On our flanks.
Then higher, higher, higher burned the old-fashioned fire
   Through the ranks!

4. Then the old-fashioned Colonel
Galloped through the white infernal
   Powder-cloud;
His broad sword was swinging,
And his brazen throat was ringing
   Trumpet loud.
   Then the blue
   Bullets flew,

And the trooper-jackets redden at the touch of the leaden
Rifle-breath,
And rounder, rounder, rounder roared the iron six
pounder,
Hurling death.

GUY HUMPHREY McMASTER.

"The Old Continentals" (1) here referred to are the soldiers of our Revolutionary war, the men of the Continental army; the "files of the Isles" (1) are the rows of British soldiers, men from the British Isles. "The banner of the rampant Unicorn" (1) is the English flag, on which appears the unicorn, a fabulous animal. "St. George's cannoneers" (3) are the British gunners, St. George being the patron saint of England. "Villainous saltpeter" (3) means gunpowder, being so called by Hotspur when in Shakespeare's "King Henry IV." he quotes the fop who was sent to demand prisoners.

## LESSON XLVII.

1. å quăt' Ic; a. frequenting water.
2. ı dĕn' tĭ fīed; v. united in interest.
3. cu pĭd' Ĭ tỹ; n. eager desire to possess something.
4. tŭs' sŏ̧k; n. a knot or bunch of grass, twigs, or the like.
5. ăs' sĭ dū' ĭ tĭęs; n. close attentions.
6. u ṣûrp' ing; v. seizing without right.
7. whĭr' ring; v. flying with a buzzing sound.
8. plăĭn' tĭve; a. sad.
9. dĕ' vĭ ou̧s; a. winding.

### Quail.

1. The quail is peculiarly a domestic bird, and is attached to his birthplace and the home of his forefathers. The various members of the aquatic families educate their children in the cool summer of the far north, and bathe their warm bosoms in July in the iced waters of Hudson Bay; but when Boreas scatters the rushes where they had builded their bed-chambers they desert their fatherland, and fly to disport in the sunny waters of the south.

2. The songsters of the woodland, when their customary crops of insects and berries are cut off in the fall, gather themselves to renew their loves and get married in more genial climes. Presently, the groves so vocal and the sky so full shall be silent and barren. The "melancholy days" will soon be here; only thou, dear Bob White, wilt remain.

3. The quail is the bird for me. He is no rover, no emigrant. He stays at home, and is identified with the soil. Where the farmer works, he lives, and loves, and whistles. In budding spring-time and in scorching summer, in bounteous autumn and in barren winter, his voice is heard from the same bushy hedge-fence and from his customary cedars. Cupidity and cruelty may drive him to the woods and to seek more quiet seats; but be merciful and kind to him, and he will visit your barn-yard and sing for you upon the boughs of the apple-tree by your gateway.

4. When warm May first wooes the young flowers to open and receive her breath, then begin the cares and responsibilities of wedded life. Away fly the happy pair to seek some grassy tussock, where, safe from the eye of the hawk and the nose of the fox, they may rear their expectant brood in peace.

5. Oats harvest arrives, and the fields are waving with yellow grain. Now be wary, O kind-hearted cradler, and tread not into those pure white eggs ready to burst with life! Soon there is a peeping sound heard, and lo! a proud mother walketh magnificently in the midst of her children, scratching and picking, and teaching them how to swallow. Happy she if she may be permitted to bring them up to maturity and uncompelled to renew her joys in another nest!

6. The assiduities of a mother have a beauty and a

sacredness about them that command respect and reverence in all animal nature, human or inhuman—what a lie does that word carry!—except, perhaps, in monsters, insects, and fish. I never yet heard of the parental tenderness of a trout, eating up his little baby, nor of the filial gratitude of a spider, nipping the life out of his gray-headed father and usurping his web.

7. But if you would see the purest, the sincerest, the most affecting piety of a parent's love, startle a young family of quails, and watch the conduct of the mother. She will not leave you. No, not she. But she will fall at your feet, uttering a noise which none but a distressed mother can make, and she will run, and flutter, and seem to try to be caught, and cheat your outstretched hand, and affect to be wing-broken and wounded, and yet have just strength to tumble along, until she has drawn you, fatigued, a safe distance from her threatened children and the young hopes of her heart; and then will she mount, whirring with glad strength, and, away through the maze of trees you have not seen before, like a close-shot bullet, fly to her skulking infants.

8. Listen now. Do you hear those three half-plaintive notes, quickly and clearly poured out? She is calling the boys and girls together. She sings not now "Bob White!" nor "Ah! Bob White!" That is her husband's love-call, or his trumpet-blast of defiance. But she calls sweetly and softly for her lost children. Hear them "Peep! peep! peep!" at the welcome voice of their mother's love! They are coming together. Soon the whole family will meet again.

9. It is a foul sin to disturb them; but retread your devious way, and let her hear your coming footsteps, breaking down the briers, as you renew the danger. She is

quiet. Not a word is passed between the fearful fugitives. Now, if you have the heart to do it, lie low, keep still, and imitate the call of the hen-quail. O mother! mother! how your heart would die if you could witness the deception! The little ones raise up their trembling heads, and catch comfort and imagined safety from the sound. "Peep! peep!" They come to you, straining their little eyes, and, clustering together and answering, seem to say, "Where is she? Mother! mother! we are here!"

"Boreas" (1) means the north-wind, a name used by the ancient Greeks. "Bob White" (2) is a familiar name for the quail, given on account of its note. "Cradler" (5) is one who uses a *cradle*, an instrument which receives the grain as it is cut by the scythe, and lays it evenly in swaths or lines. "Trumpet-blast of defiance" (8) is an allusion to the custom among the knights of old of blowing a blast on a trumpet, as a challenge, when going out to fight.

## LESSON XLVIII.

4. Ĭm pär′ tial lȳ; *adv.* not favoring one more than another.
4. broid′ ēr̆ĕd; *v.* embroidered.
6. ŭp brā̆′d′ ing; *v.* blaming; reproaching.

### The Blue and the Gray.

1. By the flow of the inland river,
    Whence the fleets of iron have fled,
  Where the blades of the grave-grass quiver,
    Asleep are the ranks of the dead,—
      Under the sod and the dew,
        Waiting the judgment day:
      Under the one, the Blue;
      Under the other, the Gray.

2. These, in the robings of glory;
    Those, in the gloom of defeat;

All, with the battle-blood gory,
  In the dusk of eternity meet,—
    Under the sod and the dew,
      Waiting the judgment day:
    Under the laurel, the Blue;
      Under the willow, the Gray.

3. From the silence of sorrowful hours
    The desolate mourners go
  Lovingly laden with flowers,
    Alike for the friend and the foe,—
      Under the sod and the dew,
        Waiting the judgment day:
      Under the roses, the Blue;
        Under the lilies, the Gray.

4. So, with an equal splendor,
    The morning sun-rays fall,
  With a touch impartially tender,
    On the blossoms blooming for all,—
      Under the sod and the dew,
        Waiting the judgment day:
      Broidered with gold, the Blue;
        Mellowed with gold, the Gray.

5. So, when the summer calleth,
    On forest and field of grain,
  With an equal murmur falleth
    The cooling drip of the rain,—
      Under the sod and the dew,
        Waiting the judgment day:
      Wet with the rain, the Blue;
        Wet with the rain, the Gray.

6. Sadly, but not with upbraiding,
    The generous deed was done;
  In the storm of the years that are fading
    No braver battle was won,—
      Under the sod and the dew,
        Waiting the judgment day:
      Under the blossoms, the Blue;
        Under the garlands, the Gray.

7. No more shall the war-cry sever
    Or the winding rivers be red;
  They banish our anger forever
    When they laurel the graves of our dead—
      Under the sod and the dew,
        Waiting the judgment day:
      Love and tears, for the Blue;
        Tears and love, for the Gray.

FRANCIS MILES FINCH.

This poem was suggested by the action of the women of Columbus, Mississippi, who on Decoration Day strewed flowers impartially on the graves of the Northern and of the Southern soldiers.

The expression "fleets of iron" (1) is an allusion to the ironclad gunboats used during our civil war; "the Blue" (1) means the soldiers of the Northern army, whose uniforms were blue, while "the Gray" (1) refers to the men of the Southern army, who wore a gray uniform. "These" (2), that is, "the Blue," and "Those" (2), "the Gray." The "laurel" (2) is a symbol of victory, while the "willow" (2) represents sorrow. "They laurel" (7), that is, decorate with laurel.

---

Be scrupulously honest because it is right to be so, and not because "honesty is the best *policy*."

Remember that all rich men are not knaves nor all poor ones angels.

Remember that a life need not necessarily be a failure because it is not crowned with wealth.

## LESSON XLIX.

1. tĕr′ rá pĭns; *n.* a kind of large sea-turtles.
1. re fĕrr&d′; *v.* given in charge.
3. pro found′; *a.* deeply felt.
3. sŏph′ ĭst rĭĕş; *n.* false reasonings.
8. In €ŏn′ tro vẽr′ tĭ blᵫ; *a.* indisputable.
8. In′ tĭ măt ĭng; *v.* hinting; referring to obscurely.
11. Il lĕġ′ Ĭ blᵫ; *a.* incapable of being read.

### Is a Turtle Fish or Game?

1. Mr. Speaker: A bill having for its object the marking and determining of the close season for catching and killing turtles and terrapins has just been introduced by the gentleman from Rockbridge, who asks that it be referred to the Committee on Game, of which I have the honor to be chairman. To this disposition of the bill the gentleman from Gloucester objects, on the ground that as turtles and terrapins are fish, and not game, it should go to the Committee on Fish and Oysters.

2. On Chesapeake Bay and its tributaries, says the honorable gentleman, turtles and terrapins are frequently captured many miles out from land in nets or with hook and line, as all other members of the finny tribe are; and that, therefore, they are fish, and nothing but fish.

3. I have profound respect for the gentleman's opinion; as a lawyer he has acquired not only a state, but a national reputation; but even I, opposing a pin's point against the shield of Pelides, take issue with him. Sir, I am no lawyer, I don't understand enough of law to keep out of its meshes, but I will answer his sophistries with a few, plain, incontrovertible facts, and, as the old saw says, "facts are stubborn things."

4. Is a turtle a fish? I imagine not. Down on the old Virginia lowlands of the Potomac River, where I come

from, the colored people have dogs trained to hunt turtles when they come up on the dry land to deposit their eggs, and when they find them they bark as if they were treeing a squirrel. Now, I ask the House, did any member ever hear of a fish being hunted with dogs?

5. Who does not know that a turtle has four legs; that those legs have feet; and that those feet are armed with claws, like a cat's, a panther's, or a lion's? Has the gentleman from Gloucester ever seen a fish with talons? I think not.

6. It is well known that a turtle can be kept in a cellar for weeks, and even months, without food or water. Can a fish live without water? Why, sir, it has grown into a proverb that it cannot. And yet the gentleman says the turtle is a fish!

7. Do we not all know that you may cut off a turtle's head, and that it won't die till the sun goes down? Suppose now a modern Joshua should point his sword at the sun and command it to stand still in the heavens; why, Mr. Speaker, the turtle would live a thousand years with its head off. And yet the gentleman says the turtle is a fish.

8. Æsop tells the fable of the race between the tortoise and the hare, and we are left to believe that it took place on dry land—the author nowhere intimating that it was a swimming-match. Did the gentleman from Gloucester ever hear of a fish running a quarter stretch and coming out winner of the silver cup?

9. I read but a short time ago, Mr. Speaker, of a man who had a lion which, he offered to wager, could whip any living thing. The challenge was accepted. A snapping turtle was then produced, which conquered the lordly king of beasts at the first bite. Can the gentleman from

Gloucester bring any fish from York River that will do the same?

10. Again, a turtle has a tail; now, what nature intended him to do with that particular member I cannot divine. He does not use it like our Darwinian ancestors, the monkeys, who swing themselves from the trees by their tails; nor like a cow or mule, as a brush in fly-time; nor yet as our household pet, the dog, who wags a welcome to us with his; nor, finally, does he use it to swim with. And, sir, if the gentleman from Gloucester ever saw a fish who didn't use his tail to swim with, then he has discovered a new and most wonderful variety.

11. Mr. Speaker, I will not take up more of the valuable time of the House by further discussion of this vexed question. I will have only one more shot at the gentleman,—to prove to him that the turtle is the oldest inhabitant of the earth. Last summer, sir, I was away up in the mountains of Giles County, some two hundred miles from the ocean. One day strolling leisurely up the mountain road, I found a land tortoise or turtle, and picking him up, I saw some quaint and curious characters engraved in the shell on his back. Through lapse of time the letters were nearly illegible, but after considerable effort I made out the inscription, and read—

ADAM. PARADISE. YEAR ONE.

Mr. Speaker, I have done. If I have not convinced every member on this floor, except the gentleman from Gloucester, that a turtle is not a fish, then I appeal to the wisdom of this House to tell me what it is!

ALEXANDER HUNTER.

This humorous debate occurred in the Virginia House of Delegates, and the "Mr. Speaker" (1) is the presiding officer, who is addressed in that way. Pelides is another name for Achilles; his shield, made by Vulcan, was almost impenetrable; hence the reference (3) means that the point of a pin would have as much effect on "the shield of Pelides" as the speaker's arguments against those of his opponent. "Saw" (3) means an old saying or proverb. "Joshua" (7) is the Protestant spelling of Josue, at whose command, as we read in the Bible, the sun stood still, thus prolonging the day, and enabling him to win a victory over his enemies. "Æsop" (8) was a Greek slave and the writer of the famous fables which bear his name. "A quarter stretch" (8), meaning a quarter of a mile, is an expression borrowed from the race-course. "Darwinian ancestors" (10) is an allusion to the condemned theory of Prof. Darwin that man is descended from the monkey. "Adam. Paradise. Year One" (11) is a bit of pleasantry intended to convey the idea that the tortoise had lived in Paradise in the time of Adam, the first man.

## LESSON L.

1. sŭp' plĭ ănçẹ; *n.* earnest petition.
1. trō' phĭẹṣ; *n.* things taken and preserved as evidence of victory.
4. Mŏṣ' lĕm; *n.* a Mussulman; a Mohammedan.
5. nûr' tūrẹd; *v.* nourished; brought up.
5. stō' rĭẹd; *a.* having a history.

### Marco Bozzaris.

1. At midnight, in his guarded tent,
   The Turk was dreaming of the hour
When Greece, her knee in suppliance bent,
   Should tremble at his power.
In dreams, through camp and court he bore
The trophies of a conqueror;
   In dreams, his song of triumph heard;
Then wore his monarch's signet-ring;
Then pressed that monarch's throne—a king;
As wild his thoughts, and gay of wing,
   As Eden's garden bird.

2. At midnight, in the forest shades,
  Bozzaris ranged his Suliote band,
 True as the steel of their tried blades,
  Heroes in heart and hand.
There had the Persian's thousands stood,
There had the glad earth drunk their blood,
  In old Platæa's day;
And now, there breathed that haunted air
The sons of sires who conquered there,
With arms to strike, and soul to dare
  As quick, as far, as they.

3. An hour passed on; the Turk awoke;
  That bright dream was his last;
He woke to hear his sentries shriek,
 "To arms! They come—the Greek! the Greek!'
He woke to die 'midst flame and smoke,
And shout, and groan, and saber-stroke,
  And death-shots falling thick and fast
As lightnings from the mountain-cloud,
And heard, with voice as trumpet loud,
  Bozzaris cheer his band:
"Strike, till the last armed foe expires!
Strike, for your altars and your fires!
Strike, for the green graves of your sires—
  God, and your native land!"

4. They fought, like brave men, long and well;
  They piled the ground with Moslem slain;
 They conquered, but Bozzaris fell,
  Bleeding at every vein.
His few surviving comrades saw
His smile when rang their proud hurrah

And the red field was won;
Then saw in death his eyelids close,
Calmly, as to a night's repose,
　　Like flowers at set of sun.

5. Bozzaris! with the storied brave
　　Greece nurtured in her glory's time,
Rest thee! there is no prouder grave,
　　Even in her own proud clime.
We tell thy doom without a sigh,
For thou art Freedom's now, and Fame's—
One of the few, the immortal names,
　　That were not born to die.
　　　　　　　　　　FITZ-GREENE HALLECK.

**Fitz-Greene Halleck** was born at Guilford, Connecticut, July 8, 1790, and died there November 17, 1867. From his boyhood he wrote verses. His style is spirited, flowing, graceful, and harmonious. His poems display much geniality and tender feeling; their humor is quaint and keen, and always refined.

**Marco Bozzaris** (2), Greek patriot, was born about 1788 at Suli, in the mountains of Epirus. On the night of August 20, 1823, during the war between the Greeks and the Turks, Bozzaris with 850 Suliotes (2), as the natives of Suli are called, fell upon a Turkish camp of 4000 men, and defeated it with great slaughter; but Bozzaris was killed while leading the attack. It is this point in his career that is narrated in the poem. "There had the Persian's thousands stood, . . . in old Platæa's day" (2) is an allusion to the army under Mardonius, a Persian, which was overthrown at Platæa, a city of Greece, in the year 479 B.C.

Let the pupils give in their own language the meaning of the seven last lines in stanza 1. Give in its natural order the sentence contained in the three last lines of stanza 4.

---

The successful men in every calling have had a keen sense of the value of time. They have been misers of minutes. Washington was so rigidly punctual that when his secretary pleaded a slow watch as an excuse for being some minutes late, he replied, "Then, sir, either you must get a new watch or I must get a new secretary."

## LESSON LI.

2. In' tĕl lĕc' tu ḳl; *a.* treating of the mind.
4. cŏm pȧct'; *a.* closely and firmly united.
4. pōr'ṭus; *a.* full of pores or very small openings.
5. e văp' o rāt ed; *v.* passed off in the form of vapor.
6. wrȯught (*rawt*); *v.* worked.
8. In' tĕr vạls; *n.* spaces of time.
9. Ŏb strŭct' ed; *v.* stopped; blocked up.
12. ăp' pȧ rā' tŭs; *n.* instruments for performing experiments.

### Teaching to Think.

This is an extract from "Locke Amsden, the Schoolmaster," and the Lesson begins at that part of the story where Locke has applied for a position as teacher in a district school. Mr. Bunker, who has the appointing power, is a man of no education, can neither read nor write, but is naturally intelligent, and by his own observation has acquired much information.

1. "Have you any questions to ask me in the other branches, sir?" asked Locke.

"Not many," replied Bunker. "There is reading, writing, grammar, etc., which I know nothing about; and as to them, I must, of course, take you by guess, which will not be much of a guess, after all, if I find you have thought well on all other matters. Do you understand philosophy?"

2. "To what branch of philosophy do you allude, sir?"

"To the only branch there is."

"But you are aware that philosophy is divided into different kinds; as, natural, moral, and intellectual."

"Nonsense! philosophy is philosophy, and means the study of the reasons and causes of the things which we see, whether it be applied to a crazy man's dreams or the roasting of potatoes. Have you attended to it?"

"Yes, to a considerable extent, sir."

3. "I will put a question or two, then, if you please. What is the reason of the fact, for it is a fact, that the damp breath of a person blown on a good knife and on a bad one, will soonest disappear from the well-tempered blade?"

"It may be owing to the difference in the polish of the two blades, perhaps," replied Locke.

4. "Ah! that is an answer that don't go deeper than the surface," rejoined Bunker, humorously. "As good a thinker as you evidently are, you have not thought on this subject, I suspect. It took me a week, in all, I presume, of hard thinking, and making experiments at a blacksmith's shop, to discover the reason of this. It is not the polish: for take two blades of equal polish, and the breath will disappear from one as much quicker than it does from the other as the blade is better. It is because the material of the blade is more compact or less porous in one case than in the other.

5. "In the first place, I ascertained that the steel was made more compact by being hammered and tempered, and that the better it was tempered the more compact it would become; the size of the pores being made, of course, less in the same proportion. Well, then, I saw the reason I was in search of, at once. For we know a wet sponge is longer in drying than a wet piece of green wood, because the pores of the first are bigger. A seasoned or shrunk piece of wood dries quicker than a green one, for the same reason.

6. "Or you might bore a piece of wood with large gimlet-holes, and another with small ones, fill them both with water, and let them stand till the water evaporated, and the difference of time it would take to do this would make the case still more plain. So with the blades: the vapor lingers longest on the worst wrought and tempered

one, because the pores, being larger, take in more of the wet particles, and require more time in drying."

7. "Your theory is at least a very ingenious one," observed Locke, "and I am reminded by it of another of the natural phenomena, of the true explanation of which I have not been able to satisfy myself. It is this: what makes the earth freeze harder and deeper under a trodden path than the untrodden earth around it? All that I have asked say it is because the trodden earth is more compact. But is that reason a sufficient one?"

8. "No," said Bunker, "but I will tell you what the reason is, for I thought that out long ago. You know that, in the freezing months, much of the warmth we get is given out by the earth, from which, at intervals, if not constantly, to some extent, ascend the warm vapors to mingle with and moderate the cold atmosphere above.

9. "Now these ascending streams of warm air would be almost wholly obstructed by the compactness of a trodden path, and they would naturally divide at some distance below it, and pass up through the loose earth on each side, leaving the ground along the line of the path, to a great depth beneath it, a cold, dead mass, through which the frost would continue to penetrate, unchecked by the internal heat, which, in its unobstructed ascent on each side, would be continually checking or overcoming the frost in its action on the earth around.

10. "That, sir, is the true philosophy of the case, you may depend upon it. But we will now drop the discussion of these matters; for I am abundantly satisfied that you have not only knowledge enough, but that you can think for yourself. And now, sir, all I wish to know further about you is, whether you can teach others to think, which is half the battle with a teacher. But as I have had

an eye on this point, while attending to the others, probably one experiment, which I will ask you to make on one of the boys here, will be all I shall want."

"Proceed, sir," said the other.

11. "Ay, sir," rejoined Bunker, turning to the open fireplace, in which the burning wood was sending up a column of smoke: "There, you see that smoke rising, don't you? Well, you and I know the reason why smoke goes upward, but my youngest boy does not, I think. Now take your own way, and see if you can make him understand it."

12. Locke, after a moment's reflection, and a glance round the room for something to serve for apparatus, took from a shelf, where he had espied a number of articles, the smallest of a set of cast-iron cart-boxes, as are usually termed the round hollow tubes in which the axle-tree of a carriage turns. Then selecting a tin cup that would just take in the box, and turning into the cup as much water as he judged, with the box, would fill it, he presented them separately to the boy, and said,

"There, my lad, tell me which of these is the heavier?"

13. "Why, the cart-box, to be sure," replied the boy, taking the cup, half-filled with water, in one hand, and the hollow iron in the other.

"Then you think this iron is heavier than as much water as would fill the place of it, do you?" resumed Locke.

"Why, yes, as heavy again, and more too—I know it is," promptly said the boy.

14. "Well, sir, now mark what I do," proceeded the former, dropping into the cup the iron box, through the hollow of which the water instantly rose to the brim of the vessel.

"There, you saw that water rise to the top of the cup, did you?"

"Yes, I did."

"Very well, what caused it to do so?"

15. "Why; I know well enough, if I could only think: why, it is because the iron is the heavier, and as it comes all around the water so it can't get away sideways, it is forced up."

"That is right; and now I want you to tell what makes that smoke rise up the chimney."

16. "Why—I guess," replied the boy, hesitating, "I guess—I guess I don't know."

"Did you ever get upon a chair to look on some high shelf, so that your head was brought near the ceiling of a heated room, in winter? and did you notice any difference between the air up there and the air near the floor?"

17. "Yes, I remember I have, and found the air up there as warm as mustard; and when I got down, and bent my head near the floor to pick up something, I found it as cold as could be."

"That is ever the case; but I wish you to tell me how the cold air always happens to settle down to the lower part of the room, while the warm air, somehow, at the same time, gets above."

18. "Why, why, heavy things settle down, and the cold air—yes, yes, that's it, I am sure—the cold air is heavier, and so settles down, and crowds up the warm air."

"Very good. You then understand that cold air is heavier than the heated air, just as that iron is heavier than the water; so now we will go back to the main question—what makes the smoke go upward?"

19. "Oh! I see now as plain as day; the cold air settles down all round, like the iron box, and drives up the

hot air as fast as the fire heats it, in the middle, like the water; and so the hot air carries the smoke along up with it, just as feathers and things in a whirlwind. Well! I have found out what makes smoke go up—isn't it curious?"

20. "Done like a philosopher!" cried Bunker. "The thing is settled. I will grant that you are a teacher among a thousand. You can not only think yourself, but can teach others to think; so you may call the position yours as quick as you please." DANIEL PIERCE THOMPSON.

## LESSON LII.

1. re coiled'; *v.* drew back in alarm.
1. ap' pa ri' tion; *n.* a ghost.
2. sôr' çĕr ess; *n.* a woman who is supposed to deal with evil spirits.
2. spĕc' u la' tion; *n.* power of sight.
6. rāl' lĭed; *v.* ridiculed; attacked with jesting language, either in good humor or with slight contempt.
7. clūe; *n.* anything serving to guide.
13. vĕr' i fĭed; *v.* proved to be true.

### A Christian Martyr. Part I.

This Lesson is an extract from Cardinal Wiseman's great story "Fabiola." The scene is at the time when a body of Roman soldiers, led by Torquatus, an apostate, and Corvinus, the son of the prefect Tertullus, are attempting to carry out a plot to capture the Christians who are attending divine worship in the Catacombs. Having been warned, however, the Christians succeed in making their escape. Torquatus suddenly falls down a neglected staircase in the Catacombs, and thus mysteriously disappears from his companions. Cæcilia, a blind girl, remains after the other Christians have escaped, to guide any of the faithful who may have been left behind.

1. Before these foiled hounds with drooping heads had reached the entrance, they recoiled before the sight of a singular apparition. At first they thought they had caught

a glimpse of daylight; but they soon perceived it was the glimmering of a lamp. This was held steadily by an upright, immovable figure, which thus received its light upon itself. It was clothed in a dark dress, so as to resemble one of those bronze statues which have the head and extremities of white marble, and startle one when first seen, so like are they to living forms.

2. "Who can it be? What is it?" the men whispered to one another.

"A sorceress," replied one.

"The *genius loci*," observed another.

"A spirit," suggested a third.

Still, as they approached stealthily toward it, it did not appear conscious of their presence: "there was no speculation in its eyes"; it remained unmoved and unscared. At length, two got sufficiently near to seize the figure by its arms.

3. "Who are you?" asked Corvinus, in a rage.

"A Christian," answered Cæcilia, with her usual cheerful gentleness.

"Bring her along," he commanded; "some one at least shall pay for our disappointment."

4. Cæcilia, already forewarned, had approached the cemetery by a different but neighboring entrance. No sooner had she descended than she snuffed the strong odor of the torches. "This is none of *our* incense, I know," she said to herself; "the enemy is already within." She hastened therefore to the place of assembly and delivered Sebastian's note; adding also what she had observed. It warned them to disperse and seek the shelter of the inner and lower galleries; and begged of the Pontiff not to leave till he should send for him, as his person was particularly sought for.

5. Pancratius urged the blind messenger to save herself too. "No," she replied, "my office is to watch the door, and guide the faithful safe."

"But the enemy may seize you."

"No matter," she answered, laughing; "my being taken may save much worthier lives. Give me a lamp, Pancratius."

"Why, you cannot see by it," observed he, smiling.

"True, but others can."

"They may be your enemies."

"Even so," she answered, "I do not wish to be taken in the dark. If my Bridegroom come to me in the night of this cemetery, must He not find me with my lamp trimmed?"

Off she started, reached her post, and hearing no noise except that of quiet footsteps, she thought they were those of friends, and held up her lamp to guide them.

6. When the party came forth with their only captive, Fulvius was perfectly furious. It was worse than a total failure: it was ridiculous—a poor mouse come out of the bowels of the earth. He rallied Corvinus till the wretch winced and foamed; then suddenly he asked, "And where is Torquatus?" He heard the account of his sudden disappearance, told in as many ways as the Dacian guard's adventure; but it annoyed him greatly. He had no doubt whatever, in his own mind, that he had been duped by his supposed victim, who had escaped into the unsearchable mazes of the cemetery. If so, this captive would know, and he determined to question her. He stood before her, therefore, put on his most searching and awful look, and said to her sternly, "Look at me, woman, and tell me the truth."

7. "I must tell you the truth without looking at you,

sir," answered the poor girl, with her cheerfullest smile and softest voice; " do you not see that I am blind?"

"Blind!" all exclaimed at once, as they crowded to look at her. But over the features of Fulvius there passed the slightest possible emotion, just as much as the wave that runs, pursued by a playful breeze, over the ripe meadow. A knowledge had flashed into his mind, a clue had fallen into his hand.

8. " It will be ridiculous," he said, " for twenty soldiers to march through the city guarding a blind girl. Return to your quarters, and I will see you are well rewarded. You, Corvinus, take my horse, and go before to your father, and tell him all; I will follow in a carriage with the captive."

" No treachery, Fulvius," he said, vexed and mortified. " Mind you bring her. The day must not pass without a sacrifice."

" Do not fear," was the reply.

9. Fulvius, indeed, was pondering whether, having lost one spy, he should not try to make another. But the placid gentleness of the poor beggar perplexed him more than the boisterous zeal of the gamester, and her sightless orbs defied him more than the restless roll of the toper's. Still, the first thought that had struck him he could yet pursue. When alone in a carriage with her, he assumed a soothing tone, and addressed her. He knew she had not overheard the last dialogue.

10. "My poor girl," he said, " how long have you been blind?"

" All my life," she replied.

" What is your history? Whence do you come?"

" I have no history. My parents were poor, and brought me to Rome when I was four years old, as they came to pray, in discharge of a vow made for my life in early sickness, to the blessed martyrs Chrysanthus and Daria. They left me in charge of a pious lame woman, at the door of the title of Fasciola, while they went to their devotions. It was on that memorable day when many Christians were buried at their tomb by earth and stones cast down upon them. My parents had the happiness to be of the number."

11. " And how have you lived since?"

" God became my only Father then, and His Catholic Church my mother. The one feeds the birds of the air, the other nurses the weaklings of the flock. I have never wanted for anything since."

" But you can walk about the streets freely, and without fear, as well as if you saw."

" How do you know that?"

" I have seen you. Do you remember very early one morning in the autumn, leading a poor lame man along the Vicus Patricius?"

12. She blushed and remained silent. Could he have seen her put into the poor old man's purse her own share of the alms?

" You have owned yourself a Christian?" he asked negligently.

" Oh, yes! how could I deny it?"

" Then that meeting was a Christian meeting?"

" Certainly; what else could it be?"

13. He wanted no more; his suspicions were verified. Agnes, about whom Torquatus had been able or willing to tell him nothing, was certainly a Christian. His game was made. She must yield, or he would be avenged.

After a pause, looking at her steadfastly, he said, " Do you know whither you are going?"

"Before the judge of earth, I suppose, who will send me to my Spouse in heaven."

"And so calmly?" he asked in surprise; for he could see no token from the soul to the countenance, but a smile.

"So joyfully rather," was her brief reply.

"The *genius loci*" (2) is a Latin expression meaning "the guardian genius of the place." The expression "If my Bridegroom come to me in the night of this cemetery, must He not find me with my lamp trimmed?" (5) refers to the parable of the ten virgins, related in St. Matthew xxv. The "Vicus Patricius" (11) was the "Patrician Street" of ancient Rome.

## LESSON LIII.

1. ĭn'çĭ dĕnt; *n.* event.
2. pre ṣûmę'; *v.* take the liberty.
4. de crēęs'; *n.* laws.
5. dāįn' tĭ lỹ; *adv.* nicely.
5. de lū'ṣions; *n.* errors.
6. dĭ vẽr' sĭ tĭęṣ; *n.* varieties.
7. prăt'tlę; *n.* trifling talk.
9. ŏb lā'tion; *n.* offering.
11. sŭf fīçę'; *v.* to be enough.
12. lĕn' ĭ tỹ; *n.* gentleness; mercy.

### A Christian Martyr. Part II.

1. Having got all that he desired, he consigned his prisoner to Corvinus at the gates of the Æmilian basilica, and left her to her fate. It had been a cold and drizzling day like the preceding evening. The weather and the incident of the night had kept down all enthusiasm; and while the prefect had been compelled to sit in-doors, where no great crowd could collect, as hours had passed away without any arrest, trial, or tidings, most of the curious had left, and only a few more persevering remained past the hour of afternoon recreation in the public gardens. But just before the captive arrived, a fresh knot of spectators came in, and stood near one of the side-doors, from which they could see all.

2. As Corvinus had prepared his father for what he was to expect, Tertullus, moved with some compassion, and imagining there could be little difficulty in overcoming the obstinacy of a poor, ignorant, blind beggar, requested the spectators to remain perfectly still, that he might try his persuasion on her, alone, as she would imagine, with him; and he threatened heavy penalties on any one who should presume to break the silence.

3. It was as he had calculated. Cæcilia knew not that any one else was there, as the prefect thus kindly addressed her:

"What is thy name, child?"

"Cæcilia."

"It is a noble name; hast thou it from thy family?"

"No; I am not noble; except because my parents, though poor, died for Christ. As I am blind, those who took care of me called me *Cæca*, and then, out of kindness, softened it into Cæcilia."

4. "But now give up all this folly of the Christians, who have kept thee only poor and blind. Honor the decrees of the divine emperors, and offer sacrifice to the gods; and thou shalt have riches, and fine clothes, and good fare; and the best physicians shall try to restore thee thy sight."

"You must have better motives to propose to me than these; for the very things for which I most thank God and His Divine Son are those which you would have me put away."

5. "How dost thou mean?"

"I thank God that I am poor and meanly clad, and fare not daintily; because by all these things I am the more like Jesus Christ, my only Spouse."

"Foolish girl!" interrupted the judge, losing patience

a little; "hast thou learnt all these silly delusions already? At least thou canst not thank thy God that He has made thee sightless."

6. "For that, more than all the rest, I thank Him daily and hourly with all my heart."

"How so? Dost thou think it a blessing never to have seen the face of a human being, or the sun, or the earth? What strange fancies are these?"

"They are not so, most noble sir. For in the midst of what you call darkness, I see a spot of what I must call light, it contrasts so strongly with all around. It is to me what the sun is to you, which I know to be local from the varying directions of its rays. And this object looks upon me as with a countenance of intensest beauty, and smiles upon me ever. And I know it to be that of Him whom I love with undivided affection. I would not for the world have its splendor dimmed by a brighter sun nor its wondrous loveliness confounded with the diversities of others' features nor my gaze on it drawn aside by earthly visions. I love Him too much not to wish to see Him always alone."

7. "Come, come! let me have no more of this silly prattle. Obey the emperors at once, or I must try what a little pain will do. That will soon tame thee."

"Pain?" she echoed innocently.

"Yes, pain. Hast thou never felt it? hast thou never been hurt by any one in thy life?"

"Oh, no! Christians never hurt one another."

8. The rack was standing, as usual, before him; and he made a sign to Catulus to place her upon it. The executioner pushed her back on it by her arms; and as she made no resistance, she was easily laid extended on its wooden couch. The loops of the ever-ready ropes were

in a moment passed round her ankles, and arms drawn over the head. The poor sightless girl saw not who did all this; she knew not but it might be the same person who had been conversing with her. If there had been silence hitherto, men now held their very breath; while Cæcilia's lips moved in earnest prayer.

9. "Once more, before proceeding further, I call on thee to sacrifice to the gods, and escape cruel torments," said the judge, with a sterner voice.

"Neither torments nor death," firmly replied the victim tied to the altar, "shall separate me from the love of Christ. I can offer up no sacrifice but to the one living God: and its ready oblation is myself."

10. The prefect made a signal to the executioner, and he gave one rapid whirl to the two wheels of the rack, round the windlasses of which the ropes were wound; and the limbs of the maiden were stretched with a sudden jerk, which, though not enough to wrench them from their sockets, as a further turn would have done, sufficed to inflict an excruciating or, more truly, a *racking* pain through all her frame. Far more grievous was this, from the preparation and the cause of it being unseen, and from that additional suffering which darkness inflicts. A quivering of her features and a sudden paleness alone gave evidence of her torture.

11. "Ha! ha!" the judge exclaimed, "thou feelest that? Come, let it suffice; obey, and thou shalt be freed."

She seemed to take no heed of his words, but gave vent to her feelings in prayer: "I thank Thee, O Lord Jesus Christ, that Thou hast made me suffer pain the first time for Thy sake. I have loved Thee in peace; I have loved Thee in comfort; I have loved Thee in joy,—and

THE CHRISTIAN MARTYR.

now in pain I love Thee still more. How much sweeter it is to be like Thee, stretched upon Thy Cross, even than resting upon the hard couch at the poor man's table!"

12. "Thou triflest with me," exclaimed the judge, thoroughly vexed, "and makest light of my lenity. We will try something stronger. Here, Catulus, apply a lighted torch to her sides."

A thrill of disgust and horror ran through the assembly, which could not help sympathizing with the poor blind creature. A murmur of suppressed indignation broke out from all sides of the hall.

13. Cæcilia, for the first time, learnt that she was in the midst of a crowd. A crimson glow of modesty rushed into her brow, her face, and neck, just before white as marble. The angry judge checked the rising gush of feeling; and all listened in silence, as she spoke again, with warmer earnestness than before:

"O my dear Lord and Spouse! I have been ever true and faithful to Thee! Let me suffer pain and torture for Thee; but spare me confusion from human eyes. Let me come to Thee at once, not covering my face with my hands in shame when I stand before Thee."

14. Another muttering of compassion was heard.

"Catulus!" shouted the baffled judge in fury, "do your duty, sirrah! what are you about, fumbling all day with that torch?"

The executioner advanced, and stretched forth his hand to her robe, to withdraw it for the torture; but he drew back, and, turning to the prefect, exclaimed in softened accents:

"It is too late. She is dead!"

"Dead!" cried out Tertullus; "dead with one turn of the wheel? Impossible!"

15. Catulus gave the rack a turn backward, and the body remained motionless. It was true: she had passed from the rack to the throne, from the scowl of the judge's countenance to her Spouse's welcoming embrace. Had she breathed out her pure soul, as a sweet perfume, in the incense of her prayer? or had her heart been unable to get back its blood, from the intensity of that first virginal blush?
CARDINAL WISEMAN.

Nicholas, Cardinal Wiseman was born at Seville, in Spain, of an Irish family settled there. Completing his education at Rome, he became eminent for his learning, and his lectures on Science and Revealed Religion were printed in many countries and many languages. In 1840 he was appointed a Coadjutor Bishop in England, and in his person as Archbishop of Westminster the English hierarchy was fully restored in 1850. He was also created a Cardinal. He was an eloquent preacher and writer; and, as one of the founders of the *Dublin Review*, and by works in various departments of literature, exercised great influence for the Catholic cause. He died in 1865, aged sixty-three.

"Cæca" (3) is the Latin for "blind." The rack was used not only as a direct torment, but also to keep the body distended for the application of other tortures. That of fire (12) was one of the most common. There are many instances in the lives of martyrs of their deaths being the fruit of prayer (15), as in the case of St. Praxedes, St. Cæcilia, St. Agatha, etc.

---

Small service is true service while it lasts;
  Of friends, however humble, scorn not one:
The daisy, by the shadow that it casts,
  Protects the lingering dew-drop from the sun.

The heights by great men reached and kept
  Were not attained by sudden flight;
But they, while their companions slept,
  Were toiling upward in the night.

## LESSON LIV.

1. cŭr' rĕnt; a. common.
1. făc tō' tŭm; n. a person employed to do all kinds of work.
1. In' dĭs pĕn' sá blẹ; a. absolutely necessary.
3. rō' tatẹ; v. to move round a center.
3. In ăd' e quatẹ; a. unequal; insufficient.
3. çĕn' tĭ pĕd; n. a venomous insect having a great number of feet.
6. pĕn' stŏċk; n. a tube of planks for conducting water.
8. chōrẹs; n. the regular or daily light work of a household, both in and out of doors; small jobs.

### A Boy on a Farm.

1. Boys in general would be very good farmers if the current notions about farming were not so very different from those they entertain. What passes for laziness is very often an unwillingness to farm in a particular way. But say what you will about boys, it is my impression that a farm without a boy would very soon come to grief. What the boy does is the life of the farm. He is the factotum, always in demand, always expected to do the thousand indispensable things that nobody else will do. Upon him fall all the odds and ends, the most difficult things.

2. After everybody else is through, he has to finish up. His work is like a woman's—perpetual waiting on others. Everybody knows how much easier it is to eat a good dinner than it is to wash the dishes afterward. Consider what a boy on a farm is required to do; things that must be done, or life would actually stop.

3. It is understood, in the first place, that he is to do all the errands, to go to the store, to the post-office, and to carry all sorts of messages. If he had as many legs as a centiped, they would tire before night. His two short limbs seem to him entirely inadequate to the task. He

would like to have as many legs as a wheel has spokes, and rotate about in the same way.

4. This he sometimes tries to do; and the people who have seen him "turning cart-wheels" along the side of the road have supposed that he was amusing himself and idling his time; he was only trying to invent a new mode of locomotion, so that he could economize his legs, and do his errands with greater dispatch.

5. He practices standing on his head, in order to accustom himself to any position. Leap-frog is one of his methods of getting over the ground quickly. He would willingly go an errand any distance if he could leap-frog it with a few other boys.

6. He has a natural genius for combining pleasure with business. This is the reason why, when he is sent to the spring for a pitcher of water, and the family are waiting at the dinner-table, he is absent so long, for he stops to poke the frog that sits on the stone, or, if there is a penstock, to put his hand over the spout, and squirt the water a little while.

7. He is the one who spreads the grass when the men have cut it; he mows it away in the barn; he rides the horse, to cultivate the corn, up and down the hot, weary rows; he picks up the potatoes when they are dug; he drives the cows night and morning; he brings wood and water, and splits kindling; he gets up the horse, and puts out the horse; whether he is in the house or out of it, there is always something for him to do.

8. Just before school in winter he shovels paths; in summer he turns the grindstone. He knows where there are lots of wintergreens and sweet flag-root, but, instead of going for them, he is to stay in-doors and pare apples and stone raisins and pound something in a mortar. And yet,

with his mind full of schemes of what he would like to do, and his hands full of occupations, he is an idle boy, who has nothing to busy himself with but school and chores!

9. He would gladly do all the work if somebody else would do the chores, he thinks; and yet I doubt if any boy ever amounted to anything in the world, or was of much use as a man, who did not enjoy the advantages of a liberal education in the way of chores.

CHARLES DUDLEY WARNER.

## LESSON LV.

2. trŭdġ´ing; *v.* going on foot.
3. hăb´ I tūdė; *n.* mode of living.
4. är´ tĭ zăng; *n.* mechanics.
4. ĕs chew´ ing; *v.* shunning.
6. cŏm´ plĕx; *a.* composed of two or more parts.
7. pīęd; *a.* spotted.
8. swąrd; *n.* turf; sod.
9. moil; *n.* grimy work

### The Barefoot Boy.

1. Blessings on thee, little man,
   Barefoot boy, with cheek of tan!
   With thy turned-up pantaloons,
   And thy merry whistled tunes;
   With thy red lip, redder still
   Kissed by strawberries on the hill;
   With the sunshine on thy face,
   Through thy torn brim's jaunty grace ·
   From my heart I give thee joy;—
   I was once a barefoot boy!

2. Prince thou art—the grown-up man
   Only is republican.
   Let the million-dollared ride—
   Barefoot, trudging at his side,

Thou hast more than he can buy,
In the reach of ear and eye:
Outward sunshine, inward joy—
Blessings on thee, barefoot boy!

3. Oh for boyhood's painless play;
Sleep that wakes in laughing day;
Health that mocks the doctor's rules;
Knowledge, never learned of schools,
Of the wild bee's morning chase,
Of the wild flower's time and place,
Flight of fowl, and habitude
Of the tenants of the wood;
How the tortoise bears his shell,
How the woodchuck digs his cell,
And the ground-mole sinks his well;
How the robin feeds her young,
How the oriole's nest is hung;

4. Where the whitest lilies blow,
Where the freshest berries grow,
Where the ground-nut trails its vine,
Where the wood-grape's clusters shine;
Of the black wasp's cunning way,
Mason of his walls of clay,
And the architectural plans
Of gray hornet artisans!—
For, eschewing books and tasks,
Nature answers all he asks;
Hand in hand with her he walks,
Face to face with her he talks,
Part and parcel of her joy,—
Blessings on the barefoot boy!

5. Oh for boyhood's time of June,
Crowding years in one brief moon,
When all things I heard or saw,
Me, their master, waited for;—
I was rich in flowers and trees,
Humming-birds and honey-bees;
For my sport the squirrel played,
Plied the snouted mole his spade;
For my taste the blackberry-cone
Purpled over hedge and stone;
Laughed the brook for my delight,
Through the day, and through the night,
Whispering at the garden wall,
Talked with me from fall to fall!

6. Mine the sand-rimmed pickerel pond,
Mine the walnut slopes beyond,
Mine on bending orchard trees
Apples of Hesperides!
Still as my horizon grew,
Larger grew my riches, too;
All the world I saw or knew
Seemed a complex Chinese toy,
Fashioned for a barefoot boy!

7. Oh for festal dainties spread,
Like my bowl of milk and bread,—
Pewter spoon and bowl of wood,
On the door-stone gray and rude!
O'er me like a regal tent,
Cloudy-ribbed, the sunset bent,
Purple-curtained, fringed with gold,
Looped in many a wind-swung fold;

While for music came the play
Of the pied frogs' orchestra;
And, to light the noisy choir,
Lit the fly his lamp of fire;
I was monarch: pomp and joy
Waited on the barefoot boy!

8. Cheerily, then, my little man,
Live and laugh, as boyhood can,
Though the flinty slopes be hard,
Stubble-speared the new-mown sward,
Every morn shall lead thee through
Fresh baptisms of the dew;
Every evening from thy feet
Shall the cool wind kiss the heat.

9. All too soon these feet must hide
In the prison-cells of pride,
Lose the freedom of the sod,
Like a colt's for work be shod,
Made to tread the mills of toil,
Up and down in ceaseless moil;
Happy if their track be found
Never on forbidden ground,—
Happy if they sink not in
Quick and treacherous sands of sin.
Ah! that thou couldst know thy joy
Ere it passes, BAREFOOT BOY!

JOHN GREENLEAF WHITTIER.

**Explain** the expressions: "the grown-up man only is republican" (2); "Mason of his walls of clay" (4); "Plied the snouted mole his spade" (5); "Like a colt's for work be shod" (9).

We read in mythology that the *Hesperides* were the daughters of Hesperus, or Night, and possessors of a garden in which golden apples grew. Hence the reference here (6) means "apples of gold."

## LESSON LVI.

4. ăs′pĕct; n. look or appearance.
6. e lăpsĕd′; v. passed away.
8. wrĭth′ ing; v. twisting with violence.
9. whĭrlĕd (hwêrled); v. turned round rapidly.
10. lū′ rĭd; a. gloomy; ghastly pale.
10. dĭf fūsĕd′; v. sent out in all directions.
10. re sūmĕd′; v. took again.
13. dĕv′ ạs tāt ing; a. destroying; laying waste.
14. răv′ ẹn ọus; a. eager for prey.
15. răv′ aġ eṣ; n. ruins.

### The Hurricane.

1. Various portions of our country have, at different times, suffered severely from the influence of violent storms of wind, some of which have been known to traverse nearly the whole of the United States, and to leave such deep impressions in their wake as will not easily be forgotten.

2. Having witnessed one of these awful scenes in all its grandeur, I will attempt to describe it. The recollection of that astonishing revolution of the airy element even now brings with it so disagreeable a sensation that I feel as if about to be affected with a sudden stoppage of the circulation of my blood.

3. I had left the village of Shewanee, situated on the banks of the Ohio, on my return from Henderson, which is also situated on the banks of the same beautiful stream. The weather was pleasant, and I thought not warmer than usual at that season. My horse was jogging quietly along, and my thoughts were, for once at least in the course of my life, entirely engaged in commercial speculations.

4. I had forded Highland Creek, and was on the eve of entering a tract of bottom-land or valley that lay between it and Canoe Creek, when suddenly I noticed a great difference in the aspect of the heavens. A hazy thickness

had overspread the country, and I for some time expected an earthquake; but my horse exhibited no inclination to stop and prepare for such an occurrence. I had nearly arrived at the verge of the valley, when I thought fit to stop near a brook, and dismounted to quench the thirst which had come upon me.

5. I was leaning on my knees, with my lips about to touch the water, when, from my proximity to the earth, I heard a distant murmuring sound of an extraordinary nature. I drank, however, and as I rose to my feet, looked toward the south-west, when I observed a yellowish oval spot, the appearance of which was quite new to me.

6. Little time was left to me for consideration, as the next moment a smart breeze began to agitate the taller trees. It increased to an unexpected height, and already the smaller branches and twigs were seen falling in a slanting direction toward the ground. Two minutes had scarcely elapsed when the whole forest before me was in fearful motion. Here and there, where one tree pressed against another, a creaking noise was produced, similar to that occasioned by the violent gusts which sometimes sweep over the country.

7. Turning toward the direction from which the wind blew, I saw, to my great astonishment, that the noblest trees of the forest bent their lofty heads for a while, and, unable to stand against the blast, were falling in pieces. First, the branches were broken off with a crackling noise, then went the upper part of the massive trunks, and in many cases whole trees of gigantic size were falling, entire, to the ground.

8. So rapid was the progress of the storm, that before I could think of taking measures to insure my safety, the hurricane was passing opposite the place where I stood.

Never can I forget the scene which at that moment presented itself. The tops of the trees were seen moving in the strangest manner, in the central current of the tempest, which carried along with it a mingled mass of twigs and foliage that completely obscured the view. Some of the largest trees were seen bending and writhing beneath the gale; others suddenly snapped across, and many, after a momentary resistance, fell uprooted to the earth.

9. The mass of branches, twigs, foliage, and dust that moved through the air was whirled onward like a cloud of feathers, and on passing disclosed a wide space filled with fallen trees, naked stumps, and heaps of shapeless ruins, which marked the path of the tempest. The space was about a fourth of a mile in breadth, and to my imagination resembled the dried-up bed of the Mississippi, with its thousands of snags and sunken logs strewed in the sand and inclined in various degrees. The horrible noise resembled that of the great cataracts of Niagara, and as it howled along in the track of the desolating tempest, it produced a feeling in my mind which it is impossible to describe.

10. The principal force of the hurricane was now over, although millions of twigs and small branches, that had been brought from a great distance, were seen following the blast, as if drawn onward by some mysterious power. They were floating in the air for some hours after, as if supported by the thick mass of dust that rose high above the ground. The sky had now a greenish lurid hue, and an extremely disagreeable odor of sulphur was diffused in the atmosphere. Having sustained no material injury, I waited in amazement, until nature at length resumed her usual aspect.

11. For some moments I felt undetermined whether I

should return to Morgantown, or attempt to force my way through the wrecks of the tempest. My business, however, being of an urgent nature, I ventured into the path of the storm, and, after encountering innumerable difficulties, succeeded in crossing it.

12. I was obliged to lead my horse by the bridle to enable him to leap over the fallen trees, whilst I scrambled over or under them the best way I could, at times so hemmed in by the broken tops and tangled branches as almost to become desperate. On arriving at my house I gave an account of what I had seen, when, to my surprise, I was told that there had been very little wind in the neighborhood, although in the streets and gardens many branches and twigs had fallen in a manner which excited great surprise.

13. Many wondrous accounts of the devastating effects of this hurricane were circulated in the country after its occurrence. Some log-houses, we were told, had been overturned, and their inmates destroyed. One person informed me that a wire-sifter had been conveyed by the gust to a distance of many miles. Another had found a cow lodged in the fork of a large half-broken tree.

14. But as I am disposed to relate only what I have myself seen, I will not lead you into the region of romance, but shall content myself with saying that much damage was done by the awful visitation. The valley is yet a desolate place, overgrown with briers and bushes thickly entangled among the tops and trunks of the fallen trees, and is the resort of ravenous animals, to which they betake themselves when pursued by man, or after they have committed their depredations on the farms of the surrounding district.

15. I have crossed the path of the storm at a distance

of a hundred miles from the spot where I witnessed its fury, and again, four hundred miles farther off, in the State of Ohio. Lastly I observed traces of its ravages on the summits of the mountains connected with the Great Pine Forest of Pennsylvania, three hundred miles beyond the place last mentioned. In all those different parts it appeared to me not to have exceeded a quarter of a mile in breadth.

JOHN J. AUDUBON.

John James Audubon was born in Louisiana in May, 1780. Even as a boy he conceived a passion for the study of birds. When about fourteen years old he was sent to Paris by his father, who was also an ardent lover of nature, to study drawing. Returning home, he devoted his time to the exploration of his native forests, and the result was his great work "The Birds of America." As a naturalist and a writer on that branch of natural science which treats of birds, as well as an artist, Audubon has no superior. He died January 27, 1851.

## LESSON LVII.

1. ĕp′ I thĕts; n. titles expressing some quality.
2. con fĭrmĕd′; v. rendered certain.
3. In sŭ′ pĕr á blę; a. incapable of being overcome.
3. cŏm′ pe tęnt; a. fit.
5. de fĭ′ cien çў; n. want.
6. pŭr sŭ′ ąnt; a. following.
8. cŏm pĕn′ dĭ ŭm; n. a short account of a subject.
8. mў thŏl′ o ġў; n. the science treating of legendary popular fables.

### The Royal Scholar.

1. Alfred, the "Shepherd of his People," the "Darling of the English," for these were the epithets given to him in the old time, was deemed the wisest man in England. Alfred was wholly ignorant of letters until he attained twelve years of age. But though he could not read, he could attend; and he listened eagerly to the verses which were recited in his father's hall by the minstrels and the glee-

men, the masters of Anglo-Saxon song. Day and night would he employ in hearkening to these poems; he treasured them in his memory, and during the whole of his life poetry continued to be his solace and amusement in trouble and care.

2. It chanced one day that Alfred's mother, Osburga, showed to him and his brothers a volume of Anglo-Saxon poetry which she possessed. "He who first can read the book shall have it," said she. Alfred's attention was attracted by the bright gilding and coloring of one of the illuminated capital letters. He was delighted with it, and inquired of his mother,—would she really keep her word? She confirmed the promise, and put the book into his hands; and he applied so steadily to his task that the book became his own.

3. The information which Alfred now possessed rendered him extremely desirous of obtaining more; but his ignorance of Latin was an insuperable obstacle. Science and knowledge could not then be acquired otherwise than from Latin books; and earnestly as he sought for instruction in that language, none could be found. Sloth had overspread the land; and there were so few "Grammarians," that is to say Latinists, in Wessex, that he was utterly unable to discover a competent teacher. In after-life Alfred was accustomed to say, that of all the hardships, privations, and misfortunes which had befallen him, there was none which he felt so grievous as this, the enforced idleness of his youth, when his intellect would have been fitted to receive the lesson and his time was unoccupied. At a more advanced period, the arduous toils of royalty and the pressure of most severe and constant pain interrupted the studies which he was then enabled to pursue, and harassed and disturbed his mind,—yet he persevered; and the unquench-

able thirst for knowledge, which the child had manifested, continued without abatement until he was removed from this stage of exertion.

4. In the eighth century, the age of Bede, Britain was distinguished for learning: the rapid decline of cultivation had been occasioned by the Danish invasions. Alfred's plans for the intellectual cultivation of his country were directed, in the first instance, to the diffusion of knowledge amongst the great body of the people. Hence he earnestly recommended the translation "of useful books into the language which we all understand; so that all the youth of England, but more especially those who are of gentle kind and at ease in their circumstances, may be grounded in letters,—for they cannot profit in any pursuit until they are well able to read English."

5. Alfred taught himself Latin by translating. You will recollect his regret at the want of masters in early life. As soon as he was settled in his kingdom he attempted to supply this deficiency, not only for himself, but also for his people, by inviting learned men from foreign parts. Asser, a native of St. David's, in Wales, whom he appointed Bishop of Sherbourne, was one of them. Great friendship and confidence prevailed between Alfred and the British priest; and to the pen of Asser we owe a biography of the Anglo-Saxon monarch, written with equal simplicity and fidelity. Grimbald, at the invitation of Alfred, left Gaul, his own country, and settled in England. A third celebrated foreigner was called Johannes *Scotus*, from his nation, or *Erigena*, the Irishman, from the place of his birth. From these distinguished men, to whom must be added Plegmund, Archbishop of Canterbury, Alfred was enabled to acquire that learning which he had so long sought.

6. Asser permits us to contemplate Alfred beginning

his literary labors. They were engaged in pleasant converse; and it chanced that Asser quoted a text or passage either from the Bible or from the works of one of the Fathers. Alfred asked his friend to write it down in a blank leaf of that collection of psalms and hymns which he always carried in his bosom; but not a blank could be found of sufficient magnitude. Pursuant therefore to Asser's proposal, a *quire*, that is to say, a sheet of vellum folded into *fours*, was produced, on which these texts were written; and Alfred, afterward working upon them, translated the passages so selected into the Anglo-Saxon tongue.

7. He continued the practice of writing down such remarkable passages as were quoted in conversation. His "handboc" or manual, however, included some matters of his own observation, anecdotes, or sayings of pious men; but the body of the collection appears to have consisted of extracts from the Scriptures, intermingled with reflections of a devotional cast. Alfred appears to have been induced to attempt a complete version of the Bible. Some writers have supposed that he completed the greater portion of the task. It seems, however, that the work was prevented by his early death.

8. We must now advert to Alfred's "Family Library," or "Library of Useful Knowledge." As far as we can judge from those portions of the plan which were carried into execution, he intended to present his subjects with a complete course of such works as were then considered the most useful and best calculated to form the groundwork of a liberal education. The chronicle of Orosius, containing a history of the world to the fifth century, was the best compendium which had yet been composed. Alfred, in the work of the Spaniard—for Orosius was a native of Seville —enlarged the text by additions of great curiosity. He

presents us with a geographical account of the natives of Germany; and the voyages of Audher toward the North Pole, and of Wulstan in the Baltic, are detailed as these travelers related them to the king. The History of Venerable Bede, also rendered into Anglo-Saxon by Alfred, instructed the learner in the annals of his own country. It is the earliest history of any of the States formed during the Middle Ages which can be read in the language of the people. In this work Alfred did not depart from his original. In translating the "Consolations of Philosophy" by Boëthius, Alfred seems to have delighted in his task. The narratives taken from ancient mythology, such as the story of Orpheus and Eurydice, are expanded by Alfred into pleasing tales, such as the gleeman recited during the intervals of his song.

FRANCIS PALGRAVE.

**Alfred the Great,** here described as the "Royal Scholar," was born about the year 849. He was a wise and thoughtful prince; systematic in his labors, giving one-third of his time to God, one-third to his subjects, and one-third to rest and recreation. Besides being a learned man he was a skillful general: he drove the Danes from England, and was the founder of a regular government in that country. He died in 901.

**Sir Francis Palgrave** was born in London in July, 1788. He was the author of many valuable historical and other works. He died July 6, 1861.

**Venerable Bede** (4), a monk of the eighth century, was born about the year 673 and died about the year 735. He was the first writer of English prose, and was eminent as scholar, historian, and divine. Though works of piety made up the bulk of his productions, he wrote treatises on philosophy, astronomy, arithmetic, grammar, and history, besides biographies, homilies, and comments on the Scripture. He was a prodigy of learning, and has left a list of forty-five different works which he composed, to which others have been added. He died on the floor of his cell chanting with his last breath the *Gloria Patri*.

"Illuminated capital letters" (2) refers to the beautiful initial letters, at the head of chapters and elsewhere, painted in gold and colors by the monks. "Of gentle kind" (4) means of noble birth.

## LESSON LVIII.

1. sēar; *a.* withered; dried up.
1. ĕd′ dў ing; *a.* moving in a circular direction.
1. gŭst; *n.* a sudden rushing of the wind.
3. ŭp′ lạnd; *n.* high or elevated land; land which is generally dry.
3. glĕn; *n.* a secluded and narrow valley.

### The Death of the Flowers.

1. The melancholy days are come, the saddest of the year,
   Of wailing winds, and naked woods, and meadows brown and sear.
   Heaped in the hollows of the grove, the autumn leaves lie dead;
   They rustle to the eddying gust, and to the rabbits' tread.
   The robin and the wren are flown, and from the shrubs the jay,
   And from the wood-top calls the crow, through all the gloomy day.

2. Where are the flowers, the fair young flowers, that lately sprang and stood
   In brighter light and softer airs, a beauteous sisterhood?
   Alas! they all are in their graves—the gentle race of flowers
   Are lying in their lowly beds, with the fair and good of ours.
   The rain is falling where they lie; but the cold November rain
   Calls not from out the gloomy earth the lovely ones again.

3. The windflower and the violet, they perished long ago,
   And the brier-rose and the orchis died amid the summer glow;

But on the hill the goldenrod, and the aster in the wood,
And the yellow sunflower by the brook in autumn beauty stood,
Till fell the frost from the clear cold heaven, as falls the plague on men,
And the brightness of their smile was gone from upland, glade, and glen.

4. And now, when comes the calm, mild day, as still such days will come,
To call the squirrel and the bee from out their winter home;
When the sound of dropping nuts is heard, though all the trees are still,
And twinkle in the smoky light the waters of the rill;
The south-wind searches for the flowers whose fragrance late he bore,
And sighs to find them in the wood and by the stream no more.

5. And then I think of one who in her youthful beauty died,
The fair, meek blossom that grew up and faded by my side:
In the cold, moist earth we laid her, when the forests cast the leaf,
And we wept that one so lovely should have a life so brief;
Yet not unmeet it was that one, like that young friend of ours,
So gentle and so beautiful, should perish with the flowers. WILLIAM CULLEN BRYANT.

**William Cullen Bryant** was born at Cummington, Massachusetts, in 1794 and died in New York City in 1878 from the effects of a sunstroke. He was a poet by nature; his "Thanatopsis," written before he was nineteen, bids fair to secure him a literary immortality. He was a careful observer of nature, "as any one may prove who will take a volume of his poems out into the woods and fields, and read the descriptions in the presence of what is described." In 1826 Bryant became editor of the New York *Evening Post*, which position he retained until his death. His writings in that paper were often very anti-Catholic.

At what time of the year do the flowers fade? Why is this time called "the melancholy days" (1)? What is meant by "the fair and good of ours" (2)? What flowers remain in bloom until the end of autumn (3)? The "one who in her youthful beauty died" (5) is an allusion to the death of the poet's sister.

## LESSON LIX.

1. greet'ed; *v.* spoke to; addressed.
2. im pōṣ'ing; *a.* exciting attention.
3. peer'ing; *v.* looking curiously.
5. nēst'led; *v.* settled.
10. queūe (kū); *n.* a tail-like twist of hair worn at the back of the head.
11. chintz; *n.* cotton cloth, printed with flowers and other designs in a number of colors.

### An Old-fashioned Girl.

This Lesson is an extract from Mrs. Alcott's "Old-fashioned Girl." Polly, the heroine of the story, who lives in the country, is on a visit to her city friend Fanny Shaw. Tom, the "dreadful boy," is Fanny's brother. Maud is a younger sister.

1. Polly hoped the "dreadful boy" would not be present; but he was, and stared at her all dinner-time in a most trying manner. Mr. Shaw, a busy-looking gentleman, said, "How do you do, my dear? Hope you'll enjoy yourself;" and then appeared to forget her entirely. Mrs. Shaw, a pale, nervous woman, greeted her little guest kindly, and took care that she wanted for nothing.

2. Madam Shaw, a quiet old lady, with an imposing cap, exclaimed, on seeing Polly, "Bless my heart! the image of her mother—a sweet woman—how is she, dear?" and kept peering at the newcomer over her glasses till, between Madam and Tom, poor Polly lost her appetite. Fanny chatted like a magpie, and little Maud fidgeted, till Tom proposed to put her under the big dish-cover, which produced such an explosion that the young lady was borne screaming away by the much-enduring Katy, the nurse.

3. It was, altogether, an uncomfortable dinner, and Polly was very glad when it was over. All went about their own affairs; and, after doing the honors of the house, Fan was called to the dressmaker, leaving Polly to amuse herself in the great drawing-room. Polly was glad to be alone for a few minutes; and, having examined all the pretty things about her, began to walk up and down over the soft, flowery carpet, humming to herself, as the daylight faded and only the ruddy glow of the fire filled the room.

4. Presently Madam came slowly in, and sat down in her arm-chair, saying, "That's a fine old tune; sing it to me, my dear. I haven't heard it this many a day." Polly didn't like to sing before strangers, for she had no teaching but such as her busy mother could give her; but she had been taught the utmost respect for old people, and, having no reason for refusing, she directly went to the piano and did as she was bid.

5. "That's the sort of music it's a pleasure to hear. Sing some more, dear," said Madam, in her gentle way, when she had done. Pleased with this praise, Polly sang away in a fresh little voice that went straight to the listener's heart and nestled there. The sweet old tunes that one is never tired of were all Polly's store. The more she

sung, the better she did it; and when she wound up with "A Health to King Charlie," the room quite rung with the stirring music made by the big piano and the little maid.

6. "That's a jolly tune! Sing it again, please," cried Tom's voice; and there was Tom's red head bobbing up over the high back of the chair where he had hidden himself. It gave Polly quite a turn, for she thought no one was hearing her but the old lady dozing by the fire. "I can't sing any more; I'm tired," she said, and walked away to Madam in the other room. The red head vanished like a meteor, for Polly's tone had been decidedly cool.

7. The old lady put out her hand, and, drawing Polly to her knee, looked into her face with such kind eyes that Polly forgot the impressive cap, and smiled at her confidently; for she saw that her simple music had pleased her listener, and she felt glad to know it. "You mustn't mind my staring, dear," said Madam, softly pinching her rosy cheek, "I haven't seen a little girl for so long, it does my old eyes good to look at you." Polly thought that a very odd speech, and couldn't help saying, "Aren't Fan and Maud little girls, too?"

8. "Oh, dear, no! not what I call little girls. Fan has been a young lady these two years, and Maud is a spoiled baby. Your mother's a very sensible woman, my child." "What a queer old lady!" thought Polly; but she said "Yes'm," respectfully, and looked at the fire. "You don't understand what I mean, do you?" asked Madam, still holding her by the chin. "No'm; not quite."

9. "Well, dear, I'll tell you. In my day, children of fourteen and fifteen didn't dress in the height of the fashion; go to parties as nearly like those of grown people as it's possible to make them; lead idle, giddy, unhealthy lives,

and get *blasé* at twenty. We were little folks till eighteen or so; worked and studied, dressed and played, like children; honored our parents; and our days were much longer in the land than now, it seems to me."

10. The old lady appeared to forget Polly at the end of her speech; for she sat patting the plump little hand that lay in her own, and looking up at a faded picture of an old gentleman with a ruffled shirt and a queue. "Was he your father, Madam?"—"Yes, my dear; my honored father. I did up his frills to the day of his death; and the first money I ever earned was five dollars which he offered as a prize to whichever of his six girls would lay the handsomest darn in his silk stockings."

11. "How proud you must have been!" cried Polly, leaning on the old lady's knee with an interested face.—"Yes; and we all learned to make bread, and cook, and wore little chintz gowns, and were as gay and hearty as kittens. All lived to be grandmothers; and I'm the last—seventy next birthday, my dear, and not worn out yet; though daughter Shaw is an invalid at forty."

12. "That's the way I was brought up, and that's why Fan calls me old-fashioned, I suppose. Tell me more about your papa, please; I like it," said Polly.—"Say 'father.' We never called him papa; and if one of my brothers had addressed him as 'governor,' as boys now do, I really think he'd have cut him off with a shilling."   LOUISA M. ALCOTT.

**Explain** the abbreviations: "aren't" (7); "Yes'm" (8); "No'm" (8); "it's" (9). "Blasé" (9) is a French word meaning *rendered incapable of continued enjoyment*. "Did up his frills" (10) means *to wash and iron the frills* which gentlemen used to wear on their shirt-bosoms. "Cut him off with a shilling" (12) is *to disinherit him*.

## LESSON LX.

8. Im' me mō' rǐ ạl; *a.* further back than can be remembered.
5. pǎr' ạ lȳzĕd; *v.* deprived of motion.
6. măn' ụ mǐs' sion; *n.* the act of giving freedom.
6. ŏb sē' quī ọus lȳ; *adv.* attentively.

8. prē ĕmp' tion; *n.* the right of a settler.
10. de mēạn' ȯr; *n.* behavior.
10. ĭm pōr' tụ natẹ; *a.* hard to be borne; overpressing in demand; troublesomely urgent.
10. cōr' vīnẹ; *a.* like a crow.

### My Garden Acquaintance.

1. Dr. Watts's statement that "birds in their little nests agree," like too many others intended to form the infant mind, is very far from being true. On the contrary, the most peaceful relation of the different species to each other is that of armed neutrality. They are very jealous of neighbors.

2. A few years ago I was much interested in the house-building of a pair of summer yellowbirds. They had chosen a very pretty site near the top of a tall white lilac, within easy eyeshot of a chamber-window. A very pleasant thing it was to see their little home growing with mutual help, to watch their industrious skill interrupted only by little flirts and snatches of endearment, frugally cut short by the common-sense of the tiny housewife.

3. They had brought their work nearly to an end, and had already begun to line it with fern-down, the gathering of which demanded more distant journeys and longer absences. But, alas! the syringa, immemorial manor of the catbirds, was not more than twenty feet away, and these "giddy neighbors" had, as it appeared, been all along jealously watchful, though silent, witnesses of what they deemed an intrusion of squatters.

4. No sooner were the pretty mates fairly gone for a new load of lining, than

"To their unguarded nest these weasel Scots
 Came stealing."

Silently they flew back and forth, each giving a vengeful dab at the nest in passing. They did not fall-to and deliberately destroy it, for they might have been caught at their mischief. As it was, whenever the yellowbirds came back, their enemies were hidden in their own sight-proof bush. Several times their unconscious victims repaired damages; but at length, after counsel taken together, they gave it up.

5. The robins, by constant attacks and annoyances, have succeeded in driving off the bluejays who used to build in our pines, their gay colors and quaint, noisy ways making them welcome and amusing neighbors. I once had the chance of doing a kindness to a household of them, which they received with very friendly condescension. I had had my eye for some time upon a nest, and was puzzled by a constant fluttering of what seemed full-grown wings in it whenever I drew nigh. At last I climbed the tree, in spite of angry protests from the old birds against my intrusion. The mystery had a very simple solution. In building the nest, a long piece of pack-thread had been somewhat loosely woven in. Three of the young had contrived to entangle themselves in it and had become full-grown without being able to launch themselves upon the air. One was unharmed; another had so tightly twisted the cord about its shank that one foot was curled up and seemed paralyzed; the third, in its struggles to escape, had sawn through the flesh of the thigh and so much harmed itself that I thought it humane to put an end to its misery.

6. When I took out my knife to cut their hempen bonds, the heads of the family seemed to divine my friendly intent. Suddenly ceasing their cries and threats, they

perched quietly within reach of my hand, and watched me in my work of manumission. This, owing to the fluttering terror of the prisoners, was an affair of some delicacy; but ere long I was rewarded by seeing one of them fly away to a neighboring tree, while the cripple, making a parachute of his wings, came lightly to the ground, and hopped off as well as he could with one leg, obsequiously waited on by his elders. A week later, I had the satisfaction of meeting him in the pine walk, in good spirits, and already so far recovered as to be able to balance himself with the lame foot. I have no doubt that in his old age he accounted for his lameness by some handsome story of a wound received at the famous Battle of the Pines, when our tribe, overcome by numbers, was driven from its ancient camping-ground.

7. Of late years the jays have visited us only at intervals; and in winter their bright plumage, set off by the snow, and their cheerful cry, are especially welcome. They would have furnished Æsop with a fable, for the feathered crest in which they seem to take so much satisfaction is often their fatal snare. Country boys make a hole with their finger in the snow-crust just large enough to admit the jay's head, and, hollowing it out somewhat beneath, bait it with a few kernels of corn. The crest slips easily into the trap, but refuses to be pulled out again, and he who came to feast remains a prey.

8. Twice have the crow-blackbirds attempted a settlement in my pines, and twice have the robins, who claim a right of pre-emption, so successfully played the part of border-ruffians as to drive them away,—to my great regret, for they are the best substitute we have for rooks. At Shady Hill (now, alas! empty of its so long-loved household) they build by hundreds, and nothing can be more cheery than their creaking clatter (like a convention of old-

fashioned tavern-signs) as they gather at evening to debate in mass-meeting their windy politics, or to gossip at their tent-doors over the events of the day. Their port is grave, and their stalk across the turf as martial as that of a second-rate ghost in "Hamlet." They never meddled with my corn, so far as I could discover.

9. For a few years I had crows; but their nests are an irresistible bait for boys, and their settlement was broken up. They grew so wonted as to throw off a great part of their shyness, and to tolerate my near approach. One very hot day I stood for some time within twenty feet of a mother and three children, who sat on an elm-bough over my head, gasping in the sultry air, and holding their wings half spread for coolness.

10. There are few things to my ear more melodious than a crow's caw of a clear winter morning as it drops to you filtered through five hundred fathoms of crisp blue air. The hostility of all smaller birds makes the moral character of the crow, for all his deaconlike demeanor and garb, somewhat questionable. He could never sally forth without insult. The golden robins, especially, would chase him as far as I could follow with my eye, making him duck clumsily to avoid their importunate bills. I do not believe, however, that he robbed any nests hereabouts, for the refuse of the gas-works, which, in our free-and-easy community, is allowed to poison the river, supplied him with dead alewives in abundance. I used to watch him making his periodical visits to the salt-marshes, and coming back with a fish in his beak to his young savages, who, no doubt, like it in that condition which makes it savory to the Kanakas and other corvine races of men.

JAMES RUSSELL LOWELL.

James Russell Lowell was born at Cambridge, Massachusetts, in

1819 and died August 12, 1891. He was known as a poet, humorist, and literary critic. That he was also a sympathetic student of nature is shown by this Lesson.

**Dr. (Isaac) Watts** (1), born 1674, died 1748, was an English Protestant minister, and a writer of hymns and other religious poems. "He who came to feast remains a prey" (7) is a parody on the line in Goldsmith's "Deserted Village": "fools who came to scoff remained to pray"; "border-ruffians" (8) were the men of either political party who respectively endeavored to exclude or to introduce slavery into Kansas, at the time of its admission as a State. "Convention of old-fashioned tavern-signs" (8) is an allusion to the old creaking signs which used to hang before taverns or inns; "Kanakas" (10) are the natives of the Sandwich Islands.

## LESSON LXI.

1. trá dĭ' tion a rȳ; *a.* relating to tradition, that is, the unwritten doctrines, belief, etc., that are handed down from father to son, or from ancestors to posterity.
1. hẽr' mĭt ąǵe; *n.* a retired residence.
3. ĕn thū' ṣĭ ăst; *n.* an ardent and imaginative person.
3. a băsh ęd'; *v.* confused.
6. re ĭt' ẽr ăt ed; *v.* repeated.
12. săl' lĭeṣ; *n.* quick rushes for the purpose of attack.
16. ăb' ju rā' tion; *n.* solemn denial.

### Venerable Joan of Arc.

Upon the death of Henry V. Charles the Dauphin laid claim to the throne of France. In consequence, England declared war, and the English forces were everywhere successful. The English at last, under the Earl of Suffolk, laid siege to Orleans, the "key of South France." The Dauphin's cause seemed lost; his friends were falling off; Orleans was on the point of surrendering, when Joan of Arc, a simple peasant girl of Domremi in the department of Vosges, "having pity on France," came forth from her obscurity, and became the savior of her country. On January 27, 1894, the Church enrolled the name of the Maid of Orleans in the ranks of those who are entitled to be called the Venerable Servants of God.

1. Joan of Arc was born about the year 1412. Her education did not differ from that of the other poor girls in

JOAN OF ARC.

the neighborhood; but she was distinguished above them all by her diligence, modesty, and piety. Domremi, like other villages, has its traditionary tales of wonder and supernatural agency. There stood at no great distance an old spreading beech-tree, under the branches of which the fairies were said to hold their nightly meetings. Near its foot ran a clear streamlet, the waters of which were believed to work astonishing cures; and a little farther off was a still more sacred spot, a solitary chapel, called the Hermitage of the Virgin.

2. Joan was accustomed to visit all these places with her companions; but the Hermitage was her favorite resort, where every Saturday she hung up a garland of flowers or burnt a taper of wax in honor of the mother of Christ. These her early habits are worthy of notice, as they probably served to impress on her mind that romantic character which it afterward exhibited.

3. The child was fond of solitude. Whatever interested her became the subject of long and serious thought; and in these day-dreams the young enthusiast learnt to invest with visible forms the creations of her own fancy. She was about twelve years old when, walking in her father's garden on a Sunday, she thought that she observed a brilliant light on one side, and heard a voice calling on her by her name. She turned and saw, as she believed, the archangel Michael, who told her to be good, dutiful, and virtuous, and God would protect her. She felt abashed in his presence, but at his departure wept, wishing that he had taken her with him.

4. At length arrived the news of the disastrous battle of Verneuil. Joan witnessed the despair of her parents and neighbors, and learned from them that there remained but one source of hope for her country, the possible accom-

plishment of a traditionary prophecy, that from Boischesnu, the adjoining forest of oaks, would come a maid destined to be the savior of France.

5. Such a prediction was likely to make a deep impression on the mind of Joan. One day when she was alone, tending her father's flock, she again heard the voice and saw the form of the archangel; but he was now accompanied by two females, the Saints Catherine and Margaret, names, it should be observed, familiar to her, for they were the patronesses of the parish church. He announced to her that she was the woman pointed out by the prophecy; that hers was the important commission to conduct her sovereign to Rheims preparatory to his coronation; that with this view she ought to apply to Baudricourt, governor of Vaucouleurs, for the means of access to the royal presence; and that Catherine and Margaret would accompany her as guides and monitors, whom it was her duty to obey.

6. She was appalled at the idea of so extraordinary a mission, and her confidence was shaken by the incredulity and disapprobation of her parents. But her "voices," as she called them, reiterated the command; they reprimanded her for her disobedience; and she began to fear that any longer delay might be a sin which would endanger her salvation.

7. At length the governor, who had deemed it his duty to communicate her history to the Dauphin, received an order to forward her to the French court. On horseback, and in male attire, with an escort of seven persons, she arrived safely at Chinon on the tenth day. An hour was fixed for the admission to the royal presence, and the poor maiden of Domremi was ushered into a spacious hall lighted up with fifty torches and filled with some hundreds of

knights, among whom Charles himself had mixed unnoticed and in plain attire.

8. Joan entered without embarrassment; the glare of the light, the gaze of the spectators, did not disconcert her. Singling out the Dauphin at the first glance, she walked up to him with a firm step, bent her knee, and said, "God give you good life, gentle king!" He was surprised, but replied, "I am not the king; he is there," pointing at the same time to a different part of the hall. "In the name of God," she exclaimed, "it is not they but you are the king. Most noble Lord Dauphin, I am Joan the maid, sent on the part of God to aid you and the kingdom, and by His order I announce to you that you will be crowned in the city of Rheims."

9. The following day "the maid" (so she was now called) made her appearance in public and on horseback. From her look she was thought to be in her sixteenth or seventeenth year; her figure was slender and graceful, and her long black locks fell in ringlets on her shoulders. She ran a course with the lance, and managed her horse with ease and dexterity. The crowd burst into shouts of admiration; they saw in her something more than human: she was a knight descended from heaven for the salvation of France.

10. Sixty bastiles or forts, erected in a circle round Orleans, had effectually intercepted all communication with the country, and the horrors of famine were already felt within the walls when it was resolved to make a desperate effort to throw a supply of provisions into the city. A strong body of men, under some of the bravest officers in France, assembled at Blois, and "the maid" solicited and obtained permission not only to join but also to direct the expedition.

11. She was received as an envoy from heaven, and began the exercise of her supernatural authority by calling on the men to prepare for combat by exercises of devotion. To Suffolk, Glasdale, and Pole, the English commanders, she sent orders in the name of God to withdraw from France, and return to their native country; to the chiefs of her own nation she promised complete success if they would cross the Loire, and march boldly through the quarters of the enemy. The promise or prediction was verified. The besiegers did not stir from their entrenchments, and the convoy entered the city.

12. From this moment it became dangerous to dispute the celestial mission of Joan. Her presence created in the soldiers a spirit of daring and a confidence of success. Day after day sallies were made, and the strongest of the English forts successively fell into the hands of the assailants. On every occasion "the maid" was to be seen in the foremost rank, with her banner displayed, and encouraging her countrymen by her voice and gestures. But at the storming of the Tournelles, whilst she was in the act of planting the first ladder against the wall, an arrow passed through an opening in her corslet, and fixed itself between the chest and the shoulder. Her companions conveyed her out of the crowd; the wound was dressed; and the heroine, after a few minutes spent in prayer, rejoined the combatants. At her appearance the assailants redoubled their efforts, and the fort was won.

13. Suffolk, disconcerted by these repeated losses, and warned by the desponding countenances of his followers, determined to raise the siege. Next day, at dawn, the English army was seen at a short distance from the walls, drawn up in battle-array, and braving the enemy to fight in the open field; but "the maid" forbade any man to

pass the gates of the city. Suffolk waited some hours in vain. At length he gave the signal; the long line of forts, the fruits of so many months' labor, was instantly in flames; and the soldiers, with feelings of shame and regret, turned their backs on the city. The French pursued, and town after town fell into their hands, till at last, as was promised, the Dauphin entered the city of Rheims.

14. The coronation was performed in the usual manner. During the ceremony "the maid of Orleans," with her banner unfurled, stood at the king's side. As soon as it was over she threw herself on her knees, embraced his feet, declared her mission accomplished, and with tears solicited his leave to return to her former station. But the king was unwilling to lose the services of one who had hitherto proved so useful; and at his earnest request she consented to remain with the army, and to strengthen that throne which she had in a great measure established.

15. But in trying to raise the siege of Compiègne "the maid" fell into the hands of the Burgundians, who sold her to their allies, the English. She was then thrown into prison, where she was treated with neglect by her friends and with cruelty by her enemies, and at last tried and condemned for witchcraft.

16. The captive was placed at the bar, and when the judge was prepared to pronounce sentence, she yielded to a sudden impulse of terror, signed an act of abjuration, and, having promised upon oath never more to wear male attire, was remanded to her former place of confinement.

17. Her enthusiasm, however, revived in the solitude of a prison; her cell was again peopled with celestial visitants, and new scenes of military glory opened to her imagination. The cruelty of her judge condemned her, on the charge of having relapsed into her former errors.

18. She was led sobbing and struggling to the stake; nor did the expectation of a heavenly deliverer forsake her till she saw the fire kindled at her feet. She then burst into loud exclamations, protesting her innocence, and invoking the aid of the Almighty; and, just before the flames enveloped her, was seen embracing a crucifix, and calling on Christ for mercy. This cruel and unjustifiable tragedy was acted in the market-place of Rouen, before an immense concourse of spectators, about twelve months after her capture. — REV. JOHN LINGARD, D.D.

**John Lingard**, the celebrated historian, was born of Catholic parents at Winchester, England, in 1771. Having finished his collegiate course, he studied theology, and was ordained a priest in April, 1795. As a writer he is best known by his "History of England." He drew the material for this work from original documents, and on many points gave new and correct views of manners, events, and characters. Cardinal Wiseman said he was "the only impartial historian" of his country. Lingard died in July, 1851.

Rheims (5) is famous for its grand cathedral, and as being the city in which in former times the kings of France were crowned. Orleans (10) is a cathedral city on the river Loire. Rouen (18), another town famous for its cathedral, is on the river Seine.

## LESSON LXII.

1. a nŏn'; *adv.* in a short time.
1. vo cā' tion; *n.* calling, profession, business.
2. wĕll; *v.* flow.
2. tärn; *n.* a small lake among the mountains.
2. fĕll; *n.* a stony hill (*Provincial English*).
2. ġills; *n.* woody glens (*Provincial English*).
7. sprāy' ing; *v.* sending the water flying in small drops.
7. tûr moil' ing; *v.* disquieting.
7. pûrl' ing; *v.* running swiftly round.

### The Cataract of Lodore.

1. "How does the water
  Come down at Lodore?"

My little boy asked me
  Thus, once on a time;
And, moreover, he tasked me
  To tell him in rhyme.
Anon at the word,
  There first came one daughter,
  And then came another,
To second and third
  The request of their brother,
And to hear how the water
Comes down at Lodore,
With its rush and its roar,
  As many a time
They had seen it before.
  So I told them in rhyme—
For of rhymes I had store;
And 'twas my vocation
For their recreation
  That so I should sing;
Because I was Laureate
  To them and the king.

2. From its sources, which well
  In the tarn on the fell;
  From its fountains
  In the mountains,
Its rills and its gills;
Through moss and through brake,
  It runs and it creeps
  For a while, till it sleeps
In its own little lake.
And thence, at departing,
Awakening and starting,

It runs through the reeds,
And away it proceeds,
Through meadow and glade,
In sun and in shade,
And through the wood-shelter,
   Among crags in its flurry,
Helter-skelter,
   Hurry-skurry.
Here it comes sparkling,
And there it lies darkling;
Now smoking and frothing
In tumult and wrath in,
Till, in this rapid race
   On which it is bent,
It reaches the place
   Of its steep descent.

3. The cataract strong
  Then plunges along,
  Striking and raging,
  As if a war waging
Its caverns and rocks among;
  Rising and leaping,
  Sinking and creeping,
  Swelling and sweeping,
  Showering and springing,
  Flying and flinging,
  Writhing and ringing,
  Eddying and whisking,
  Spouting and frisking,
  Turning and twisting,
  Around and around
  With endless rebound;

Smiting and fighting,
A sight to delight in;
Confounding, astounding,
Dizzying, and deafening the ear with its sound,

4. Collecting, projecting,
Receding and speeding,
And shocking and rocking,
And darting and parting,
And threading and spreading,
And whizzing and hissing,
And dripping and skipping,
And hitting and splitting,
And shining and twining,
And rattling and battling,
And shaking and quaking,
And pouring and roaring,
And waving and raving,
And tossing and crossing,
And flowing and going,
And running and stunning,
And foaming and roaming,
And dinning and spinning,
And dropping and hopping,
And working and jerking,
And guggling and struggling,
And heaving and cleaving,
And moaning and groaning,

5. And glittering and frittering,
And gathering and feathering,
And whitening and brightening,
And quivering and shivering,

   And hurrying and skurrying,
   And thundering and floundering;

6. Dividing and gliding and sliding,
 And falling and brawling and sprawling,
 And driving and riving and striving,
 And sprinkling and twinkling and wrinkling,
 And sounding and bounding and rounding,
 And bubbling and troubling and doubling,
 And grumbling and rumbling and tumbling,
 And chattering and battering and shattering;

7. Retreating and beating and meeting and sheeting,
Delaying and straying and playing and spraying,
Advancing and prancing and glancing and dancing,
Recoiling, turmoiling, and toiling and boiling,
And gleaming and streaming and steaming and beaming,
And rushing and flushing and brushing and gushing,
And flapping and rapping and clapping and slapping,
And curling and whirling and purling and twirling,
And thumping and plumping and bumping and jumping,
And dashing and flashing and splashing and clashing;
And so never ending, but always descending,
Sounds and motions forever and ever are blending,
 All at once, and all o'er, with a mighty uproar:
 And this way the water comes down at Lodore.
         ROBERT SOUTHEY.

**Robert Southey,** at one time Poet Laureate of England, was born at Bristol, England, in 1774 and died in 1843. He was a voluminous writer, and at once a poet, scholar, critic, historian, and an antiquary. His greatest poetical work is "The Curse of Kehama," founded on Hindoo mythology. Several selections from Southey's writings will be found in the Catholic National Sixth Reader.

Lodore (1) is a cascade on Derwent River, Cumberland, England.

This Lesson will prove admirable for practice on the termination *-ing*.

## LESSON LXIII.

2. sery'tĭ nў; *n.* critical examination.
5. bōŵl' dẽrs; *n.* masses of rock.
5. ŏb' vĭ ȯŭs lў; *adv.* plainly.
7. seeth' ing; *v.* boiling.
8. in cŭm' brançę; *n.* troublesome load.
10. rĕṣ' o nạnt; *a.* resounding.
11. In' tẽr mĭt' tạnt; *a.* ceasing at intervals.
11. pro tū' bẽr ạnçę; *n.* anything prominent beyond the surrounding surface.
12. prŏm' on to rў; *n.* a high point of land or rock projecting beyond the line of coast.
17. shāle; *n.* a fine-grained rock.

### Beneath the Falls of Niagara.

1. On the first evening of my visit, I met, at the head of Biddle's Stair, the guide to the Cave of the Winds. He was in the prime of manhood—large, well-built, firm, and pleasant in mouth and eye. My interest in the scene stirred up his, and made him communicative. Turning to a photograph, he described, by reference to it, a feat which he had accomplished some time previously, and which had brought him almost under the green water of the Horseshoe Fall.

2. "Can you lead me there to-morrow?" I asked.

He eyed me inquiringly, weighing, perhaps, the chances of a man of light build, and with gray in his whiskers, in such an undertaking.

"I wish," I added, "to see as much of the Fall as can be seen, and where you lead I will endeavor to follow."

His scrutiny relaxed into a smile, and he said, "Very well; I shall be ready for you to-morrow."

3. On the morrow, accordingly, I came. In the hut at the head of Biddle's Stair I redressed—drawing on two pairs of woolen pantaloons, three woolen jackets, two pairs of socks, and a pair of felt shoes. Even if wet, my guide assured me that the clothes would keep me from being chilled, and he was right. A suit and hood of yellow oil cloth covered all. Most laudable precautions were taken by the young assistant of the guide to keep the water out, but his devices broke down immediately when severely tested.

4. We descended the stair; the handle of a pitchfork doing, in my case, the duty of an alpenstock. At the bottom, the guide inquired whether we should go first to the Cave of the Winds or to the Horseshoe, remarking that the latter would try us most. I decided to get the roughest done first, and he turned to the left over the stones. They were sharp and trying.

5. The base of the first portion of the cataract is covered with huge bowlders, obviously the ruins of the limestone ledge above. The water does not distribute itself uniformly among these, but seeks for itself channels through which it pours with the force of a torrent. We passed some of these with wet feet, but without difficulty. At length we came to the side of a more formidable current. My guide walked along its edge until he reached its least turbulent portion. Halting, he said, "This is our greatest difficulty; if we can cross here, we shall get far toward the Horseshoe."

6. He waded in. It evidently required all his strength to steady him. The water rose above his loins, and it foamed still higher. He had to search for footing, amid unseen bowlders, against which the torrent rose violently. He struggled and swayed, but he struggled successfully,

and finally reached the shallower water at the other side. Stretching out his arm, he said to me, "Now come on!"

7. I looked down the torrent as it rushed to the river below, which was seething with the tumult of the cataract. Even where it was not more than knee-deep, its power was manifest. As it rose around me, I sought to split the torrent by presenting a side to it; but the insecurity of the footing enabled it to grasp the loins, twist me fairly round, and bring its impetus to bear upon the back. Further struggle was impossible; and feeling my balance hopelessly gone, I turned, flung myself toward the bank just quitted, and was instantly swept into shallower water.

8. The oil-cloth covering was a great incumbrance; it had been made for a much stouter man, and, standing upright after my submersion, my legs occupied the center of two bags of water. My guide exhorted me to try again. Instructed by the first misadventure, I once more entered the stream. Had the alpenstock been of iron, it might have helped me; but, as it was, the tendency of the water to sweep it out of my hands rendered it worse than useless. I however clung to it from habit.

9. Again the torrent rose, and again I wavered; but by keeping the left hip well against it, I remained upright, and at length grasped the hand of my leader at the other side. He laughed pleasantly. The first victory was gained, and he enjoyed it. "No traveler," he said, "was ever here before." Soon afterward, by trusting to a piece of driftwood which seemed firm, I was again taken off my feet, but was immediately caught by a protruding rock.

10. We clambered over the bowlders toward the thickest spray, which soon became so weighty as to cause us to stagger under its shock. For the most part nothing could be seen; we were in the midst of bewildering

tumult, lashed by the water, which sounded at times like the cracking of innumerable whips. Underneath this was the deep resonant roar of the cataract. I tried to shield my eyes with my hands and look upward, but the defense was useless. My guide continued to move on, but at a certain place he halted, desiring me to take shelter in his lee, and observe the cataract.

11. The spray did not come so much from the upper ledge as from the rebound of the shattered water when it struck the bottom. Hence the eyes could be protected from the blinding shock of the spray, while the line of vision to the upper ledges remained to some extent clear. On looking upward over the guide's shoulder I could see the water bending over the ledge, while the Terrapin Tower loomed fitfully through the intermittent spray-gusts. We were right under the tower. A little farther on, the cataract, after its first plunge, hit a protuberance some way down, and flew from it in a prodigious burst of spray; through this we staggered.

12. We rounded the promontory on which the Terrapin Tower stands, and moved, amid the wildest commotion, along the arm of the Horseshoe, until the bowlders failed us, and the cataract fell into the profound gorge of the Niagara River.

13. Here my guide sheltered me again, and desired me to look up; I did so, and could see as before the green gleam of the mighty curve sweeping over the upper ledge, and the fitful plunge of the water, as the spray between us and it alternately gathered and disappeared.

14. We returned, clambering at intervals up and down, so as to catch glimpses of the most impressive portions of the cataract. We passed under ledges formed by tabular masses of limestone, and through some curious openings

formed by the falling together of the summits of the rocks. At length we found ourselves beside our enemy of the morning. My guide halted for a minute or two, scanning the torrent thoughtfully. I said that, as a guide, he ought to have a rope in such a place; but he retorted that, as no traveler had ever thought of coming there, he did not see the necessity of keeping a rope.

15. He waded in. The struggle to keep himself erect was evident enough; he swayed, but recovered himself again and again. At length he slipped, gave way, did as I had done, threw himself flat in the water toward the bank, and was swept into the shallow. Standing in the stream near its edge, he stretched his arm toward me. I retained the pitchfork handle, for it had been useful among the bowlders. By wading some way in the staff could be made to reach him, and I proposed his seizing it.

16. "If you are sure," he replied, "that in case of giving way you can maintain your grasp, then I will certainly hold you."

I waded in and stretched the staff to my companion. It was firmly grasped by both of us. Thus helped, though its onset was strong, I moved safely across the torrent. All danger ended here.

17. We afterward roamed sociably among the torrents and bowlders below the Cave of the Winds. The rocks were covered with organic slime, which could not have been walked over with bare feet, but the felt shoes effectually prevented slipping. We reached the cave and entered it, first by a wooden way carried over the bowlders, and then along a narrow ledge, to the point eaten deepest into the shale. When the wind is from the south, the falling water, I am told, can be seen tranquilly from this

spot; but when we were there, a blinding hurricane of spray was whirled against us.   JOHN TYNDALL.

"Horseshoe Fall" (1) has been so worn away by the action of the water that the horseshoe form has disappeared. "Terrapin Tower" (11) stood on a rock just above the American Fall. "Organic slime" (17) is a sticky mud containing the lowest form of animal life.

## LESSON LXIV.

1. knŏll; *n.* a little round hill.
1. wŏe'-be gŏne'; *a.* crushed by grief.
2. in crŭst'ed; *v.* covered with a crust.
2. roist'ẽrs; *n.* bold, blustering fellows.
3. găm'bŏl; *n.* a frolic.
3. tĕn'drĭls; *n.* thread-like shoots of a plant that wind round another body for support.
6. ăd'dlĕd; *v.* confused.
8. con nū'bĭ ạl; *a.* relating to marriage.

### Rip Van Winkle. Part I.

Rip Van Winkle is described as a good-natured, lazy fellow, a favorite of the village children, and more fond of drinking and of hunting than of hard work. According to the story, he one day went into the Kaatskill Mountains to shoot squirrels, and growing tired, lay down for a nap. He wakened from his sleep to see some odd-looking dwarfish men playing at ninepins and drinking from large cups or flagons. At their invitation Rip joined them in one drink after another until at last, growing drowsy, he fell into a deep sleep, from which he did not awake for twenty years. What followed his awakening is here described.

1. On waking he found himself on the green knoll from whence he had first seen the old man of the glen. He rubbed his eyes—it was a bright sunny morning. The birds were hopping and twittering among the bushes, and the eagle was wheeling aloft, and breasting the pure mountain breeze. "Surely," thought Rip, "I have not slept here all night." He recalled the occurrences before he fell asleep. The strange man with the keg of liquor—the

mountain ravine—the wild retreat among the rocks—the woe-begone party at ninepins—the flagon—" Oh, that wicked flagon!" thought Rip—" what excuse shall I make to Dame Van Winkle?"

2. He looked round for his gun, but in place of the clean well-oiled fowling-piece he found an old firelock lying by him, the barrel incrusted with rust, the lock falling off, and the stock worm-eaten. He now suspected that the grave roisters of the mountain had put a trick upon him, and, having dosed him with liquor, had robbed him of his gun. Wolf, too, had disappeared, but he might have strayed away after a squirrel or partridge. He whistled after him, and shouted his name, but all in vain; the echoes repeated his whistle and shout, but no dog was to be seen.

3. He determined to revisit the scene of the last evening's gambol, and if he met with any of the party to demand his dog and gun. As he rose to walk, he found himself stiff in the joints, and wanting in his usual activity. "These mountain beds do not agree with me," thought Rip, " and if this frolic should lay me up with a fit of the rheumatism, I shall have a blessed time with Dame Van Winkle." With some difficulty he got down into the glen; he found the gully up which he and his companion had ascended the preceding evening; but to his astonishment a mountain stream was now foaming down it, leaping from rock to rock, and filling the glen with babbling murmurs. He, however, made shift to scramble up its sides, working his toilsome way through thickets of birch, sassafras, and witch-hazel; and sometimes tripped up or entangled by the wild grape-vines that twisted their coils and tendrils from tree to tree, and spread a kind of network in his path.

4. At length he reached to where the ravine had

opened through the cliffs to the amphitheater; but no traces of such opening remained. The rocks presented a high impenetrable wall, over which the torrent came tumbling in a sheet of feathery foam, and fell into a broad, deep basin, black from the shadows of the surrounding forest. Here, then, poor Rip was brought to a stand. He again called and whistled after his dog; he was only answered by the cawing of a flock of idle crows, sporting high in air about a dry tree that overhung a sunny precipice; and who, secure in their elevation, seemed to look down and scoff at the poor man's perplexities. What was to be done? The morning was passing away, and Rip felt famished for want of his breakfast. He grieved to give up his dog and gun; he dreaded to meet his wife; but it would not do to starve among the mountains. He shook his head, shouldered his rusty firelock, and with a heart full of trouble and anxiety turned his steps homeward.

5. As he approached the village he met a number of people, but none whom he knew, which somewhat surprised him, for he had thought himself acquainted with every one in the country round. Their dress, too, was of a different fashion from that to which he was accustomed. They all stared at him with equal marks of surprise, and whenever they cast eyes upon him, invariably stroked their chins. The constant recurrence of this gesture induced Rip, involuntarily, to do the same, when to his astonishment he found his beard had grown a foot long!

6. He had now entered the skirts of the village. A troop of strange children ran at his heels, hooting after him, and pointing at his gray beard. The dogs, too, not one of which he recognized for an old acquaintance, barked at him as he passed. The very village was altered; it was larger and more populous. There were rows of houses which he

had never seen before, and those which had been his familiar haunts had disappeared. Strange names were over the doors—strange faces at the windows—everything was strange. His mind now misgave him; he began to doubt whether both he and the world around him were not bewitched. Surely this was his native village, which he had left but a day before. There stood the Kaatskill Mountains—there ran the silver Hudson at a distance—there was every hill and dale precisely as it had always been. Rip was sorely perplexed—" That flagon last night," thought he, " has addled my poor head sadly!"

7. It was with some difficulty that he found the way to his own house, which he approached with silent awe, expecting every moment to hear the shrill voice of Dame Van Winkle. He found the house gone to decay—the roof fallen in, the windows shattered, and the doors off the hinges. A half-starved dog, that looked like Wolf, was skulking about it. Rip called him by name, but the cur snarled, showed his teeth, and passed on. This was an unkind cut indeed. " My very dog," sighed poor Rip, " has forgotten me!"

8. He entered the house, which, to tell the truth, Dame Van Winkle had always kept in neat order. It was empty, forlorn, and apparently abandoned. This desolateness overcame all his connubial fears—he called loudly for his wife and children—the lonely chambers rang for a moment with his voice, and then all again was silence.

---

Sloth makes all things difficult, but Industry all easy; and he that riseth late must trot all day, and shall scarce overtake his business at night; while Laziness travels so slowly, that Poverty soon overtakes him.—FRANKLIN.

## LESSON LXV.

1. mĕt' ȧ mōr' phosĕd; v. changed into a different form.
1. scĕp' tẽr; n. a staff borne by kings on solemn occasions.
2. dĭs' pu tā' tious; a. inclined to dispute.
2. phlĕgm (flĕm); n. dullness; want of interest.
2. hȧ răngū' ing; v. speaking to a large crowd.
2. jär' gŏn; n. confused, unintelligible talk.
3. ȧ kĭm' bo; a. with the hand on the hip, and the elbow turned outward.
4. rĕf' ȯ ģee'; n. one who flees to a place of safety.
5. eŭl' prĭt; n. a person accused of a crime.
9. coun' tẽr pärt'; n. copy.

### Rip Van Winkle. Part II.

1. He now hurried forth, and hastened to his old resort, the village inn—but it too was gone. A large rickety wooden building stood in its place, with great gaping windows, some of them broken, and mended with old hats and petticoats, and over the door was painted, "The Union Hotel, by Jonathan Doolittle." Instead of the great tree that used to shelter the quiet little Dutch inn of yore, there now was reared a tall naked pole, with something on the top that looked like a red nightcap, and from it was fluttering a flag, on which was a singular assemblage of stars and stripes—all this was strange and incomprehensible. He recognized on the sign, however, the ruby face of King George, under which he had smoked so many a peaceful pipe, but even this was singularly metamorphosed. The red coat was changed for one of blue and buff, a sword was held in the hand instead of a scepter, the head was decorated with a cocked hat, and underneath was painted in large characters, GENERAL WASHINGTON.

2. There was, as usual, a crowd of folk about the door, but none that Rip recollected. The very character of the

people seemed changed. There was a busy, bustling, disputatious tone about it, instead of the accustomed phlegm and drowsy tranquillity. He looked in vain for the sage Nicholas Vedder, with his broad face, double chin, and fair long pipe, uttering clouds of tobacco-smoke instead of idle speeches; or Van Bummel, the schoolmaster, doling forth the contents of an ancient newspaper. In place of these, a lean, bilious-looking fellow, with his pockets full of handbills, was haranguing vehemently about rights of citizens— election—members of Congress—liberty—Bunker Hill— heroes of seventy-six—and other words that were a perfect Babylonish jargon to the bewildered Van Winkle.

3. The appearance of Rip, with his long, grizzled beard, his rusty fowling-piece, his uncouth dress, and the army of women and children that had gathered at his heels soon attracted the attention of the tavern politicians. They crowded round him, eying him from head to foot with great curiosity. A knowing, self-important old gentleman, in a sharp cocked hat, made his way through the crowd, putting them to the right and left with his elbows as he passed, and planting himself before Van Winkle, with one arm akimbo, the other resting on his cane, his keen eyes and sharp hat penetrating, as it were, into his very soul, demanded in an austere tone what brought him to the election with a gun on his shoulder, and a mob at his heels, and whether he meant to breed a riot in the village.

4. "Alas! gentlemen," cried Rip, somewhat dismayed, "I am a poor, quiet man, a native of the place, and a loyal subject of the King, God bless him!"

Here a general shout burst from the by-standers—"A tory! a tory! a spy! a refugee! Hustle him! away with him!"

5. It was with great difficulty that the self-important

man in the cocked hat restored order; and having assumed a tenfold austerity of brow, demanded again of the unknown culprit what he came there for, and whom he was seeking. The poor man humbly assured him that he meant no harm, but merely came there in search of some of his neighbors, who used to keep about the tavern.

6. "Well—who are they?—name them."

Rip bethought himself a moment, and inquired, "Where's Nicholas Vedder?"

There was a silence for a little while, when an old man replied, in a thin, piping voice, "Nicholas Vedder? why, he is dead and gone these eighteen years! There was a wooden tombstone in the church-yard that used to tell all about him, but that's rotten and gone too."

7. "Where's Brom Dutcher?"

"Oh, he went off to the army in the beginning of the war; some say he was killed in the storming of Stony Point—others say he was drowned in the squall at the foot of Anthony's Nose. I don't know—he never came back again."

"Where's Van Bummel, the schoolmaster?"

"He went off to the wars, too; was a great militia general, and is now in Congress."

8. Rip's heart died away at hearing of these sad changes in his home and friends, and finding himself thus alone in the world. Every answer puzzled him, too, by treating of such enormous lapses of time, and of matters which he could not understand—war—Congress—Stony Point!—he had no courage to ask after any more friends, but cried out in despair, "Does nobody here know Rip Van Winkle?"

"Oh, Rip Van Winkle!" exclaimed two or three. "Oh, to be sure! that's Rip Van Winkle yonder, leaning against the tree."

9. Rip looked, and beheld a precise counterpart of himself as he went up the mountain; apparently as lazy, and certainly as ragged. The poor fellow was now completely confounded. He doubted his own identity, and whether he was himself or another man. In the midst of his bewilderment the man in the cocked hat demanded who he was, and what was his name.

"God knows!" exclaimed he, at his wit's end; "I'm not myself—I'm somebody else—that's me yonder—no—that's somebody else got into my shoes—I was myself last night, but I fell asleep on the mountain, and they've changed my gun, and everything's changed, and I'm changed, and I can't tell what's my name or who I am!"

"Babylonish jargon" (2) is a reference to the confusion of tongues which God sent upon the children of Adam to punish their pride at the building of the tower of Babel. "Anthony's Nose" (7), a bold promontory on the east side of the Hudson River, Putnam County, New York.

## LESSON LXVI.

1. sĭg nĭf′ ĭ cạnt lỹ; *adv.* with meaning.
1. pre çĭp′ ĭ tā′ tion; *n.* great hurry.
1. cóme̱′ lỹ (*kŭm′ lỹ*); *a.* handsome.
6. vẽrsẹd; *a.* acquainted.
6. cõr rŏb′ o rāt ed; *v.* established the truth of.
6. ăf fĭrmẹd′; *v.* declared.
7. dĭt tō; *n.* the same thing.
7. he rĕd′ ĭ ta rỹ; *a.* inheritable.
8. cro̱′ nĭẹṣ; *n.* familiar friends.

### Rip Van Winkle. Part III.

1. The by-standers began now to look at each other, nod, wink significantly, and tap their fingers against their foreheads. There was a whisper, also, about securing the gun, and keeping the old fellow from doing mischief; at

the very suggestion of which, the self-important man with the cocked hat retired with some precipitation. At this critical moment a fresh, comely woman passed through the throng to get a peep at the gray-bearded man. She had a chubby child in her arms, which, frightened at his looks, began to cry. "Hush, Rip," cried she, "hush, you little fool; the old man won't hurt you." The name of the child, the air of the mother, the tone of her voice, all awakened a train of recollections in his mind.

2. "What is your name, my good woman?" asked he.

"Judith Gardenier."

"And your father's name?"

"Ah, poor man, his name was Rip Van Winkle; it's twenty years since he went away from home with his gun, and never has been heard of since—his dog came home without him; but whether he shot himself, or was carried away by the Indians, nobody can tell. I was then but a little girl."

3. Rip had but one question more to ask; but he put it with a faltering voice.

"Where's your mother?"

Oh, she too had died but a short time since; she broke a blood-vessel in a fit of passion at a New England peddler.

There was a drop of comfort, at least, in this intelligence. The honest man could contain himself no longer. He caught his daughter and her child in his arms. "I am your father!" cried he—"Young Rip Van Winkle once—old Rip Van Winkle now! Does nobody know poor Rip Van Winkle?"

4. All stood amazed until an old woman, tottering out from among the crowd, put her hand to her brow, and, peering under it in his face for a moment, exclaimed: "Sure enough! it is Rip Van Winkle—it is himself. Wel-

come home again, old neighbor. Why, where have you been these twenty long years?"

5. Rip's story was soon told, for the whole twenty years had been to him but as one night. The neighbors stared when they heard it; some were seen to wink at each other, and put their tongues in their cheeks; and the self-important man in the cocked hat, who, when the alarm was over, had returned to the field, screwed down the corners of his mouth, and shook his head—upon which there was a general shaking of the head throughout the assemblage.

6. It was determined, however, to take the opinion of old Peter Vanderdonk, who was seen slowly advancing up the road. He was a descendant of the historian of that name, who wrote one of the earliest accounts of the province. Peter was the most ancient inhabitant of the village, and well versed in all the wonderful events and traditions of the neighborhood. He recollected Rip at once, and corroborated his story in the most satisfactory manner. He assured the company that it was a fact, handed down from his ancestor the historian, that the Kaatskill Mountains had always been haunted by strange beings. That it was affirmed that the great Hendrick Hudson, the first discoverer of the river and country, kept a kind of vigil there every twenty years with his crew of the Half-Moon, being permitted in this way to revisit the scenes of his enterprise, and keep a guardian eye upon the river and the great city called by his name. That his father had once seen them in their old Dutch dresses playing at ninepins in a hollow of the mountain; and that he himself had heard, one summer afternoon, the sound of their balls, like distant peals of thunder.

7. To make a long story short, the company broke up,

and returned to the more important concerns of the election. Rip's daughter took him home to live with her; she had a snug, well-furnished house, and a stout, cheery farmer for a husband, whom Rip recollected for one of the urchins that used to climb upon his back. As to Rip's son and heir, who was the ditto of himself, seen leaning against the tree, he was employed to work on the farm; but evinced a hereditary disposition to attend to anything else but his business.

8. Rip now resumed his old walks and habits; he soon found many of his former cronies, though all rather the worse for the wear and tear of time; and preferred making friends among the rising generation, with whom he soon grew into great favor. WASHINGTON IRVING.

**Washington Irving**, the first to win European respect for American literature, was born at New York in 1783. His graceful style, his sense of humor, and the graphic power shown in his more serious works, will long retain the popularity which his early writings obtained. He died at Sunnyside, on the Hudson, in 1859.

## LESSON LXVII.

1. ăs sĭgnĕd'; *v.* appointed; selected.
2. ĕm' ū lāte; *v.* imitate, with a view to equal.
2. bărds; *n.* poets.
2. sāġ' eṣ; *n.* wise men.
3. cŏm mūn' ion; *n.* intercourse.
3. fĭc' tion; *n.* that which is invented or imagined.
3. cŏn vĭc' tion; *n.* strong belief.

### What I Live for.

1. I live for those who love me,
   Whose hearts are kind and true;
   For the heaven that smiles above me,
   And awaits my spirit, too;
   For all human ties that bind me.

For the task by God assigned me,
For the hopes not left behind me,
   And the good that I can do.

2. I live to learn their story
   Who've suffered for my sake;
To emulate their glory,
   And follow in their wake;
Bards, patriots, martyrs, sages,
The noble of all ages,
Whose deeds crown history's pages,
   And time's great volume make.

3. I live to hold communion
   With all that is divine;
To feel there is a union
   'Twixt nature's heart and mine;
To profit by affliction,
Reap truths from fields of fiction,
Grow wiser from conviction,
   And fulfill each grand design.

4. I live to hail that season
   By gifted minds foretold,
When men shall live by reason,
   And not alone by gold;
When man to man united,
And every wrong thing righted,
The whole world shall be lighted
   As Eden was of old.

5. I live for those who love me,
   For those who know me true;
For the heaven that smiles above me,
   And awaits my spirit, too;

For the cause that lacks assistance,
For the wrong that needs resistance,
For the future in the distance,
   And the good that I can do.

G. Linnæus Banks.

Try to give the sense of the poem in prose form, making a separate paragraph of each stanza.

## LESSON LXVIII.

1. făc' tŏrs; *n.* circumstances or influences which help to produce a result.
1. cўn'Ic ạl; *a.* snarling; fault-finding.
3. stĭm' u lātẹ; *v.* encourage; urge.
4. hŏb' bў; *n.* a favorite subject of thought or effort.
4. ḡe ŏl' o ḡĭst; *n.* one who understands the science which treats of the earth, its physical features, and its history.
5. wạl' low; *v.* roll, as in mud.

### Books.

1. Books are resources and consolation; study is a resource and consolation. Both are strong factors in the best home-life; and the man who can look back with gratitude to the time when, around the home-lamp, he made one of the circle about his father's table, has much to be thankful for; and we venture to assert that the coming man whose father will give him such a remembrance to be thankful for can never be an outcast, or grow cold, or bitter, or cynical.

2. But the taste for books does not come always by nature: it must be cultivated. And everything between covers is not a book; and a taste for books cannot be cultivated in a bookless house. It may be said that there is no Catholic literature, or that it is very expensive to buy books, or that it is difficult to get a small number of the best books, or to be sure that one has the best in a small compass.

3. None of these things is true—none of them. There is a vast Catholic literature, and a vast literature not professedly Catholic which is good and pure, which will stimulate a desire for study, and help to cultivate every quality of the mind and heart. Does anybody realize how many good books twelve or fifteen dollars will buy nowadays? And, after all, there are not fifty really *great* books in all languages. If one have fifty books, one has the best literature in all languages. A book-shelf thus furnished is a treasure which neither adversity nor fatigue nor sickness itself can take away.

4. Each child may even have his own book-shelf, with his favorites on it, and such volumes as treat of his favorite hobby—for every child old enough should have a hobby, even if it be only the collecting of pebbles, and every chance should be given him to enjoy his hobby and to develop it into a serious study. A little fellow who used to range his pebbles on the table in the lamplight, and get such hints as he could about them out of an old text-book, is a great geologist. And a little girl who used to hang over her very own copy of Adelaide Procter's poems is spoken of as one of the cleverest newspaper men (though she is a woman) in the city of New York. The taste of the early days, encouraged in a humble way, became the talent which was to make their future.

5. There should be no bookless house in all this land —least of all among Catholics, whose ancestors in Christ preserved all that is great in literature. Let the trashy novels, paper-backed, soiled, borrowed or picked up, be cast out. Let the choosing of books not be left to mere chance. A little brains put into it will be returned with more than its first value. What goes into the precious minds of the young ought not to be carelessly chosen.

And it is true that, in the beginning, it is the easiest possible thing to interest young people in good and great books. But if one lets them wallow in whatever printed stuff happens to come in their way, one finds it hard to conduct them back again. Let the books be carefully chosen—a few at a time—be laid within the circle of the evening lamp—and God bless you all!

MAURICE FRANCIS EGAN.

## LESSON LXIX.

3. ŏm' ĭ noŭs; *a.* foreboding evil.
4. shroud; *n.* clothes; especially the dress of the dead.
6. thătch; *n.* straw or other substance used to cover the roof of a building for securing it from rain.
10. dĭ shĕv' ĕlĕd; *a.* disordered; disarranged.
10. spĕc' tĕr; *n.* an appearance; a ghost.
11. lĭv' ĭd; *a.* lead color.
14. twāin; *n.* two.
18. cŏr' mo rănt; *n.* a sea-raven; a great glutton.

### The Poor Fisher Folk.

1. 'Tis night; within the close-shut cabin door
    The room is wrapped in shade, save where there fall
   Some twilight rays that creep along the floor
    And show the fisher's nets upon the wall.

2. Five children on the long low mattress lie,—
    A nest of little souls, it heaves with dreams;
   In the high chimney the last embers die,
    And redden the dark roof with crimson gleams.

3. The mother kneels and thinks, and, pale with fear,
    She prays alone, hearing the billows shout;
   While to wild winds, to rocks, to midnight drear,
    The ominous old ocean sobs without.

4. Janet is sad: her husband is alone,
    Wrapped in the black shroud of this bitter night:
His children are so little, there is none
    To give him aid.—"Were they but old, they might."—
Ah, mother! when they too are on the main,
    How wilt thou weep, "Would they were young again!"

5. She takes her lantern,—'tis his hour at last;
    She will go forth, and see if the day breaks,
And if his signal-fire be at the mast;—
    Ah no,—not yet!—no breath of morning wakes.

6. Sudden her anxious eyes, that peer and watch
    Through the deep shade, a neighbor's dwelling find.
No light within,—the thin door shakes,—the thatch
    O'er the green walls is twisted of the wind,

7. Yellow and dirty as a swollen rill.
    "Ah me!" she saith, "here doth that widow dwell:
Few days ago my goodman left her ill;
    I will go in and see if all be well."

8. She strikes the door, she listens; none replies,
    And Janet shudders. "Husbandless, alone,
And with two children,—they have scant supplies,—
    'Good neighbor!'—she sleeps heavy as a stone."

9. She calls again, she knocks: 'tis silence still,—
    No sound, no answer! Now she opes the door;
She enters; and her lantern's gleam lights ill
    The house so mute but for the wild waves' roar.

10. Half clothed, dark-featured, motionless lay she,
    The once strong mother, now devoid of life ;
  Disheveled specter of dead misery,—
    All that the poor leave after their long strife.

11. The cold and livid arm, already stiff,
    Hung o'er the soaked straw of her wretched bed.
  The mouth lay open horribly, as if
    The parting soul with a great cry had fled,—

12. That cry of death which startles the dim ear
    Of vast Eternity. And all the while
  Two little children, in one cradle near,
    Slept face to face, on each sweet face a smile.

13. The dying mother o'er them, as they lay,
    Had cast her gown and wrapped her mantle's fold ;
  Feeling chill death creep up, she willed that they
    Should yet be warmed while she was lying cold.

14. Rocked by their own weight, sweetly sleep the twain,
    With even breath, and foreheads calm and clear ;
  So sound that the last trump might call in vain,—
    For, being innocent, they have no fear.

15. Ah, why does Janet pass so fast away?
    What hath she stolen from the awful dead?
  What foldeth she beneath her mantle gray,
    And hurries home, and hides it in her bed?

16. The dawn was whitening over the sea's verge
    As she sat pensive, touching broken chords
  Of half-remorseful thought, while the hoarse surge
    Howled a sad concert to her broken words.

17. "Ah, my poor husband! we had five before;
    Already so much care, so much to find,
For he must work for all. I give him more.—
    What was that noise? His step? Ah no, the wind.

18. "That I should be afraid of him I love!
    I have done ill. If he should beat me now,
I would not blame him.—Did not the door move?
    Not yet, poor man."—She sits with careful brow,
Wrapped in her inward grief; nor hears the roar
    Of winds and waves that dash against his prow,
Nor the black cormorant shrieking on the shore.

19. Sudden the door flies open wide, and lets
    Noisily in the daylight scarcely clear;
And the good fisher, dragging his damp nets,
    Stands on the threshold with a joyous cheer.

20. How gay their hearts that wedded love made light!
    "What weather was it?" "Hard."—"Your fishing?" "Bad.
The sea was like a nest of thieves to-night;
    But I embrace thee, and my heart is glad.

21. "There was a demon in the wind that blew:
    I tore my net, caught nothing, broke my line,
And once I thought the bark was broken too.—
    What did you all the night long, Janet mine?"

22. She, trembling in the darkness, answered, "I?
    Oh, naught! I sewed, I watched, I was afraid;
The waves were loud as thunders from the sky:
    But it is over." Shyly then she said:—

23. "Our neighbor died last night; it must have been
       When you were gone.  She left two little ones,
   So small, so frail,—William and Madeline;
       The one just lisps, the other scarcely runs."

24. The man looked grave, and in the corner cast
       His old fur bonnet, wet with rain and sea;
   Muttered a while, and scratched his head,—at last,
       "We have five children, this makes seven," said he.

25. "Already in bad weather we must sleep
       Sometimes without our supper.  Now—  Ah, well,
   'Tis not my fault.  These accidents are deep;
       It was the good God's will.  I cannot tell.

26. "Why did He take the mother from those scraps,
       No bigger than my fist?  'Tis hard to read;
   A learned man might understand, perhaps;—
       So little, they can neither work nor need.

27. "Go fetch them, wife; they will be frightened sore,
       If with the dead alone they waken thus;—
   The storm was God's hand knocking at our door,
       And we must take the children home to us.

28. "Brother and sister shall they be to ours,
       And they shall learn to climb my knee at even.
   When He shall see these strangers in our bowers,
       More fish, more food will give the God of heaven.

29. "I will work harder; I will drink no wine—
       Go fetch them.  Wherefore dost thou linger, dear?
   Not thus were wont to move these feet of thine."
       She drew the curtain, saying,—"They are here!"

SHE DREW THE CURTAIN, SAYING "THEY ARE HERE!"

**Explain** the expressions: "The room is wrapped in shade" (1); "the last embers die" (2); "old ocean sobs" (3); "wrapped in the black shroud of this bitter night" (4); "the hoarse surge howled a sad concert" (16). "If his signal-fire be at the mast" (5) is an allusion to the custom formerly existing among French fishermen to light a signal-fire at the masthead to announce their coming. "The last trump" (14), that is, the last trumpet, on judgment-day, calling the dead to rise.

Who was kneeling in the fisherman's cottage (8)? What time was it (1)? How many children had the woman (2)? Where were they (2)? Where was her husband (4)? Why does she take her lantern and go out (5)? What does she find in her neighbor's cottage (10)? What does her husband say when he hears what has happened (27)? What does she show him (29)?

## LESSON LXX.

1. feūd' al; *a.* holding as payment for military services.
1. dĕs' pŏts; *n.* tyrants.
2. răp' Ine; *n.* the seizing and carrying away of things by force.
2. fŏr sōōth'; *adv.* in truth.
2. sĕrv' Ile; *a.* meanly submissive; befitting a servant or slave.
3. līm' nēr; *n.* one who draws or paints.
3. cŏrse; *n.* the dead body of a human being.

### Rienzi's Address to the Romans.

1. I come not here to talk. You know too well
   The story of our thralldom. We are slaves!
   The bright sun rises to his course, and lights
   A race of slaves! he sets, and his last beam
   Falls on a slave!—not such as, swept along
   By the full tide of power, the conqueror leads
   To crimson glory and undying fame,
   But base, ignoble slaves—slaves to a horde
   Of petty tyrants; feudal despots; lords,
   Rich in some dozen paltry villages,
   Strong in some hundred spearmen; only great
   In that strange spell—a name.

2.                          Each hour dark fraud,
   Or open rapine, or protected murder,
   Cry out against them.  But this very day,
   An honest man, my neighbor (there he stands),
   Was struck—struck like a dog, by one who wore
   The badge of Ursini, because, forsooth,
   He tossed not high his ready cap in air
   Nor lifted up his voice in servile shouts
   At sight of that great ruffian!  Be we men,
   And suffer such dishonor?—men, and wash not
   The stain away in blood?

3.                          Such shames are common
   I have known deeper wrongs.  I that speak to you,
   I had a brother once (a gracious boy),
   Full of gentleness, of calmest hope,
   Of sweet and quiet joy: there was the look
   Of heaven upon his face, which limners give
   To the beloved disciple.  How I loved
   That gracious boy!  Younger by fifteen years,
   Brother at once and son!  He left my side,
   A summer bloom on his fair cheek, a smile
   Parting his innocent lips: in one short hour,
   The pretty, harmless boy was slain!  I saw
   The corse, the mangled corse, and then I cried
   For vengeance!

4.                          Rouse ye, Romans! rouse ye, slaves!
   Have ye brave sons?  Look, in the next fierce brawl,
   To see them die.  Have ye fair daughters?  Look
   To see them live, torn from your arms, distained,
   Dishonored; and, if ye dare call for justice,
   Be answered by the lash.

5.                    Yet this is Rome,
That sat on her seven hills, and, from her throne
Of beauty, ruled the world! Yet we are Romans!
Why, in that elder day, to be a Roman
Was greater than a king! And, once again,
(Hear me, ye walls, that echoed to the tread
Of either Brutus!) once again, I swear,
The Eternal City shall be free!

MARY RUSSELL MITFORD.

This scene is taken from the drama of "Rienzi."

**Cola di Rienzi**, the famous Roman tribune, was born of humble parentage, at Rome, in 1313. He distinguished himself by freeing, for a time, his native city from the barbarous thralldom of the nobles. His triumph was short-lived, however, and he was eventually killed by the very people for whom he had labored.

The expression "crimson glory" (1) means a "bloody battle-field." The "Ursini" (2) were among the most distinguished of Italian noble families, and were opposed to Rienzi. The "beloved disciple" (3) is St. John the Evangelist.

## LESSON LXXI.

2. ĕf' fĭ cā' cious; *a.* producing the effect intended.
3. plī' å blĕ; *a.* easy to be bent.
4. ŏb' lŏng; *a.* having greater length than breadth.
5. tĕn' tĕr-housĕ; *n.* a house stretched tightly.
3. sĕr' rā tĕd; *a.* notched on the edge like a saw.
7. dĕn tīc' u lā' tĕd; *a.* notched into little tooth-like projections.
9. sū' turĕ; *n.* the seam or joint which unites the bones of the skull.
11. ăb nôr' măl; *a.* irregular.
11. vĕr' te bræ; *n.* joints of the back-bone.

### The Clothing of some Animals.

1. It is very interesting to observe the wonderful way in which the Creator has clothed and ornamented His

various creatures. Some live in the water, some on land, some pass their time partly in the water or on land, some exist partly in the air, on the water, and on the land. All are beautifully and wonderfully constructed. I propose to make a few remarks on the external coverings of some of these.

2. In the scales of the fish we find plates of thin horn. These plates are set in a soft pocket of the true skin, and overlap one another so as to form a complete suit of armor —giving origin, no doubt, to the idea of scale armor as worn by our ancestors at the time when arrows were used in battle. The scales in the fish are not all of the same size; they are beautifully fitted, like enamel plates, on to the body, so that while they afford the most efficacious protection, they do not interfere in the least with the movements of the fish, which in many instances are exceedingly rapid.

3. Passing on from the fish to the crocodile, we again find a scale-formed armor. The scales are let into the skin in a different manner from those of the fish, and they are capable of absorbing a considerable amount of water. This I found out by soaking a crocodile's skin in water. Before the skin was soaked, it was as hard and inflexible as a board. Having been soaked a few hours, it became as pliable and soft as a wet towel. This is evidently an arrangement to enable the crocodile to pass his time with comfort both in the water and out of the water. A crocodile also has lungs, not gills, and we never find true scales, like those of a fish, unaccompanied by gills. When the crocodile is basking in the sun, his scales are much harder than when they are in the water.

4. If we look for scales in land animals, we shall find them more especially in the armadillo and the tortoise.

In the armadillo we find a series of scales of peculiar shape, not let into pockets as in the fish, but each connected with its neighbor by soft skin, so that the armadillo's skin may be said to be a series of oblong-headed nails (such as are used to tack on furniture fringes) fastened into a covering which forms the skin of the animal. The armadillo has to roll himself into a ball as occasion requires; therefore the studs of his armor are so beautifully fitted, as to size and shape, that he can roll them up into a ball without the slightest appearance of crease or wrinkle.

5. In the case of the armadillo, who lives under a covering of horny flexible skin, please to observe that his backbone, and all other bones, as well as his lungs, heart, and other viscera, are all underneath this flexible roof to his body. In the tortoise we find quite another arrangement. Take a tortoise-shell and boil it, and you will find that you can pick off the scales one by one, and that underneath the scales is a tenter-house of solid-formed bone.

6. This dome-shaped house is not composed of a continuous mass of bone, as a tea-cup is made of a continuous plate of pottery, but rather of a series of small bones, all properly arched to suit the original curve, and jointed together in a most marvelous manner. The edges of each bone are deeply serrated, and the serrations fit in such a workmanlike manner one into another that an amount of solidity is gained which could not have been equaled if the whole dome had been cast in a single piece.

7. But how is a tortoise to live in his house? Where are his ribs to go? Let us examine. In ordinary animals, the backbone forms an attachment for the ribs, and there are plenty of muscles outside the ribs. In the tortoise, the ribs themselves are actually used to form part of the dome, or roof. By examining the inside of a tortoise-shell, the

fact will at once become apparent. The ribs will be seen forming the girders of this wonderful roof, and they are connected together by means of the above-mentioned plates of bone and denticulated edges, while the center portion of the bone sends down an arch to form a canal, in which the spinal marrow is contained.

8. The tortoise therefore lives inside a house which is composed of his own ribs formed into a dome, and he rests upon his breast-bone, which is flattened out into a broad plate, to serve, first, for the attachment of the ribs, and, secondly, as a kind of supporting foot or basement. Can there possibly be a more beautiful piece of design than this, which combines economy of material and great strength with lightness?

9. We often find the same design in created things utilized for various purposes. It is, therefore, highly interesting to find that the kind of denticulated suture as adopted in the tortoise is present also in our own skulls. A bony box is required to carry and protect the brain; the human skull, therefore, is formed of bones, each being jointed to its neighbor by identically the same kind of union as that in the tortoise. There is in the human skull another meaning for this: the interposition of several lines of sutures all over the skull prevents a fracture of one of the bones of the skull spreading to its neighbor, just as the woodwork in a window-frame prevents the fracture of an individual square of glass spreading to the adjoining squares.

10. In the common hedgehog we find a very curious bit of mechanism. The hedgehog has no horny studs fastened into the skin as in the armadillo, nor yet has he a bone-formed dome, covered with horny scales, as in the tortoise. Instead of this his horny covering assumes the form of spines, or bristles, each set firmly into the skin at

one end, and very sharply pointed at the other end. These bristles the owner can erect in groups, with all the points outward, presenting a formidable array of weapons; but the hedgehog has also power to lay back all these sharp-pointed spines in one direction, namely, from his head downward.

11. The muscles which command these spines are fine strings or fibers similar to the "frowning muscle" in our own foreheads; in fact, when a hedgehog curls himself up, he begins work with a tremendous frown as he tucks his head inward. The muscles that work the spines are attached to the spines which project from the back-bone, and also more especially on to the ribs, which I find to be of unusual strength and abnormal width for so small an animal. The vertebræ are attached to the ribs in a very peculiar manner, and each of the back-bones fits on to its neighbor by a wonderful joint which keeps the chain of bones quite stiff when the animal is walking, but which enables him to coil up into a ball on the slightest provocation.   FRANCIS T. BUCKLAND.

What do we find in the scales of the fish (2)? How are these plates set (2)? What suggested the idea of the scale armor worn in olden times (2)? What effect has soaking on the skin of the crocodile (3)? What has the crocodile instead of gills (3)? What always accompany true scales (3)? What may be said of the armadillo's skin (4)? What do we find if we boil a tortoise-shell (5)? Of what is the dome-shaped house of the tortoise constructed (6)? What is meant by "dome-shaped" (6)? To what are the ribs of the tortoise attached (7)? Of what is the human skull formed (9)? What form does the horny covering of the hedgehog assume (10)? What can the hedgehog do with its bristles (10)? How does the hedgehog begin when about to curl itself up (11)? How are its vertebræ attached to its ribs (11)?

## LESSON LXXII.

8. lōw'ing; *e.* bellowing.
8. fra'grance; *n.* perfume.

11. ăb rŭpt'; *a.* sudden; unexpected.

### An April Day.

1. All day the low-hung clouds have dropped
    Their garnered fullness down;
  All day that soft gray mist hath wrapped
    Hill, valley, grove, and town.

2. There has not been a sound to-day
    To break the calm of nature;
  Nor motion, I might almost say,
    Of life, or living creature:

3. Of waving bough, or warbling bird,
    Or cattle faintly lowing;—
  I could have half believed I heard
    The leaves and blossoms growing.

4. I stood to hear—I love it well—
    The rain's continuous sound,
  Small drops, but thick and fast they fell,
    Down straight into the ground;

5. For leafy thickness is not yet
    Earth's naked breast to screen,
  Though every dripping branch is set
    With shoots of tender green.

6. Sure, since I looked at early morn,
    Those honeysuckle buds
  Have swelled to double growth; that thorn
    Hath put forth larger studs;

7. That lilac's cleaving cones have burst,
　　The milk-white flowers revealing;
　E'en now, upon my senses first
　　Methinks their sweets are stealing.

8. The very earth, the steamy air,
　　Are all with fragrance rife;
　And grace and beauty everywhere
　　Are flushing into life.

9. Down, down they come—those fruitful stores!
　　Those earth-rejoicing drops!
　A momentary deluge pours,
　　Then thins, decreases, stops;

10. And ere the dimples on the stream
　　Have circled out of sight,
　Lo! from the west a parting gleam
　　Breaks forth of amber light.

11. But yet behold—abrupt and loud
　　Comes down the glittering rain:
　The farewell of a passing cloud,
　　The fringes of her train.　　　CHAUCER.

**Geoffrey Chaucer**, known as the "Father of English Poetry," was born, it is supposed, in London about the year 1328. Very little is known of his early life. His greatest work is "The Canterbury Tales," a collection of stories in verse, and a careful picture of the manners of his time. Chaucer died in 1400.

**Explain** the expressions: "have dropped their garnered fullness down" (1); "leafy thickness is not yet earth's naked breast to screen" (5); "a parting gleam breaks forth of amber light" (10).

What kind of cattle "low" (3)? What is the shape of a "cone" (7)? What other expression could be used for "steamy air" (8)? Why are the rain-drops called "fruitful stores" (9)?

## LESSON LXXIII.

1. eŏn′ stĕr na′ tion; *n.* alarm.
2. re prieve′; *n.* the delaying for a time of punishment.
4. re vēal′; *v.* to make known.
6. be wĭl′ dẽr mȧnt; *n.* the state of being puzzled.
7. pro tĕst′ ĕd; *a.* declared solemnly.
7. rāng′ ing; *v.* wandering; passing over.
12. re sŭs′ çĭ tāt ĕd; *v.* raised to life again.
12. ehrўs′ a lĭs; *n.* a form into which the caterpillar passes, and from which the perfect insect, after a while, comes forth.

### The Seven Sleepers.

1. The Emperor Decius, who persecuted the Christians, having come to Ephesus, ordered the erection of temples in the city, that all might come and sacrifice before him, and he commanded that the Christians should be sought out and given their choice either to worship the idols or to die. So great was the consternation in the city that the friend denounced his friend, the father his son, and the son his father.

2. Now there were in Ephesus seven Christians—Maximian, Malchus, Marcian, Dionysius, John, Serapion, and Constantine by name. These refused to sacrifice to the idols, and remained in their houses praying and fasting. They were accused before Decius, and they confessed themselves to be Christians. However, the Emperor gave them a little time to consider what line they would adopt. They took advantage of this reprieve to dispense their goods among the poor, and then they retired, all seven, to Mount Celion, where they determined to conceal themselves.

3. One of their number, Malchus, in the disguise of a physician, went to the town to obtain victuals. Decius, who had been absent from Ephesus for a little while, re-

turned, and gave orders for the seven to be sought. Malchus, having escaped from the town, fled, full of fear, to his comrades, and told them of the Emperor's fury. They were much alarmed; and Malchus handed them the loaves he had bought, bidding them eat, that, fortified by the food, they might have courage in the time of trial. They ate, and then, as they sat weeping and speaking to one another, by the will of God they fell asleep.

4. The Pagans sought everywhere, but could not find them, and Decius was greatly irritated at their escape. He had their parents brought before him, and threatened them with death if they did not reveal the place of concealment; but they could only answer that the seven young men had distributed their goods to the poor, and that they were quite ignorant as to their whereabouts. Decius, thinking it possible that they might be hiding in a cavern, blocked up the mouth with stones that they might perish of hunger.

5. Three hundred and sixty years passed, and in the thirtieth year of the reign of Theodosius there broke forth a heresy denying the resurrection of the dead. Now it happened that an Ephesian was building a stable on the side of Mount Celion, and finding a pile of stones handy, he took them for his edifice, and thus opened the mouth of the cave. Then the seven sleepers awoke, and it was to them as if they had slept but a single night. They began to ask Malchus what decision Decius had given concerning them.

6. "He is going to hunt us down, so as to force us to sacrifice to the idols," was his reply. "God knows," replied Maximian, "we shall never do that." Then exhorting his companions, he urged Malchus to go back to the town to buy some more bread, and at the same time to obtain fresh information. Malchus took five coins and left

the cavern. On seeing the stones he was filled with astonishment; however, he went on toward the city; but what was his bewilderment, on approaching the gate, to see over it a cross! He went to another gate, and there he beheld the same sacred sign; and so he observed it over each gate of the city. He believed that he was suffering from the effects of a dream.

7. Then he entered Ephesus, rubbing his eyes, and walked to a baker's shop, and laid down his money. The baker, examining the coin, inquired whether he had found a treasure, and began to whisper to some others in the shop. The youth, thinking that he was discovered, and that they were about to conduct him to the Emperor, implored them to let him alone, offering to leave loaves and money if he might only be suffered to escape. But the shopman, seizing him, said, " Whoever you are, you have found a treasure; show us where it is, that we may share it with you, and then we will hide you." Malchus was too frightened to answer. So they put a rope round his neck, and drew him through the streets into the market-place. The news soon spread that the young man had discovered a great treasure, and there was presently a vast crowd about him. He stoutly protested his innocence. No one recognized him, and his eyes ranging over the faces which surrounded him, could discover not even one which he had known, or which was in the slightest degree familiar to him.

8. So Martin, the bishop, and Antipater, the governor, having heard of the excitement, ordered the young man to be brought before them, along with the bakers. The bishop and the governor asked him where he had found the treasure, and he replied that he had found none, but that the few coins were from his own purse. He was next

asked whence he came. He replied that he was a native of Ephesus, "if this be Ephesus."

9. "Send for your relations—your parents if they live here," ordered the governor.

"They live here, certainly," replied the youth; and he mentioned their names. No such names were known in the town. Then the governor exclaimed, "How dare you say that this money belonged to your parents, when it dates back three hundred and seventy-seven years, and is as old as the beginning of the reign of Decius, and is utterly unlike our modern coinage? Do you think to impose on the old men and sages of Ephesus? Believe me, I shall make you suffer the severities of the law unless you show where you made the discovery."

10. "I implore you," cried Malchus, "in the name of God, answer me a few questions, and then I will answer yours. Where is the Emperor Decius gone to?"

The bishop answered, "My son, there is no emperor of that name; he who was thus called died long ago."

Malchus replied, "All I hear perplexes me more and more. Follow me, and I will show you my comrades who fled with me into a cave of Mount Celion only yesterday, to escape the cruelty of Decius. I will lead you to them."

11. Then they followed, and a great crowd after them. And Malchus entered first into the cavern to his companions, and the bishop after him. And there they saw the martyrs seated in the cave, with their faces fresh and blooming as roses; so all fell down and glorified God. The bishop and the governor sent notice to Theodosius, and he hurried to Ephesus. All the inhabitants met him and conducted him to the cavern.

12. As soon as the saints beheld the Emperor their faces shone like the sun, and the Emperor gave thanks

unto God, and embraced them, and said, "I see you, as though I saw the Saviour restoring Lazarus." Maximian replied, "Believe us, for the faith's sake, God has resuscitated us before the great resurrection-day, in order that you may believe firmly in the resurrection of the dead. For as the insect is in its chrysalis living and not suffering, so have we lived without suffering, fast asleep." And having thus spoken, they bowed their heads, and their souls returned to their Maker. — BARING GOULD.

The Emperor Trajan Decius (1) reigned during the years 249–251 and was unceasing in his persecution of the Christians. He was slain in a battle with the Goths, against whom he had undertaken a war. Ephesus (1) was an ancient city of Asia Minor. The Emperor Theodosius (5), here referred to, was probably Theodosius II., although the dates do not agree, as he reigned in the East from 408 to 450.

**Explain** the expression "what line they would adopt" (2). Let the pupils write out the legend in their own language.

## LESSON LXXIV.

1. throe; n. agony.
1. strife; n. struggle for victory.
5. trend; n. direction.
7. brunt; n. violence; shock.
8. swath; n. the whole sweep of a scythe in mowing.
8. stead'fast; a. firm; firmly tied.

### The Ride of Collins Graves.

On Saturday morning, May 16, 1874, occurred the great flood at Mill River Valley, Hampshire County, Massachusetts, caused by the breaking of a mill-dam. Four villages were swept away, and nearly two hundred lives were lost in the calamity. Collins Graves, a milkman, mounted his horse and spurred through the villages, warning the inhabitants and saving hundreds of lives.

1. No song of a soldier riding down
   To the raging fight from Winchester town;
   No song of a time that shook the earth
   With the nation's throe at the nation's birth;

But the song of a brave man free from fear
As Sheridan's self or Paul Revere;
Who risked what they risked, free from strife
And its promise of glorious pay—his life!

2. The peaceful valley has waked and stirred,
And the answering echoes of life are heard:
The dew still clings to the trees and grass,
And the early toilers smiling pass,
As they glance aside at the white-walled homes
Or up the valley, where merrily comes
The brook that sparkles in diamond rills
As the sun comes over the Hampshire hills.

3. What was it that passed like an ominous breath—
Like a shiver of fear, or a touch of death?
What was it? The valley is peaceful still,
And the leaves are afire on top of the hill.
It was not a sound—nor thing of sense—
But a pain, like the pang of the short suspense
That thrills the being of those who see
At their feet the gulf of Eternity!

4. The air of the valley has felt the chill:
The workers pause at the door of the mill;
The housewife, keen to the shivering air,
Arrests her foot on the cottage stair,
Instinctive taught by the mother-love,
And thinks of the sleeping ones above.
Why start the listeners? Why does the course
Of the mill-stream widen? Is it a horse—
Hark to the sound of his hoofs, they say—
That gallops so wildly Williamsburg way?

5. Ah! what was that like a human shriek
   From the winding valley? Will nobody speak?
   Will nobody answer those women who cry
   As the awful warnings thunder by?
   Whence came they? Listen! And now they hear
   The sound of the galloping horse-hoofs near;
   They watch the trend of the vale, and see
   The rider who thunders so menacingly,
   With waving arms and warning scream
   To the home-filled banks of the valley stream.

6. He draws no rein, but he shakes the street
   With a shout and the ring of the galloping feet;
   And this the cry he flings to the wind:
   "To the hills for your lives! The flood is behind!"
   He cries and is gone; but they know the worst—
   The breast of the Williamsburg dam has burst!
   The basin that nourished their happy homes
   Is changed to a demon—It comes! it comes!

7. A monster in aspect, with shaggy front
   Of shattered dwellings, to take the brunt
   Of the homes they shatter—white-maned and hoarse,
   The merciless Terror fills the course
   Of the narrow valley, and rushing raves,
   With death on the first of its hissing waves,
   Till cottage and street and crowded mill
   Are crumbled and crushed.

8.             But onward still,
   In front of the roaring flood is heard
   The galloping horse and the warning word.
   Thank God! the brave man's life is spared!
   From Williamsburg town he nobly dared

To race with the flood and take the road
In front of the terrible swath it mowed.
For miles it thundered and crashed behind,
But he looked ahead with a steadfast mind;
"They must be warned!" was all he said,
As away on his terrible ride he sped.

9. When heroes are called for, bring the crown
To this Yankee rider: send him down
On the stream of time with the Curtius old;
His deed as the Roman's was brave and bold,
And the tale can as noble a thrill awake,
For he offered his life for the people's sake.

JOHN BOYLE O'REILLY.

The "song of a soldier riding down to the raging fight from Winchester" (1) is an allusion to T. Buchanan Reed's poem of "Sheridan's Ride." "Paul Revere's (1) Ride" is a well-known poem by Longfellow. "A time that shook the earth with the nation's throe at the nation's birth" (1) means the time of the Revolution.

**Explain** the expressions: "What was it that passed like an ominous breath—like a shiver of fear or a touch of death?" (3); "at their feet the gulf of Eternity" (3); "the merciless terror" (7).

According to a Roman tradition the earth in the Forum gave way, about the year B.C. 362, and a great chasm appeared which, it was claimed, could be closed only by casting into it the most precious treasure of the city. Thereupon Marcus Curtius (9), a noble youth, declaring that the city held no greater treasure than a brave citizen, sprang to his horse and rode into the yawning gulf; his words were verified, for the earth at once closed over him.

---

Now, blessings light on him that first invented sleep! It covers a man all over, thoughts and all, like a cloak; it is meat for the hungry, drink for the thirsty, heat for the cold, and cold for the hot.—*Don Quixote.*

## LESSON LXXV.

### The Bold Dragoon.

1. Once, in a merry tavern in Brabant,
    A jolly dozen of dragoons were boasting
    Of their past feats in many a Flemish hosting.
  "How, now," at length cried one, "friend Gaspar! can't
  You brush your memory up, and give us some
    Exploit of yours?" The query was addressed
  To a dragoon who had as yet been dumb.
    "Oh," answered Gaspar, "I am silent, lest
  You might suppose me lying, or might call
  Me braggart."—"No, no, no, we won't!" cried all.
  "Well, then, the time we lay in camp near Seville
  I—I—" "Ay! hear him! Gaspar Schnapps forever!"—
  "I cut ten troopers' legs off, clean and clever!"

2. "Their legs!" cried six or eight. "By all that's civil!
  What made you cut their legs off, prithee, brother?"
  "What made me cut their legs off?" said the other.
  "Ay! had you cut their heads off, then, in truth,
    That would have been the right way to astound them."
  "Oh, but you see," said Schnapps, "the fact is—I—
  I—*couldn't* cut their heads off."—"No? and why?"
  "Because," responded the redoubted youth,
    "Their heads had been cut off before I found them!"

Brabant (1), formerly a province of the Netherlands, now belongs partly to Holland, partly to Belgium; "hosting" (1) is an obsolete word meaning "battle."

---

Waste neither time nor money, but make the best use of both.

## LESSON LXXVI.

1. ca prī' çioŭs lỹ; *adv.* curiously shaped.
1. ȯr nāte̯'; *a.* finely cultivated.
4. thwa̯rt'ĕd; *v.* defeated.
8. e mā' çi at ĕd; *a.* thin.
8. cŏn' cou̯rse̯; *n.* assembly.
9. lŭs' tĕr; *n.* splendor.
9. mo mĕn' tou̯s; *a.* important.
14. quoth (*kwŏth*); *v.* said.

### The Meeting with the Master.

1. It was early morning, in the thirty-second year of the Christian era, when a handsome, soldier-like, and majestic man, wearing the costume of a Roman legatus, or general, stood on Mount Olivet, southeast-by-east of Jerusalem. He was looking west. The Syrian sun had climbed out of the Arabian sands behind him, and it flung his tall shadow level and far over the scanty herbage among the numerous sad-colored twigs of the olive-shrub. Opposite, just below him, across the deep ravine of the Kedron brook, better known by the awful name attached to that with which it blends, "The Josaphat Vale," shone the fiery splendor of God's temple. Its glorious eastern front, here milk-white with marble, there breast-plated with gold, its pinnacles of gold, its half-Greek, half-Roman architecture capriciously and fancifully varied by the ornate genius of the Asiatic builders whom Herod the Idumæan had employed, were of a character to arrest the least curious eye, and to fill the most stupid and indifferent spectator with astonishment and admiration. And yet this was but the second temple—how inferior to, how different from, the first!

2. This was Mount Moriah, the hill of God. On the left, as the Roman general gazed, facing westward, was Mount Zion, the city of David, now the palace of Herod the tetrarch, encompassed by the mansions of Hebrew nobles.

3. "Here I stand at last," thought Paulus, "after so many checkered fortunes, looking down upon the most beautiful, the most dazzling, and the most mysterious of cities! To see Rome thus may be the lot of an eagle as it soars over it, but has never been granted to human eyes. And even could Rome be viewed in this way, it would want the unity, the whiteness. Ah! strange city! Wondrous Mount of Zion! wondrous Hill of Moriah! wonderful temple! Not temple of Jupiter, or of Venus, or of Janus, or of this or that monster or hero, but Temple, say they, of God! *The Temple of God!* And this is the land of the prophets whom I have at last read; yonder, beyond the wall, north, is Jeremiah's grotto! This, too, is the age, the time, the day, the hour, to which they all point, when the God of whom they speak, and of whom the Sibyls also sang, is to come down into a visibly ruined and corrupted world, and to perform that which to do is in itself surely God-like.

4. "But one thing is dark even in the glooms of mystery. How can a God suffer?—be thwarted, be overcome, at least apparently so, by His own creatures, and these the very worst of them? What can these cries of grief and horror which the prophets utter, mean?"

5. As Paulus thus mused, some one passed him, going down the Mount of Olives, and in passing looked at him; and until Paulus died he never ceased to see that glance, and in dying he saw it yet, and with a smile thanked his Maker that he saw it then also—especially then.

6. The person who thus passed our hero was more than six feet in height. He was fair in complexion. His hair was light auburn, and large locks of it fell with a natural wave and return upon His neck. His head was bare. His dress was the long flowing robe of the Jews, girdled at the waist, and, as Paulus afterward fancied, the

color of it was red. He was in the bloom of life. Our hero could see, as this person passed, that He was the very perfection of health, beauty, vigor, elegance, and of all the faculties of physical humanity; and even the odd, and strange, and wild, and somewhat mysterious thought flashed through Paulus's mind:

7. "My God," thought he, "if there were a new Adam to be created, to be the natural, or rather the supernatural, king of the human race, would not his appearance surely be as the appearance and the bearing of this person?"

8. And the person who passed was moreover thin, and a little emaciated. And He would have seemed wan, only that the most delicate, faint blood-color mantled in His cheeks. And He looked at the hero Paulus with the look of Him out of whose hand none hath power to take those whom He picks from a vast concourse and elects. And Paulus felt glad, and calm, and without anxiety for the future, and free from all bitterness for the past, and firm, yet grave; and, when his mind went actually forth to look upon the things that were around it, he saw nothing but the face and the glance.

9. And now I come to the strangest particular of all. Paulus felt that this beautiful and vigorous new Adam, fit to be the natural and even supernatural king of the world, was one who never could have laughed, and probably had never smiled. But no smile was so sweet as His gravity. And Paulus remembered another extraordinary and unparalleled circumstance: it was this—those beautiful and benignant eyes were so full of terror that it seemed they could scarcely hold in an equal degree any other expression in them except that which shone therein with what seemed to Paulus a celestial and divine luster; I· mean, first, love, and, next, unconquerable, and everlasting, and victorious

courage. As though there was a work to do which none but He (from the creation to the day of doom) could ever accomplish—a dreadful work, a work unspeakable in shame, and in pain, and in horror, and yet a work entirely indispensable, and the most important and real and momentous that had ever been performed. And the subject or hero of this tale, Paulus, wondered how in the same look and eyes, and in a single glance of them, two things so opposite as ineffable terror and yet God-like, adorable courage, could be combined.

10. But, nevertheless, they were both there; and with this mighty and mysterious mental combination Paulus also saw a sweetness so inexpressibly awful that, at once (and as if he had heard words formed within his own heart), the reflection arose within him: "How much more terrible would be the wrath of the lamb than the rage of the lion!"

And the figure of this person passed onward, and was hidden from poor Paulus beyond the olive groves.

11. Our hero sat down on a jutting stone, half-covered with herbage, and fell into a vague and somewhat sorrowful meditation. A rustle of the olives near him caused him to turn his head, and who, of all men in the world, should be at his side but Longinus the centurion!

12. "Why," cried Paulus, "I thought you were at Rome!"

"I have just arrived, my tribune," returned the brave man, "with orders to report myself to Pontius Pilate, the Procurator of Judea, or Governor of Jerusalem. Cornelius, of the Italian band, also a centurion, as you know, my tribune, has been ordered to Cæsarea, and is there stationed."

"Well," said Paulus, "I am delighted to meet you again. How is Thellus?"

THE MEETING WITH THE MASTER.

"Curiously enough," returned Longinus, "he too is here, stationed in Jerusalem. He was tired of too much quiet."

"Good!" exclaimed Paulus. "We must all often see each other, and talk of old days."

13. After a few more words interchanged, they began to descend Mount Olivet together.

"Did you meet any one," says Paulus to Longinus, "as you came up the hill.?"

"I did," said Longinus very gravely; "but I know not who he is."

They proceeded silently in company till, in the valley of Josaphat, at the bottom of the Mount of Olives, not far from the Golden Gate of the Temple, a most beautiful youth, with rich fair locks, worn uncovered (like him whom Paulus had just seen), met them.

14. "Friends," quoth the stranger, "have you seen the Master coming down from the Hill of Olives?"

"I think," said Paulus, after a little reflection, "that I must have seen him whom you mean." And he described the person who had looked at him.

"That is he," said the beautiful youth. "Pray, which way was he going?"

Paulus told him, and the other, after thanking him, was moving swiftly away when Paulus cried after him:

"Stay one moment," said he. "What is the name of him you call *The Master?*"

15. "Know you not?" replied the youth, with a smile. "Why, you are, I now observe by your dress, a Roman. His name is *Iesous*."

"What!" cried Paulus. "Then it is a reality. There is some one of that name who has appeared among men, and appeared at this time, and appeared in this land! I will, this very day, send off a letter to Dionysius, at Athens. And pray, fair youth, what is your own name?"

"Ah!" returned the other, "I am nobody; but they call me *John*. Yet," added he, "I ought not lightly to name such a name, for the greatest and holiest of mere men, now a prisoner of Herod's, is likewise called John; I mean John the Baptist, John the Prophet; yea, more than a prophet: 'John the Angel of God.'"

MILES GERALD KEON in "Dion and the Sibyls."

**Miles Gerald Keon**, the last male descendant of an old Irish family, was born February 20, 1821, on the banks of the Shannon. As a boy he entered the Jesuit College at Stonyhurst, England, where he won many honors. On quitting college he served for a short time with the French army in Algiers, afterward studied law, and finally turned his attention to literature, and to this profession devoted his life. He became favorably known as a magazine-writer, and was attached, from time to time, to the editorial staff of one or another of the London papers. In 1859 he was appointed Colonial Secretary at Bermuda, which position he held until his death, June 3, 1875. It was while at Bermuda, in 1866, that he published "Dion and the Sibyls," a classic Christian novel, which has been declared by competent judges the equal of "Fabiola" and one of the two or three *great* English Catholic novels.

LESSON LXXVII.

4. sŭb'stĭ tūt ĕd; *v.* put in the place of.
5. re pĕls'; *v.* drives back.
8. zĭg'zăg; *a.* running this way and that.
8. spīrēs; *n.* steeples.
10. cŏm' mŏnş; *n.* public grounds.
10. fī' bērs; *n.* fine, slender threads or thread-like substances.
12. ĕd'ĭ fĭç eş; *n.* buildings.
12. shrouds; *n.* a set of ropes reaching from the mast-heads to the sides of a vessel to support the masts.

Electricity. Part I.

1. So long ago as the time of the Greeks it was already known that amber, when rubbed, will attract or draw

toward it bits of straw and other light bodies; and it is from the Greek word *electron*,—amber,—that our word "electricity" is taken.

2. Until the sixteenth century, however, no one had made any careful experiments upon this curious fact; and it was Dr. Gilbert, an English physician, who first discovered that other bodies besides amber will, when rubbed, attract straws, thin shavings of metals, and other substances; and he also proved that the attraction was stronger when the air is dry and cold than when it is warm and moist.

3. You can easily try this for yourself by rubbing the end of a stick of common sealing-wax on a piece of dry flannel, and then holding the rubbed end near to some small pieces of light paper or feathers. You will find that these substances will spring toward the sealing-wax, and cling to it a short time.

4. After Gilbert's time very little notice was taken of these facts, till Guericke invented the first rude electrical machine in 1672. He made a globe of sulphur which turned in a wooden frame, and by pressing a cloth against it with his hand as it went round he caused the sulphur to become charged with electricity. His apparatus was very rough, but it led to better ones being made; and, some years later, a man named Hawksbee substituted a glass globe for the sulphur and a piece of silk for the cloth, and in this way electrical machines were made much like those we now use.

5. Guericke also discovered that an electrical body attracts one that is not electrified, but repels it again as soon as it has filled it with electricity like its own. He was also the first to notice the spark of fire and crackling sound which are produced by electricity when it passes between two bodies which do not touch each other.

6. Soon after this, a Frenchman named Du Fay showed that substances filled with *different* kinds of electricity *attract* each other. Both these men thought that electricity was a fluid which was created by the rubbing, and which was not in bodies at other times.

7. But about the middle of the last century Benjamin Franklin began to pay attention to these experiments in electricity, and to make experiments himself. He soon saw clearly that *all* bodies have more or less electricity in them, which the rubbing only brings out. Franklin began to consider how many of the effects of lightning were the same as those of electricity.

8. Lightning travels in a zigzag line, said he, and so does an electric spark; electricity sets things on fire, so does lightning; electricity melts metals, so does lightning. Animals can be killed by both, and both cause blindness. Electricity always finds its way along the best conductor, or the substance which carries it most easily, so does lightning; pointed bodies attract the electric spark, and in the same way lightning strikes spires and trees and mountaintops. " Is it not probable," thought he, " that lightning is nothing more than electricity passing from one cloud to another, just as an electric spark passes from one substance to another?"

9. Franklin's idea was, that if he could send an iron rod up into the clouds to meet the lightning, it would become charged with the electricity which he believed was there, and would send it down a thread attached to it, so that he might be able to feel it. He took, therefore, two light strips of cedar fastened crosswise, upon which he stretched a silk handkerchief tied by the corners to the ends of the cross; and to the top of this kite he fixed a sharp-pointed iron wire more than a foot long. He then

put a tail and a string to his kite; and at the end of the string near his hand he tied some silk (which is a bad conductor), to prevent the electricity from escaping into his body. Between the string and the silk he tied an iron key (the metals being the very best conductors), in which the electricity might be collected.

10. When his kite was ready he waited eagerly for a heavy thunder-storm; and, as soon as it came, he went out with his son to the commons near Philadelphia, and let his kite fly. It mounted up among the dark clouds; but at first no electricity came down, for the string was too dry to conduct it. But by and by the heavy rain fell, the kite and string both became thoroughly wet, and the fibers of the string stood out as threads do when electricity passes along them.

11. As soon as Franklin saw this, he knew that his experiment had succeeded: he put his finger to the key, and drew out a strong bright spark,—the most welcome rap upon the knuckles that any man ever received. Franklin soon put his discovery to practical use. Whenever you see a lightning-rod guarding a building from destruction, remember that we owe that invention to him and to his kite-flying.

12. Franklin proposed to fix on the highest points of edifices upright rods of iron made as sharp as a needle, and gilded to prevent rusting, and extending down the outside of the building into the ground, or down round one of the shrouds of a ship, and down the side till it reaches the water.

13. It has since been found that rods of copper form the best conductors. These are now set into the masts of ships, passing down which they pierce the keel, and are fastened underneath by copper bolts in contact with the water.

**Benjamin Franklin** (7), patriot, statesman, author, philosopher, and scientist, was born in Boston, on January 17, 1706, and died April 17, 1790. He took an active part in the struggle for American independence, and was sent as our Minister to France. It was mainly by his efforts that the aid and sympathy of France were obtained for the American Colonies.

From what is the word "electricity" taken (1)? How can we excite electricity in a simple way (3)? How and when was the first electrical machine made (4)? What was substituted for the sulphur globe (4)? What do substances filled with different kinds of electricity do (6)? Who discovered that electricity is in all bodies (7)? What did Franklin begin to consider (7)? At what conclusions did he arrive (9)? How did he experiment (9)? What was the result of his experiments (10)? What form the best conductors (13)?

## LESSON LXXVIII.

6. çĭr′ cŭit; *n.* a continuous electrical communication between the two poles of a battery.
9. de prĕss′ ĕṣ; *v.* presses down; lowers.
10. ŏp′ ẽr ā′ tŏr; *n.* one who works an instrument.
11. ū′ nĭ sŏn; *n.* agreement.
14. çlī′ ĕnt; *n.* one who applies to a lawyer for advice.
14. ac count′ ĕd; *v.* considered.

### Electricity. Part II.

1. Only a few months before Franklin died, a new fact was discovered about electricity by Galvani, professor of anatomy at Bologna. One day as Madame Galvani was skinning frogs for a soup, one of Galvani's assistants was working an electrical machine near her. Just as the flow of electricity was going on rapidly, this young man happened to touch a nerve of the leg of one of the frogs with a dissecting-knife; and to his great surprise the leg began to move and struggle as if it were alive.

2. Madame Galvani was so much struck by this that she told her husband of it; and he repeated the experi-

ment many times, and found that whenever the flow of electricity from the machine was brought near the nerve of the frog's leg it produced convulsions. This discovery of Galvani soon became spoken of far and wide, under the name of *galvanism*.

3. Among the celebrated men who were attracted by it was Volta, professor of natural philosophy at Pavia. Not satisfied with merely reading about Galvani's experiments, he tried them himself; and he began to suspect that the electricity was produced by the metal, acted on by the moisture of the flesh. As a result of his experiments Volta discovered that two different metals when joined together in contact with moisture, and separated from other substances, produce a current of electricity.

4. This may easily be tried in its very simplest form. If you take a piece of copper and a piece of zinc, placing one above your tongue and the other below it, you will feel nothing remarkable so long as the metals are kept separate; but as soon as you let them touch each other at the ends a tingling sensation will pass through your tongue, proving to you that an electrical current is passing between the metals. If you put the zinc under your upper lip, so that the copper may remain outside, you may, perhaps, even see a slight flash when the two metals meet.

5. Volta found that some acid put in the water between the two metals greatly increased the strength of the electricity. We know now, what Volta did not know, that a change is going on between the zinc and the acid water; but we do not yet know what electricity itself is. Such was Volta's discovery, and we owe to it all the powerful *voltaic* batteries with which our most valuable experiments are now made.

6. Franklin had proved the real action of electricity,

had shown it to be the same as lightning, and had brought it down from the sky. Galvani had proved its existence in animals, and led the way to Volta's discoveries; and Volta had produced it in such enormous quantities by means of two metals and acid water, that he could keep up a constant flow of electricity, *which would travel any distance so long as the circuit was not broken.*

7. Here, you will see, was the first step toward the electric telegraph. Ever since Volta showed that an electric current can be sent for any distance along a wire the two ends of which are joined to the poles of a battery, scientific men had thought it might be possible to use this current for making signals at a distance. But there was always the difficulty of how to make the signs at the other end.

8. An electric telegraph was patented by Professor Wheatstone and Mr. Cooke in 1837; and during the same year Dr. Steinheil, of Munich, and Professor Morse, an American, both invented telegraphs.

9. Telegraph stations are connected by an electrified wire, the ends of which enter the ground, the earth (which is a good conductor) completing the circuit. When one operator wants to send a message to another, he alternately depresses and raises a button at his end of the wire. This action alternately breaks and completes the electric circuit, and this breaking and completing of the circuit is instantly perceptible at the other end of the wire. The different letters of the alphabet are indicated by the number and length of these interruptions of the circuit.

10. Some machines record the dots and lines of the telegraphic alphabet on paper tapes, and some even print the message in letters; but a skillful operator becomes so accustomed to the various sounds that the clicking of the

instrument is readily understood by him through the sense of hearing alone.

11. The telegraph is now used for many other purposes besides the sending of messages. By its means alarm-bells and time-bells are rung, and clock-hands at points remote from each other are moved in unison.

12. Little as we yet know of what electricity *is*, we are learning every year how to make it more and more useful to us. Successful experiments have been made in moving boats and cars by this great power; all our most beautiful metal-plating (*electro*-plating, as it is called) is done by it, and whole cities are brilliantly lighted by it at night.

13. But perhaps the most interesting of recent electrical discoveries is the telephone. Just as the word *telegraph* is made up of two words which mean " writing at a distance," so *telephone* means " hearing at a distance "; and this is just what the telephone helps us to do,—to hear what a person miles away is saying. It was found that by placing at each end of an electrified wire a speaking-trumpet and an ear-trumpet, as we may call them, words uttered at one end could be understood at the other.

14. This invention, although very recent, has come into great use. Hardly a city of any size but has its system of telephones with all their network of centering wires, bringing together without the delays of time and travel, office and factory, lawyer and client, physician and patient, buyer and seller. Surely a discovery that will do all these things must be accounted one of the chief wonders of this wonderful age. ARABELLA B. BUCKLEY.

How was galvanism first brought to notice (1) ? What came from Volta's experiments (3) ? Describe a simple way of showing that two metals when connected by moisture produce a current of electricity (4). What else did Volta find (5) ? To what do we owe the *voltaic* batteries (5)? Give the names of some of the inventors of the telegraph (8). Describe in your own words how a telegraph works (9). How does a skillful operator learn the message sent by a telegraph (10)? For what other purposes besides sending messages is a telegraph used (11)? What is the meaning of the word "telegraph" (13)? What does the word "telephone" mean (13)? How is a telephone arranged (13)?

## LESSON LXXIX.

1. con çĕp' tion; n. idea.
1. stōre; n. supply.
1. In' ŏx hau̇st' I ble; a. unfailing.
1. dôr' mant; a. sleeping.
2. pē' rĭ ŏd' ĭc ạl ly̆; adv. at stated times.
2. stĭg' mȧ tȧ; n. marks resembling the wounds on the crucified body of Our Saviour.
2. lăç' ĕr ā' tions; n. wounds made by tearing.
4. ăm' phĭ thē' ȧ tĕr; n. a circular building having rows of seats, one above another, around an open space called the arena, and used by the ancient Romans for combats of gladiators and wild beasts.
4. e lĭç' It ed; v. drew out.

### Miracles.

1. The Catholic Church, from east to west, from north to south, is, according to our conception, hung with miracles. The store of relics is inexhaustible; they are multiplied through all lands, and each particle of each has in it, at least a dormant, perhaps an energetic, virtue of supernatural operation. At Rome there is the True Cross, the crib of Bethlehem, and the chair of St. Peter; portions of the crown of thorns are kept at Paris; the holy coat is shown at Treves; the winding-sheet at Turin; at Monza, the iron crown is formed out of a Nail of the Cross; and another Nail is claimed for the Duomo of Milan; and pieces of Our Lady's habit are to be seen in the Escurial.

2. The Agnus Dei, blessed medals, the scapular, the cord of St. Francis, all are the medium of divine manifestations and graces. Crucifixes have bowed the head to the

suppliant, and Madonnas have bent their eyes upon assembled crowds. St. Januarius's blood liquefies periodically at Naples, and St. Winifred's Well is the scene of wonders, even in an unbelieving country. Women are marked with the sacred stigmata; blood has flowed on Fridays from their five wounds, and their heads are crowned with a circle of lacerations. Relics are ever touching the sick, the diseased, the wounded, sometimes with no result at all, at other times with marked and undeniable efficacy.

3. Who has not heard of the abundant favors gained by the intercession of the Blessed Virgin, and of the marvelous consequences which have attended the invocation of St. Anthony of Padua? These phenomena are sometimes reported of Saints in their lifetime as well as after death, especially if they were evangelists or martyrs.

4. The wild beasts crouched before their victims in the Roman amphitheater; the axman was unable to sever St. Cecilia's head from her body, and St. Peter elicited a spring of water for his jailer's baptism in the Mamertine. St. Francis Xavier turned salt water into fresh for five hundred travelers; St. Raymond was transported over the sea on his cloak; St. Andrew shone brightly in the dark; St. Scholastica gained by her prayers a pouring rain; St. Paul was fed by ravens; and St. Frances saw her guardian angel. CARDINAL NEWMAN.

Treves (1) is a city of Germany; Turin (1), Monza (1), and Milan (1) are cities of Italy. The "Duomo" (1) of Milan is, next to St. Peter's in Rome, the most magnificent cathedral of Italy. St. Winifred's Well (2) is a holy place in Wales. The Mamertine (4) is the prison in Rome in which St. Peter was confined.

---

If you would hit the mark, you must aim above it; every arrow that flies feels the attraction of the earth.

## LESSON LXXX.

1. pē′rī; n. an imaginary being, represented as a descendant of fallen angels, excluded from Paradise until penance is accomplished.
1. dĭs cŏn′ so lătė; a. filled with grief.
2. glĭs′ tėnėd; v. shone.
3. nўmph (nĭmf); n. a lovely young girl.
4. hāzė; n. dimness.
6. bōon; n. present.
8. I mä′ rĕt; n. a lodging-house for Mohammedan pilgrims.
9. mĭn′ å rĕts; n. slender, high steeples on the mosques or churches of Mohammedan countries, and surrounded by one or more projecting balconies, from which the people are called to prayer by the muezzin, a crier appointed for that purpose.
13. här′ bĭn ġĕr; n. forerunner.

### Paradise and the Peri.

1. One morn a Peri at the gate
Of Eden stood, disconsolate;
And as she listened to the springs
   Of life within, like music flowing,
And caught the light upon her wings
   Through the half-open portal glowing,
She wept to think her recreant race
Should e'er have lost that glorious place!
" How happy," exclaimed this child of air,
" Are the holy spirits who wander there
   'Mid flowers that never shall fade or fall;
Though mine are the gardens of earth and sea
And the stars themselves have flowers for me,
   One blossom of Heaven outblooms them all."

2. The glorious Angel who was keeping
The gates of light beheld her weeping;
And, as he nearer drew and listened
To her sad song, a tear-drop glistened

Within his eyelids, like the spray
   From Eden's fountain when it lies
On the blue flower, which Brahmins say,
   Blooms nowhere but in Paradise.

3. "Nymph of a fair but erring line,"
   Gently he said, " one hope is thine:
   'Tis written in the Book of Fate,
      *The Peri yet may be forgiven*
   *Who brings to this eternal gate*
      *The gift that is most dear to Heaven!*
   Go, seek it, and redeem thy sin:
   'Tis sweet to let the pardoned in."

4. Downward the Peri turns her gaze,
   And, through the war-field's bloody haze,
   Beholds a youthful warrior stand
      Alone beside his native river,
   The red blade broken in his hand,
      And the last arrow in his quiver.
   "Live," said the conqueror, "live to share
   The trophies and the crowns I bear!"
   Silent that youthful warrior stood:
   Silent he pointed to the flood
   All crimson with his country's blood,
   Then sent his last remaining dart,
   For answer, to the invader's heart.

5. False flew the shaft, though pointed well:
   The tyrant lived, the hero fell!—
   Yet marked the Peri where he lay,
      And, when the rush of war was past,
   Swiftly descending on a ray
      Of morning light, she caught the last,

Last glorious drop his heart had shed,
　　　Before his free-born spirit fled!

6. "Be this," she cried, as she winged her flight,
　　"My welcome gift at the gates of light.
　　*　　　*　　　*　　　*　　　*　　　*
　　"Sweet," said the Angel, as she gave
　　　　The gift into his radiant hand,
　　"Sweet is our welcome of the brave
　　　　Who die thus for their native land.
　　But see—alas!—the crystal bar
　　Of Eden moves not—holier far
　　Than even this drop the boon must be
　　That opes the gates of Heaven for thee!"
　　*　　　*　　　*　　　*　　　*　　　*

7. Now, upon Syria's land of roses
　　Softly the light of eve reposes,
　　And, like a glory, the broad sun
　　Hangs over sainted Lebanon;
　　Whose head in wintry grandeur towers,
　　　　And whitens with eternal sleet,
　　While summer, in a vale of flowers,
　　　　Is sleeping rosy at his feet.

8. But naught can charm the luckless Peri:
　　Her soul is sad, her wings are weary.
　　When, o'er the vale of Baalbec winging
　　　　Slowly, she sees a child at play,
　　Among the rosy wild-flowers singing,
　　　　As rosy and as wild as they,
　　Chasing, with eager hands and eyes,
　　The beautiful blue damsel-flies,
　　That fluttered round the jasmine stems,
　　Like wingèd flowers or flying gems·

And, near the boy, who tired with play
Now nestling 'mid the roses lay,
She saw a wearied man dismount
   From his hot steed, and on the brink
Of a small imaret's rustic fount
   Impatient fling him down to drink.
Then swift his haggard brow he turned
   To the fair child, who fearless sat,
Though never yet hath day-beam burned
   Upon a brow more fierce than that.

9. But, hark! the vesper-call to prayer,
   As slow the orb of daylight sets,
Is rising sweetly on the air
   From Syria's thousand minarets.
The boy has started from the bed
Of flowers, where he had laid his head,
And down upon the fragrant sod
   Kneels with his forehead to the south,
Lisping the eternal name of God
   From purity's own cherub mouth.

10. And how felt he, the wretched man
Reclining there—while memory ran
O'er many a year of guilt and strife,
Flew o'er the dark flood of his life,
Nor found one sunny resting-place,
Nor brought him back one branch of grace?
"There was a time," he said, in mild,
Heart-humbled tones, " thou blessed child!

11. "When, young and haply pure as thou,
I looked and prayed like thee—but now"—

He hung his head—each nobler aim,
   And hope, and feeling, which had slept
From boyhood's hour, that instant came
   Fresh o'er him, and he wept—he wept.

12. And now behold him kneeling there
By the child's side, in humble prayer,
While the same sunbeam shines upon
The guilty and the guiltless one,
And hymns of joy proclaim through Heaven
The triumph of a soul forgiven!

13. 'Twas when the golden orb had set,
While on their knees they lingered yet,
There fell a light more lovely far
Than ever came from sun or star
Upon the tear that, warm and meek,
Dewed that repentant sinner's cheek.
To mortal eye this light might seem
A northern flash or meteor beam;
But well the enraptured Peri knew
'Twas a bright smile the Angel threw
From Heaven's gate, to hail that tear
Her harbinger of glory near!

"Joy, joy forever! my task is done:
The gates are passed, and Heaven is won."

MOORE.

**Thomas Moore** was born in Dublin in 1779 and died in 1852. His widest and most enduring reputation is as the author of the "Irish Melodies," a collection of about 124 lyrics, adapted to Irish national airs of great beauty. His most pretentious work is his Oriental romance "Lalla Rookh," a string of stories told in sparkling verse. Moore was distinguished by the grace of his thoughts and sentiments, his wit and fancy, and the melody and refinement of his versification.

Eden (1), though properly the garden in which Adam and Eve first dwelt, in this case means *heaven*. Lebanon (7) is a mountain of Syria. "Whose head in wintry grandeur towers, and whitens with eternal sleet, while summer, in a vale of flowers, is sleeping rosy at his feet" (7) means that while the mountain-tops are white with snow the valleys are covered with fertile orchards, vineyards, and corn-fields. Baalbec (8) is a town of Syria. "The orb of day-light" (9) means the *sun*. "Cherub mouth" (9), that is, the mouth of a beautiful child, from the fact that modern artists have represented cherubs as beautiful children.

## LESSON LXXXI.

3. gāǵe̱; *n.* a challenge to combat.
3. prĕs' tĭǵe̱; *n.* influence.
3. vŭl' nẽr á blĕ; *a.* capable of being wounded.
4. de spŏnd' e̱n çў; *n.* abandonment of hope.
6. făth' ŏme̱d; *v.* got to the bottom of.
7. çĭt' á dĕl; *n.* stronghold.
9. tăl' ĭṣ măn; *n.* something that produces extraordinary effects.
9. ŭn' dĭs' çĭ plĭne̱d; *a.* not instructed and exercised.
10. cŏm pēe̱rs'; *n.* companions; comrades.
14. vĭ çĭs' sĭ tūde̱s; *n.* changes.

### A Hundred Years of American Independence.

This eloquent and patriotic tribute to the greatness, the freedom, the liberality of our country is from an oration delivered July 4, 1876, in New York City. The date will account for what might be considered misstatements, as, for instance, when "thirty-eight States and Territories" (12) are spoken of.

1. You have all read the Declaration of Independence. A hundred years ago it was a new revelation, startling with new terror kings on their thrones, and bidding serfs, in their poor huts, arise and take heart, and look up, with new hope of deliverance. It asserted that all men, kings and peasants, master and servant, rich and poor, were born equal, with equal rights, inheritors of equal claim to protection from the law; that governments derived their just

powers, not from conquest or force, but from the consent of the governed, and existed only for their protection and to make them happy. These were the truths eternal but long unspoken—truths that few dared to utter, which Providence ordained should be revealed here in America, to be the political creed of the peoples all over the earth. Like a trumpet-blast blown in the night, it pealed through the dark abodes of misery, and aroused men to thought and hope and action.

2. And that trumpet-blast still is pealing and will peal, still summons whatever of manhood remains in mankind to assert itself. Still, at that sound, the knees of tyrants will be loosened with fear, and the hopes of freemen will rise, and their hearts beat faster and higher as long as this earth hangs poised in air, and men live upon it whose souls are alive with memories of the past.

3. The Declaration of American Independence was a declaration of war with Great Britain, war to the knife, and the knife to the hilt. There were fearful odds against the Colonies when they threw down the gage of battle. On one side was England—strong in the consciousness of wealth and power, strong in the prestige of sovereignty, fully armed and equipped for war, insolent, haughty, scorning even to entertain the idea of possible check or defeat. On the other side, the Thirteen Colonies, stretching, for the most part, along the seaboard, vulnerable at a hundred points, and open to attack by sea and land, without army, without navy, without money or ammunition or material of war, having for troops only crowds of undisciplined citizens, who had left for a while plow and anvil and hurried to the front with what arms they could lay hands on to fight the veterans of King George, skilled in their terrible trade by long service in European wars.

4. On the second of July, 1776, the Continental Congress was in session in Philadelphia. There were about forty-nine delegates present. That day was a day of gloom. The air was dark and heavy with ill news: ill news from the North—Montgomery had fallen at Quebec, and the expedition against Canada had miserably failed; ill news from the South—a fleet of British men-of-war had crossed the bar of Charleston, South Carolina; ill news from New York—Lord Howe's ships were riding in the Lower Bay, and a British army of thirty thousand men menaced the city with attack. From all sides came ill tidings. Everywhere doubt and suspicion and despondency. It was a dark and gloomy time, when even the boldest might well be forgiven for losing heart.

5. Such was the hour when Congress entered upon the consideration of the great question on which hung the fate of a continent. There were some who clung still to British connection. The King might relent—conciliation was not impossible—a monarchical form of government was dear to them. The past of England was their past, and they were loath to lose it. Then, war was a terrible alternative. They saw the precipice, and they shuddered and started back appalled.

6. But on the other side were the men of the hour— the men of the people, who listened to the voice of the people and felt the throbbing of the people's great heart. They, too, saw the precipice. Their eyes fathomed all the depth of the black abyss, but they saw beyond the glorious vision of the coming years. They saw countless happy homes stretching far and wide across a continent, wherein should dwell for ages generation after generation of men nurtured in strength and virtue and prosperity by the light and warmth of freedom.

7. Remember that between the Thirteen Colonies there were then but few ties. They differed in many things: in race, religion, climate, productions, and habits of thought, as much then as they do now. One grand purpose alone knit their souls together, North to South, Adams of Massachusetts to Jefferson of Virginia—the holy purpose of building up here, for them and their children, a free nation, to be the example, the model, the citadel of freedom; or, failing in that, to die and be forgotten, or remembered only with the stain of rebellion on their names.

8. The counsel of these brave and generous men prevailed. Some light from the better world illumined their souls and strengthened their hearts. Behind them surged and beat the great tide of popular enthusiasm. The people, ever alive to heroic purpose; the people, whose honest instincts are often the wisest statesmanship—the people waited but for the word: ready to fight, ready to die, if need be, for independence. And so God's will was done upon the earth.

9. The word was spoken, the "Declaration" was made that gave life and name to the "United States of America," and a new nation breathed and looked into the future, daring all the best or the worst that future might bring. If that declaration became a signal of rescue and relief to countries far away, what word can describe the miracles it has wrought for this people here at home? It was a spell, a talisman, an armor of proof, and a sword of victory. The undisciplined throng of citizen-soldiers, taught in the stern school of hardship and reverse, soon grew to be a great army, before which the veterans of Britain recoiled.

10. Europe, surprised into sympathy with rebellion, sent her best and bravest here to fight the battle of freedom, and Lafayette of France, De Kalb of Germany, Kosciusko of

Poland, and their compeers, drew their bright swords in the ranks of the young republic. Best support of all was that calm, fearless, steadfast soul, which, undismayed in the midst of peril and disaster, undaunted amid wreck and ruin, stood like a tower, reflecting all that was best and noblest in the character of the American people, and personifying its resolute will. Happy is that nation to whom, in its hour of need, bountiful Heaven provides a leader so brave and wise, so fitted to guide and rule, as was, in that early crisis of the American republic, its foremost man— George Washington.

11. Thus, from the baptism of blood, the young nation came forth purified, triumphant, free. Then the mystic influence, the magic of her accomplished freedom, began to work, and the thoughts of men, and the powers of earth and air and sea, began to do her bidding and cast their treasures at her feet.

12. From the thirteen parent Colonies thirty-eight great States and Territories have been born. At first a broad land of forest and prairie stretched far and wide, needing only the labor of man to render it fruitful. Men came; across the Atlantic, breasting its storms, sped mighty fleets, carrying hither brigades and divisions of the grand army of labor. On they came, in columns mightier than ever king led to battle—in columns millions strong—to conquer a continent, not to havoc and desolation, but to fertility and wealth, and order, and happiness.

13. They came from field and forest in the noble German land—from where, amid corn-field and vineyard and flowers, the lordly Rhine flows proudly toward the sea. From Ireland—from heath-covered hill and grassy valley —from where the giant cliffs standing as sentinels for Europe meet the first shock of the Atlantic and hurl back

its surges, broken and shattered in foam. From France and Switzerland, from Italy and Sweden, from all the winds of heaven, they came; and as their battle-line advanced, the desert fell back subdued, and in its stead sprang up corn and fruit, the olive and the vine, and gardens that blossomed like the rose.

14. Of triumphs like these who can estimate the value? The population of three millions a hundred years ago has risen to forty-three millions to-day. We have great cities, great manufactures, great commerce, great wealth, great luxury and splendor. Seventy-four thousand miles of railway conquer distance, and make all our citizens neighbors to one another. All these things are great and good, and can be turned to good. But they are not all. Whatever fate may befall this republic, whatever vicissitudes or disasters may be before her, this praise, at least, can never be denied to her, this glory she has won forever, that for one hundred years she has been hospitable and generous; that she gave to the stranger a welcome—opened to him all the treasures of her liberty, gave him free scope for all his ability, a free career, and fair play.

15. And this it is that most endears this republic to other nations, and has made fast friends for her in the homes of the peoples all over the earth; not her riches not her nuggets of gold, not her mountains of silver, not her prodigies of mechanical skill, great and valuable though these things be. It is this that most of all makes her name beloved and honored: that she has been always broad and liberal in her sympathies; that she has given homes to the homeless, land to the landless; that she has secured for the greatest number of those who have dwelt on her wide domain a larger measure of liberty and peace and happiness, and for a greater length of time, than has

ever been enjoyed by any other people on this earth. For this reason, the peoples all over the earth, and through all time, will call this republic blessed.

RICHARD O'GORMAN.

## LESSON LXXXII.

1. hau'teur' (hō' tûr'); n. haughty manner.
1. pá trī' çian; a. belonging to a person of high birth.
1. těn' sion (-shŭn); n. extreme strain of mind.
4. In vŏlve' mĕnt; n. the act of being entangled.
5. pär' ạl lĕl Ịṣm; n. equal distance.
8. ĕe çĕn' trĭe; a. irregular.
9. plăç' Id; a. contented.

### The Chariot Race. Part I.

This Lesson is taken from General Lewis Wallace's great story of "Ben-Hur." According to the story, Ben-Hur, a Jew, and Messala, a Roman, were friends when boys, but jealousy and a desire to secure part of the Jew's estate led the Roman to take sides against his former friend. Ben-Hur, on a charge of attempting to murder the Roman governor, is sent to the galleys for life, from which, however, he finally escapes. In the Chariot Race there are six competitors, Ben-Hur and Messala being the principal rivals.

1. The race was on; the souls of the racers were in it; over them bent the myriads.

When the dash for position began, Ben-Hur was on the extreme left of the six. For a moment, like the others, he was half blinded by the light in the arena; yet he managed to catch sight of his antagonists and divine their purpose. At Messala, who was more than an antagonist to him, he gave one searching look. The air of passionless hauteur characteristic of the fine patrician face was there as of old, and so was the Italian beauty, which the helmet rather increased; but more—it may have been a jealous fancy, or the effect of the brassy shadow in which the features were at the moment cast, still the Israelite thought he saw the soul of the man as through a glass, darkly : cruel, cunning, desperate ; not so excited as determined—a soul in a tension of watchfulness and fierce resolve.

2. In a time not longer than was required to turn to his four again, Ben-Hur felt his own resolution harden to a like temper. At whatever costs, at all hazards, he would humble this enemy ! Prize, friends, wagers, honor—everything that can be thought of as a possible interest in the race was lost in the one deliberate purpose. Regard for life, even, should not hold him back. Yet there was no passion on his part ; no blinding rush of heated blood from heart to brain, and back again ; no impulse to fling himself upon Fortune : he did not believe in Fortune—far otherwise. He had his plan, and confiding in himself, he settled to the task, never more observant, never more capable.

3. When not half-way across the arena, he saw that Messala's rush would, if there was no collision, and the rope fell, give him the wall ; that the rope would fall he ceased as soon to doubt ; and further, it came to him, a sudden flash-like insight, that Messala knew it was to be let drop at the last moment (prearrangement with the editor could safely reach that point in the contest) ; and it suggested, what more Roman-like than for the official to lend himself to a countryman who, besides being so popular, had also so much at stake ? There could be no other accounting for the confidence with which Messala pushed his four forward the instant his competitors were prudentially checking their fours in front of the obstruction—no other except madness.

4. It is one thing to see a necessity, and another to act upon it. Ben-Hur yielded the wall for the time.

The rope fell, and all the four but his sprang into the course under urgency of voice and lash. He drew head to the right, and with all the speed of his Arabs darted across the trails of his opponents, the angle of movement being such as to lose the least time and gain the greatest possible advance. So, while the spectators were shivering at the Athenian's mishap, and the Sidonian, Byzantine, and Corinthian were striving, with such skill as they possessed, to avoid involvement in the ruin, Ben-Hur swept around and took the course neck and neck with Messala, though on the outside. The marvelous skill shown in making the change thus from the extreme left across to the right without appreciable loss did not fail the sharp eyes upon the benches; the circus seemed to rock and rock again with prolonged applause. Then Esther clasped her hands in glad surprise; then Sanballat, smiling, offered his hundred sestertii a second time without a taker; and then the Romans began to doubt, thinking Messala might have found an equal, if not a master, and that in an Israelite!

5. And now, racing together side by side, a narrow interval between them, the two neared the second goal.

The pedestal of the three pillars there, viewed from the west, was a stone wall in the form of a half-circle, around which the course and opposite balcony were bent in exact parallelism. Making this turn was considered in all respects the most telling test of a charioteer; it was, in fact, the very feat in which Orestes failed. As an involuntary admission of interest on the part of the spectators, a hush fell over all the circus, so that for the first time in the race the rattle and clang of the cars plunging after the tugging steeds were distinctly heard. Then, it would seem, Messala observed Ben-Hur, and recognized him; and at once the audacity of the man flamed out in an astonishing manner.

6. "Down Eros, up Mars!" he shouted, whirling his

lash with practiced hand. "Down Eros, up Mars!" he repeated, and caught the well-doing Arabs of Ben-Hur a cut the like of which they had never known.

The blow was seen in every quarter, and the amazement was universal. The silence deepened; up on the benches behind the consul the boldest held his breath, waiting for the outcome. Only a moment thus; then, involuntarily, down from the balcony, as thunder falls, burst the indignant cry of the people.

7. The four sprang forward affrighted. No hand had ever been laid upon them except in love; they had been nurtured ever so tenderly; and as they grew, their confidence in man became a lesson to men beautiful to see. What should such dainty natures do under such indignity but leap as from death?

8. Forward they sprang as with one impulse, and forward leaped the car. Past question, every experience is serviceable to us. Where got Ben-Hur the large hand and mighty grip which helped him now so well? Where but from the oar with which so long he fought the sea! And what was this spring of the floor under his feet to the dizzy, eccentric lurch with which in the old time the trembling ship yielded to the beat of staggering billows, drunk with their power? So he kept his place, and gave the four free rein, and called to them in soothing voice, trying merely to guide them round the dangerous turn; and before the fever of the people began to abate, he had back the mastery. Nor that only; on approaching the first goal he was again side by side with Messala, bearing with him the sympathy and admiration of every one not a Roman. So clearly was the feeling shown, so vigorous its manifestation, that Messala, with all his boldness, felt it unsafe to trifle further.

9. As the cars whirled round the goal Esther caught

sight of Ben-Hur's face—a little pale, a little higher raised, otherwise calm, even placid.

Immediately a man climbed on the entablature at the west end of the division-wall, and took down one of the conical wooden balls. A dolphin on the east entablature was taken down at the same time.

In like manner, the second ball and second dolphin disappeared, and then the third ball and third dolphin.

The "editor" (3) here mentioned was the superintendent of the races; the "Athenian's mishap" (4) is an allusion to an accident which happened to the Athenian's chariot at the beginning of the race. Sanballat (4) is a friend of Ben-Hur's, and is betting on him; "sestertii" (4) is the plural of "sestertium," an ancient Roman coin worth about forty dollars, hence a hundred sestertii equal about four thousand dollars. Among the ancient Greeks Eros was the god of Love, Mars the god of War; hence, "Down Eros, up Mars" (6) is another way of saying, "Love is nothing, war everything." The taking down of a wooden ball and a wooden dolphin (9) signified that a round run had been made; seven wooden balls and seven pieces of wood cut to represent dolphins were set on entablatures in the circus: the entablature is the upper part of a column.

### LESSON LXXXIII.

1. clăm′ or; *n.* loud and continued shouting.  |  9. shĕik; *n.* a chief among the Arabians and the Moors.

### The Chariot Race. Part II.

1. Three rounds concluded; still Messala held the inside position, still Ben-Hur moved with him side by side, still the other competitors followed as before. The contest began to have the appearance of one of the double races which became so popular in Rome during the later Cæsarean period—Messala and Ben-Hur in the first, the Corinthian, Sidonian, and Byzantine in the second. Meantime the ushers succeeded in returning the multitude to their

seats, though the clamor continued to run the rounds, keeping, as it were, even pace with the rivals in the course below.

2. In the fifth round the Sidonian succeeded in getting a place outside Ben-Hur, but lost it directly.

The sixth round was entered upon without change of relative position.

Gradually the speed had been quickened; gradually the blood of the competitors warmed with the work. Men and beasts seemed to know alike that the final crisis was near, bringing the time for the winner to assert himself.

3. The interest, which from the beginning had centered chiefly in the struggle between the Roman and the Jew, with an intense and general sympathy for the latter, was fast changing to anxiety on his account. On all the benches the spectators bent forward motionless, except as their faces turned following the contestants. Ilderim quitted combing his beard, and Esther forgot her fears.

"A hundred sestertii on the Jew!" cried Sanballat to the Romans under the consul's awning.

There was no reply.

"A talent—or five talents—or ten; choose ye!"

He shook his tablets at them defiantly.

4. "I will take thy sestertii," answered a Roman youth, preparing to write.

"Do not so," interposed a friend.

"Why?"

"Messala hath reached his utmost speed. See him lean over his chariot-rim, the reins lying loose as flying ribbons. Look then at the Jew."

The first one looked.

"By Hercules!" he replied, his countenance falling. "The dog throws all his weight on the bits. I see! I see!

If the gods help not our friend, he will be run away with by the Israelite. No, not yet. Look! Jove with us! Jove with us!"

The cry, swelled by every Latin tongue, shook the *velaria* over the consul's head.

5. If it were true that Messala had attained his utmost speed, the effort was with effect; slowly but certainly he was beginning to forge ahead. His horses were running with their heads low down; from the balcony their bodies appeared actually to skim the earth; their nostrils showed blood-red in expansion; their eyes seemed straining in their sockets. Certainly the good steeds were doing their best! How long could they keep the pace? It was but the commencement of the sixth round. On they dashed. As they neared the second goal, Ben-Hur turned in behind the Roman's car.

The joy of the Messala faction reached its bound; they screamed and howled and tossed their colors, and Sanballat filled his tablets with wagers of their tendering.

6. Malluch, in the lower gallery over the Gate of Triumph, found it hard to keep his cheer. He had cherished the vague hint dropped to him by Ben-Hur of something to happen in the turning of the western pillars. It was the fifth round, yet the something had not come, and he had said to himself, the sixth will bring it; but lo! Ben-Hur was hardly holding a place at the tail of his enemy's car.

7. Over in the east end, Simonides' party held their peace. The merchant's head was bent low. Ilderim tugged at his beard, and dropped his brows till there was nothing of his eyes but an occasional sparkle of light. Esther scarcely breathed. Iras alone appeared glad.

8. Along the home-stretch—sixth round—Messala

leading, next him Ben-Hur, and so close it was the old story :

> "First flew Eumelus on Pheretian steeds ;
> With those of Tros bold Diomed succeeds ;
> Close on Eumelus' back they puff the wind,
> And seem just mounting on his car behind ;
> Full on his neck he feels the sultry breeze,
> And, hovering o'er, their stretching shadow sees."

Thus to the first goal, and round it. Messala, fearful of losing his place, hugged the stony wall with perilous clasp ; a foot to the left, and he had been dashed to pieces ; yet when the turn was finished, no man, looking at the wheel-tracks of the two cars, could have said here went Messala, there the Jew. They left but one trace behind them.

9. As they whirled by, Esther saw Ben-Hur's face again, and it was whiter than before.

Simonides, shrewder than Esther, said to Ilderim, the moment the rivals turned into the course, "I am no judge, good sheik, if Ben-Hur be not about to execute some design. His face hath that look."

To which Ilderim answered, "Saw you how clean they were and fresh ? By the splendor of God, friend, they have not been running ! But now watch !"

A "talent" (3) was a denomination of money. The Attic talent was worth about $1180 ; the Hebrew talent, from $1600 to $1900. "Jove with us" (4) means "Jove [another name for Jupiter, the chief god of the Romans] is on our side" ; "velaria" (4) is a Latin word meaning "coverings, the awnings on the top of a theater." Malluch (6), Simonides (7), and Ilderim (9) are friends of Ben-Hur's ; it is from Ilderim that the hero of the story borrows the horses for the race. The lines beginning "First flew Eumelus," etc., are from Homer's "Iliad."

## LESSON LXXXIV.

1. făc'tions (-shŭns); n. parties.
2. In junc'tion; n. command.
2. băl'us trāde'; n. a row of small columns topped by a railing.
3. In ĕf'fȧ blȳ; adv. in a manner not to be expressed in words.
3. sŭf fūs̟ĕd'; v. overspread, as with excitement.
3. pŏr tĕnd'ĕd; v. foretold.
3. Ar' ȧ mā' ic; a. relating to the language of Syria and Mesopotamia.
5. străt'e ġȳ; n. generalship.
6. mŭrk'ȳ; a. dark.

### The Chariot Race. Part III.

1. One ball and one dolphin remained on the entablatures; and all the people drew a long breath, for the beginning of the end was at hand.

First, the Sidonian gave the scourge to his four, and, smarting with fear and pain, they dashed desperately forward, promising for a brief time to go to the front. The effort ended in promise. Next, the Byzantine and Corinthian each made the trial, with like result, after which they were practically out of the race. Thereupon, with a readiness perfectly explicable, all the factions except the Romans joined hope in Ben-Hur, and openly indulged their feeling.

"Ben-Hur! Ben-Hur!" they shouted, and the blent voices of the many rolled overwhelmingly against the consular stand.

2. From the benches above him as he passed, the favor descended in fierce injunction.

"Speed thee, Jew!"

"Take the wall now!"

"On! loose the Arabs! Give them rein and scourge!"

"Let him not have the turn on thee again. Now or never!"

Over the balustrade they stooped low, stretching their hands imploringly to him.

3. Either he did not hear or could not do better, for half-way round the course and he was still following; at the second goal even still no change!

And now, to make the turn, Messala began to draw in his left-hand steeds, an act which necessarily slackened their speed. His spirit was high; more than one altar was richer of his vows; the Roman genius was still president. On the three pillars only six hundred feet away were fame, increase of fortune, promotions, and a triumph ineffably sweetened by hate, all in store for him! That moment, Malluch, in the gallery, saw Ben-Hur lean forward over his Arabs and give them the reins. Out flew the many-folded lash in his hand; over the backs of the startled steeds it writhed and hissed, and hissed and writhed again and again, and, though it fell not, there were both sting and menace in its quick report; and as the man passed thus from quiet to resistless action, his face suffused, his eyes gleaming, along the reins he seemed to flash his will; and instantly not one, but the four as one, answered with a leap that landed them alongside the Roman's car. Messala, on the perilous edge of the goal, heard, but dared not look to see what the awakening portended. From the people he received no sign. Above the noises of the race there was but one voice, and that was Ben-Hur's. In the old Aramaic, as the sheik himself, he called to the Arabs:

4. "On, Atair! On, Rigel! What, Antares! dost thou linger now? Good horse—oho, Aldebaran! I hear them singing in the tents. I hear the children singing, and the women—singing of the stars, of Atair, Antares, Rigel, Aldebaran, victory!—and the song will never end. Well done! Home to-morrow, under the black tent-home!

THE CHARIOT RACE.

On, Antares! The tribe is waiting for us, and the master is waiting! 'Tis done! 'tis done! Ha, ha! We have overthrown the proud. The hand that smote us is in the dust. Ours the glory! Ha, ha! steady! The work is done—soho! Rest!"

5. There had never been anything of the kind more simple; seldom anything so instantaneous.

At the moment chosen for the dash, Messala was moving in a circle round the goal. To pass him Ben-Hur had to cross the track, and good strategy required the movement to be in a forward direction—that is, on a like circle limited to the least possible increase. The thousands on the benches understood it all; they saw the signal given—the magnificent response—the four close outside Messala's outer wheel—Ben-Hur's inner wheel behind the other's car; all this they saw. Then they heard a crash loud enough to send a thrill through the circus, and, quicker than thought, out over the course a spray of shining white and yellow flinders flew. Down on its right side toppled the bed of the Roman's chariot. There was a rebound as of the axle hitting the hard earth; another, and another; then the car went to pieces, and Messala, entangled in the reins, pitched forward headlong.

6. To increase the horror of the sight by making death certain, the Sidonian, who had the wall next behind, could not stop or turn out. Into the wreck full speed he drove; then over the Roman, and into the latter's four, all mad with fear. Presently, out of the turmoil, the fighting of horses, the resound of blows, the murky cloud of dust and sand, he crawled, in time to see the Corinthian and Byzantine go on down the course after Ben-Hur, who had not been an instant delayed.

7. The people arose, and leaped upon the benches, and

shouted and screamed. Those who looked that way caught glimpses of Messala, now under the trampling of the fours, now under the abandoned cars. He was still; they thought him dead; but far the greater number followed Ben-Hur in his career. They had not seen the cunning touch of the reins by which, turning a little to the left, he caught Messala's wheel with the iron-shod point of his axle, and crushed it; but they had seen the transformation of the man, and themselves felt the heat and glow of his spirit, the heroic resolution, the maddening energy of action with which, by look, word, and gesture, he so suddenly inspired his Arabs. And such running! It was rather the long leaping of lions in harness; but for the lumbering chariot, it seemed the four were flying. When the Byzantine and Corinthian were half-way down the course, Ben-Hur turned the first goal.

*And the race was* WON! LEWIS WALLACE.

Atair (4), Rigel (4), Antares (4), and Aldebaran (4) are the names of the horses.

## LESSON LXXXV.

1. crest; *n.* the highest part of a hill.
1. săg'ging; *a.* settling; sinking in the middle.
3. sĭl'hou ĕttĕ'; *n.* the outlines of an object filled in with a black color; hence, a shadow.
3. couch'ant; *a.* lying down.
3. ănd' ī rŏns; *n.* utensils of brass or iron for supporting wood in a fireplace.
3. sĭm'mered; *v.* boiled gently.
5. clăp' boards; *n.* narrow boards thicker at one edge than at the other — used for covering the outside of houses.

### A Winter's Night.

1. As night drew on, and, from the crest
Of wooded knolls that ridged the west,
The sun, a snow-blown traveler, sank
From sight beneath the smothering bank,

We piled, with care, our nightly stack
Of wood against the chimney-back:
The oaken log, green, huge, and thick,
And on its top the stout backstick;
The knotty forestick laid apart,
And filled between, with curious art,
The ragged brush; then, hovering near,
We watched the first red blaze appear;
Heard the sharp crackle, caught the gleam
On whitewashed wall and sagging beam,
Until the old, rude-furnished room
Burst, flower-like, into rosy bloom.

2. Shut in from all the world without,
We sat the clean-winged hearth about,
Content to let the north-wind roar
In baffled rage at pane and door,
While the red logs before us beat
The frost-line back with tropic heat;
And ever, when a louder blast
Shook beam and rafter as it passed,
The merrier up its roaring draught
The great throat of the chimney laughed.

3. The house-dog, on his paws outspread,
Laid to the fire his drowsy head;
The cat's dark silhouette on the wall
A couchant tiger's seemed to fall;
And, for the winter fireside meet,
Between the andirons' straddling feet,
The mug of cider simmered slow,
The apples sputtered in a row;

And, close at hand, the basket stood
With nuts from brown October's wood.

4. At last the great logs, crumbling low,
Sent out a dull and duller glow;
The bull's-eye watch, that hung in view,
Ticking its weary circuit through,
Pointed, with mutely-warning sign,
Its black hand to the hour of nine.
That sign the pleasant circle broke:
My uncle ceased his pipe to smoke,
Knocked from its bowl the refuse gray,
And laid it tenderly away,
Then roused himself to safely cover
The dull red brands with ashes over.
And while with care our mother laid
Her work aside, her steps she stayed
One moment, seeking to express
Her grateful sense of happiness
For food and shelter, warmth and health,
And love's contentment, more than wealth.

5. Within our beds awhile we heard
The wind that round the gables roared,
With now and then a ruder shock,
Which made our very bedsteads rock.
We heard the loosened clapboards tost,
The board-nails snapping in the frost;
And on us, through the unplastered wall,
Felt the light-sifted snow-flakes fall.
But sleep stole on, as sleep will do
When hearts are light and life is new;
Faint and more faint the murmurs grew,

Till, in the summer-land of dreams,
They softened to the sound of streams,
Low stir of leaves, and dip of oars,
And lapsing waves on quiet shores.

      JOHN GREENLEAF WHITTIER.

**Explain** the expressions: "the ragged brush" (1); "burst . . . into rosy bloom" (1); "tropic heat" (2); "the great throat of the chimney laughed" (2); "ticking its weary circuit through" (4); "the refuse gray" (4); "when hearts are light and life is new" (5).

## LESSON LXXXVI.

1. glănd; *n.* cell.
1. ōoz' eş; *v.* flows gently.
1. glū' tĭ noŭs; *a.* sticky.
1. dĭs' sĭ pā' tĕd; *v.* scattered.
1. bŏgs; *n.* marshes; wet, spongy ground.
3. sà văn' nàs; *n.* extensive open plains or meadows.
3. ċon sẽrv' à to rĭeş; *n.* greenhouses.
4. cŏn' vĕx; *a.* swelling into a rounded form.
5. wąn' tŏn nĕss; *n.* recklessness; playfulness.
6. ċar nĭv' o roŭs; *a.* feeding on flesh.

### How Certain Plants Capture Insects.

1. All species of Sundew have their leaves, and some their stalks also, beset with bristles tipped with a gland from which oozes a drop of clear but very glutinous liquid, making the plant appear as if studded with dewdrops. These remain, glistening in the sun, long after dewdrops would have been dissipated. Small flies, gnats, and such-like insects, seemingly enticed by the glittering drops, stick fast upon them and perish by starvation, one would suppose without any benefit whatever to the plant. But in the broad-leaved wild species of our bogs, such as the common Round-leaved Sundew, the upper face and edges of the blade of the leaf bear stronger bristles tipped with a

larger glutinous drop, and the whole forms what we must allow to be a veritable fly-trap.

2. For when a small fly alights on the upper face and is held by some of the glutinous drops long enough for the leaf to act, the surrounding bristles slowly bend inward, so as to bring their glutinous tips also against the body of the insect. The different species of Sundew offer all gradations, between those with merely scattered and motionless dewy-tipped bristles, to which flies may chance to stick, and this more complex arrangement which we cannot avoid regarding as intended for fly-catching. Moreover, in both of our commoner species the blade of the leaf itself incurves, so as to fold round its victim.

3. And a most practiced observer, whose observations are not yet published, declares that the leaves of the common Round-leaved Sundew act differently when different objects are placed upon them. For instance, if a particle of raw meat be substituted for the living fly, the bristles will close upon it in the same manner; but to a particle of chalk or wood they remain nearly indifferent. If any doubt should still remain whether the fly-catching in Sundews is accidental or intentional—in other words, whether the leaf is so constructed and arranged in order that it may capture flies—the doubt may perhaps disappear upon the contemplation of another, and even more extraordinary, plant of the same family of the Sundew—namely, Venus's Fly-trap. This plant abounds in the low savannas around Wilmington, North Carolina, and is native nowhere else. It is not very difficult to cultivate—at least, for a time—and it is kept in many choice conservatories as a vegetable wonder.

4. The trap is the end of the leaf. It is somewhat like the leaf of Sundew, only larger, about an inch in diameter,

with bristles still stouter, but only round the margin, like a fringe, and no clammy liquid or gland at their tips. The leaf folds on itself as if hinged at the midrib. Three more delicate bristles are seen on the face upon close inspection. When these are touched by the finger or the point of a pencil, the open trap shuts with a quick motion, and after a considerable interval it reopens. When a fly or other insect alights on the surface and brushes against these sensitive bristles, the trap closes promptly, generally imprisoning the intruder. It closes at first with the sides convex and the bristles crossing each other, like the fingers of interlocked hands or the teeth of a steel trap, but soon the sides of the trap flatten down and press firmly upon the victim, and it now requires a very considerable force to open the trap. If nothing is caught, the trap presently reopens of itself and is ready for another attempt.

5. When a fly or any similar insect is captured, it is retained until it perishes—is killed, indeed, and consumed; after which it opens for another capture. But after the first or second it acts sluggishly and feebly, it ages and hardens, at length loses its sensibility, and slowly decays. It cannot be supposed that plants, like boys, catch flies for pastime or in objectless wantonness; living beings though they are, yet they are not of a sufficiently high order for that. It is equally incredible that such an exquisite apparatus as this should be purposeless. And in the present case the evidence of the purpose and of the meaning of the strange action is well-nigh complete.

6. The face of this living trap is thickly sprinkled with glands large enough to be clearly discerned with a hand-lens; these glands, soon after an insect is closed upon, give out a saliva-like liquid which moistens the insect, and in a short time (within a week) dissolves all its soft parts, and

the liquid, with the animal matter it has dissolved, is reabsorbed into the leaf. We are forced to conclude, therefore, that this plant is really carnivorous.

7. That, while all plants are food for animals, some few should, in turn and to some extent, feed upon them, will appear more credible when it is considered that whole tribes of plants of the lowest grade (Mold-Fungi and the like) habitually feed upon living plants and living animals, or upon their juices when dead. ASA GRAY.

What flows from the gland on the Sundew (1)? What happens to the insects that are attracted by the glittering drops (1)? Describe the Round-leaved Sundew (1). What happens when a small fly alights on the upper face of that plant (2)? Describe how the leaves act when different articles are placed on them (3). Of what part of the country is Venus's Fly-trap a native (3)? Describe the leaf of the plant (4). What happens when its bristles are touched by the finger (4)? What if an insect touches the bristles (4)? What if nothing is caught (4)? How does the plant act when it captures an insect (5)? What do the glands of this trap give out when an insect is caught (6)? To what conclusions are we forced (6)? Why is it credible that some plants feed upon animals (7)?

## LESSON LXXXVII.

1. e văc′ u ā′ tion; *n.* the act of emptying.
4. be drăg′ glĕd; *v.* soiled.
5. In çĕs′ sănt; *a.* continuing without interruption.
6. Im pōsĕd; *v.* put.

6. shăm′ blĕs; *n.* places for slaughtering animals.
7. quĭk; *n.* living.
7. de pōṣ′ It ed; *v.* thrown down.
7. eŏn sĭgnĕd; *v.* delivered.

### The Massacre of Cawnpore.

In 1857 the Sepoys or native troops in India broke out in mutiny, on the pretext that the English, by issuing to them cartridges mixed with pig's fat, meant to insult and despise their religion. Brutal massacres of Europeans took place. At Cawnpore the English General, Sir Hugh Wheeler, asked a chief named Nana Sahib, who lived near Cawnpore and professed to be friendly to the

English, to come and help him. Nana came with his guns and soldiers, but only to join the insurgents and turn his guns against the English. The English, men, women, and children, took refuge in an old hospital with mud walls, and here continued to repel the constant attacks of the mutineers, until Nana Sahib offered to all who would lay down their arms a safe passage to Allahabad. The terms were accepted; but the English found themselves the victims of a fiendish act of treachery.

1. The time for the evacuation of the garrison came. The boats were in readiness on the Ganges. The long procession of men, women, and children passed slowly down. Some of the chief among Nana's counselors took their stand in a little temple on the margin of the river, to superintend the embarkation and the work that was to follow it. Nana's lieutenant, Tantia Topee, had given orders, it seems, that when a trumpet sounded, some work, for which he had arranged, should begin.

2. The wounded and the women were got into the boats, which were covered with roofs of straw. The officers and men were scrambling in after them. Suddenly the blast of a trumpet was heard. The moment the bugle sounded, the straw of the boat-roofs blazed up, and the native rowers began to make precipitately for the shore. They had set fire to the thatch, and were now escaping from the flames. At the same moment there came from both shores of the river thick showers of grapeshot and musketry. The banks of the Ganges seemed, in an instant, alive with shot, a very rain of bullets poured in upon the devoted inmates of the boats. To add to the horror of the moment, nearly all the boats stuck fast in the mud banks, and the occupants became fixed targets for the fire of their enemies. Only three of the boats floated. Two of these drifted to the Oude shore, and those on board them were killed at once.

3. A party of twelve men went ashore to attack the enemy, hand to hand, but only four of that gallant little party finally escaped, after most extraordinary and perilous adventures.

4. And now the firing ceased. The women and children—one hundred and twenty-five in number—who were still alive, were brought ashore and carried in forlorn procession back again through the town. They were bedraggled and disheveled, these poor Englishwomen; their clothes were in tatters; some of them were wounded, and the blood was trickling from their feet and legs. They were led into a small building and locked up there, except when some of them were taken out in the evening and set to the work of grinding corn for the use of their captors.

5. But Havelock was now moving forward from Allahabad with six cannon and about a thousand English soldiers. He was almost at the gates of Cawnpore when it was intimated to the prisoners that they were to die. Among them were three or four men. They were called out and shot. Then some sepoys were sent to the house where the women still were, and ordered to fire volleys through the windows. In the evening, five men—two Hindoo peasants, two Mohammedan butchers, and one wearing the red uniform of Nana's body-guard—were sent up to the house, and entered it. Incessant shrieks were heard to come from that fearful house. The Mohammedan soldier came out to the door holding in his hand a sword-hilt from which the blade had been broken off, and exchanged his now useless weapon for a new one. Twice this performance took place.

6. The task imposed on these men was evidently hard work for the sword-blades. After a while the five men came out of the now quiet house, and locked the doors

behind them. During that time they had killed nearly all the English women and children. They had slaughtered them like beasts in the shambles. In the morning the five men came to clear out the house of the captives. Their task was to tumble all the bodies into a dry well beyond some trees that grew near. Then it was seen by some of the spectators that certain of the women and children were not yet quite dead. Of the children, some were alive, and even tried to get away. But the same well awaited them all.

7. Some witnesses were of opinion that the Nana's officials took the trouble to kill the still living, before they tossed them down into the well; others do not think they stopped for any such work of humanity, but flung them down just as they came to hand, the quick and the dead together. At all events they were all deposited in the well. Any of the bodies that had clothes worth taking were carefully stripped before being consigned to this open grave.

8. When Cawnpore was afterward taken by the English, those who had to look down into that well saw a sight the like of which no man in modern days has ever seen elsewhere. The well of horrors has been filled up, and a memorial chapel, surrounded by a garden, built upon the spot. It was right to banish all trace of that hideous crime, and to replace the house and well by "a fair garden and a graceful shrine." JUSTIN MCCARTHY.

Justin McCarthy, journalist, novelist, historian, and Member of Parliament, was born in Cork in 1830. He has been a very prolific writer and a very successful one. His writings are full of thought and his thoughts are clothed in harmonious, smooth, and appropriate language. He is to-day one of the foremost men in Ireland, and in politics is a pronounced Nationalist.

Cawnpore is one of the principal military stations in India, about one hundred miles northwest of Allahabad on the west bank of the

Ganges, which here separates the Northwest Provinces from the province of Oude. The Ganges (1) is a river nearly 2000 miles long, flowing from the Himalaya Mountains to the Bay of Bengal, India.

**Sir Henry Havelock** (5), eminent as an English general, was born in 1795. He served with distinction in several wars. During the Mutiny in India he defeated Nana Sahib, took Cawnpore, and afterward relieved Lucknow, where he died in 1857 of cholera. Allahabad (5), the capital of the Northwest Provinces, India, situated at the junction of the Ganges and the Jumna, is considered sacred by the natives. It was held by English troops at the time of the massacre of Cawnpore.

## LESSON LXXXVIII.

1. a ā' rĭ ạl; *a.* belonging to the air.
1. spī' rạl; *a.* winding like a screw.
3. brụ' ĭn; *n.* a bear.
3. se rĕn' ĭ tỹ; *n.* undisturbed state.
4. ō' vẽr whĕlm'; *v.* immerse and bear down.
5. mŏn' o chrō' mĭst; *n.* one who paints in a single color.
5. pŏl ỹ chrō' ĭc; *a.* given to the use of many colors.
7. rĭv' u lĕts; *n.* small rivers.

### An Iceberg.

1. We have just passed a fragment of an iceberg that bore the resemblance of a huge polar bear reposing upon the base of an inverted cone, with a twist of a sea-shell, and whirling slowly round and round. The ever-attending green water, with its aerial clearness, enabled us to see its spiral folds and horns as they hung suspended in the deep.

2. The bear, a ten-foot mass in tolerable proportion, seemed to be regularly beset by a pack of hungry little swells. First, one would take him on the haunch, then whip back into the sea over his tail and between his legs. Presently a bolder swell would rise and pitch into his back with a ferocity that threatened instant destruction. It only washed his satin fleece the whiter.

3. While Bruin was turning to look the daring assailant in the face, the rogue had pitched himself back into his cave. No sooner that, than a very bulldog of a billow would attack him in the face. The serenity with which the impertinent assault was borne was complete. It was but a puff of silvery dust, powdering his mane with fresher brightness. Nothing would be left of bull but a little froth of all the foam displayed in the fierce onset. He too would turn and scud into his hiding-place.

4. Persistent little waves! After a dash, singly, all around, upon the common enemy, as if by some silent agreement under water, they would all rush on at once, with their loudest roar and shaggiest foam, and overwhelm poor bear so completely that nothing less might be expected than to behold him broken in four quarters, and floating helplessly asunder. Mistaken spectators! Although, by his momentary rolling and plunging, he was evidently aroused, yet neither Bruin nor his burrow were at all the worse for all the wear and washing.

5. The deep fluting, the wrinkled folds and cavities over and through which the green and silvery water rushed back into the sea, rivaled the most exquisite sculpture. And Nature not only gives her marbles, with the finest lines, the most perfect lights and shades, she colors them also. She is no monochromist, but polychroic, imparting such touches of dove-tints, emerald, and azure as she bestows upon her gems and skies.

6. We are bearing up under the big berg as closely as we dare. To our delight, what we have been wishing and watching for is actually taking place: loud explosions, with heavy falls of ice, followed by the cataract-like roar, and the high, thin seas, wheeling away beautifully crested with sparkling foam. If it is possible, imagine the effect upon

the beholder: this precipice of ice, with tremendous cracking, is falling toward us with a majestic and awful motion.

7. Down sinks the long water-line into the black deep; down go the porcelain crags and galleries of glassy sculptures, a speechless and awful baptism. Now it pauses, and returns: up rise sculptures and crags streaming with the shining white brine; up comes the great encircling line, followed by things new and strange, crags, niches, balconies, and caves; up, up it rises, higher, and higher still, crossing the very breast of the grand ice, and all bathed with rivulets of gleaming foam. Over goes the summit, ridge, pinnacles, and all, standing off obliquely in the opposite air. Now it pauses in its upward roll: back it comes again, cracking, cracking, cracking, "groaning out harsh thunder" as it comes, and threatening to burst, like a mighty bomb, into millions of glittering fragments. The spectacle is terrific and magnificent. Emotion is irrepressible, and peals of wild hurrah burst forth from all.

8. As we recede the upper portions of the solid ice have a light and aerial effect, a description of which is simply impossible. Peaks and spires rise out of the strong and apparently unchanging base with the light activity of flame. A mighty structure on fire, all in ice!

Louis L. Noble.

Great floating masses of ice become detached from the polar ice-fields, and form "icebergs." These bergs or mountains of ice are sometimes more than 250 feet above the sea-level, and it is calculated that the part of the berg below the surface is eight times that of the protruding part.

---

The talent of success is nothing more than doing what you can do well without a thought of fame.

## LESSON LXXXIX.

1. ĕl'e ġў; n. a mournful poem.
1. cûr' few; n. a bell which is rung at nightfall.
2. drŏn'ĭng; a. humming.
5. clăr' ĭ ŏn; n. a clear, shrill note.
7. glēbĕ; n. ground.
7. jŏc' ŭnd; a. merry.
12. prĕg' nănt; a. filled.
12. ĕc' stă sў; n. excessive and overmastering joy.
13. pĕn' u rў; n. poverty.

### Elegy Written in a Country Churchyard. Part I.

1. The curfew tolls the knell of parting day,
    The lowing herd winds slowly o'er the lea;
The plowman homeward plods his weary way,
    And leaves the world to darkness and to me.

2. Now fades the glimmering landscape on the sight,
    And all the air a solemn stillness holds,
Save where the beetle wheels his droning flight,
    And drowsy tinklings lull the distant folds,—

3. Save that from yonder ivy-mantled tower
    The moping owl does to the moon complain
Of such as, wandering near her secret bower,
    Molest her ancient, solitary reign.

4. Beneath those rugged elms, that yew-tree's shade,
    Where heaves the turf in many a moldering heap,
Each in his narrow cell forever laid,
    The rude forefathers of the hamlet sleep.

5. The breezy call of incense-breathing morn,
    The swallow twittering from the straw-built shed,
The cock's shrill clarion, or the echoing horn,
    No more shall rouse them from their lowly bed.

6. For them no more the blazing hearth shall burn,
    Or busy housewife ply her evening care;
   No children run to lisp their sire's return,
    Or climb his knees the envied kiss to share.

7. Oft did the harvest to their sickle yield,
    Their furrow oft the stubborn glebe has broke;
   How jocund did they drive their team a-field!
    How bowed the woods beneath their sturdy stroke!

8. Let not Ambition mock their useful toil,
    Their homely joys, and destiny obscure;
   Nor Grandeur hear with a disdainful smile
    The short and simple annals of the poor.

9. The boast of heraldry, the pomp of power,
    And all that beauty, all that wealth e'er gave,
   Await alike the inevitable hour:—
    The paths of glory lead but to the grave.

10. Nor you, ye proud, impute to these the fault,
     If Memory o'er their tomb no trophies raise,
    Where through the long-drawn aisle and fretted vault
     The pealing anthem swells the note of praise.

11. Can storied urn or animated bust
     Back to its mansion call the fleeting breath?
    Can Honor's voice provoke the silent dust,
     Or Flattery soothe the dull, cold ear of Death?

12. Perhaps in this neglected spot is laid
     Some heart once pregnant with celestial fire;
    Hands that the rod of empire might have swayed,
     Or waked to ecstasy the living lyre:—

13. But Knowledge to their eyes her ample page,
    Rich with the spoils of time, did ne'er unroll;
  Chill Penury repressed their noble rage,
    And froze the genial current of the soul.

14. Full many a gem of purest ray serene,
    The dark, unfathomed caves of ocean bear;
  Full many a flower is born to blush unseen,
    And waste its sweetness on the desert air.

Curfew (1) is derived from two French words which mean "to cover the fire." According to law the curfew bell was rung at eight o'clock in the evening. It is generally believed that the practice was introduced into England by William the Conqueror. It was common in France, Spain, Italy, and probably in other parts of continental Europe. In England the law obliged the people not only to cover their fires, but also to put out their lights, and any one found out-of-doors after the ringing of the curfew was liable to be arrested. Whether the object in introducing the practice into England was to prevent secret meetings of the people at night; to protect from fire, as most of the houses were of wood; or to do away with the robberies and murders at that time so frequent after dark, is a matter of dispute.

The line "The plowman homeward plods his weary way" (1) is an excellent exercise for transposition; let the pupils try in how many ways they can express the same idea in the same words, but differently arranged.

Let the pupils find synonyms for, or express in other words, the following: "turf" (4); "narrow cell" (4); "hamlet" (4); "sturdy" (7); "the inevitable hour" (9); "anthem" (10); "silent dust" (11).

---

No time is thine but the present. The time gone comes no more; the time to come may find thee gone when it comes.

Help somebody worse off than yourself, and you will find that you are better off than you fancied.

## LESSON XC.

3. çǐr′ çŭm serībĕd; v. limited.
4. ĭn ġĕn′ u ŏŭs; a. frank; open; upright.
1. mūṣe; n. one of the fabled goddesses who preside over literary, artistic, and scientific matters; in this case the Muse of Poetry is referred to.
5. se quĕs′ tēred; v. shut apart from others.
6. ŭn eoŭth′; a. clumsy.
6. trĭb′ ute; n. a personal contribution made in token of that which is due.
8. prē′ çĭnets; n. boundaries.
12. pōre; v. look with steady, continued attention.

### Elegy Written in a Country Churchyard. Part II.

1. Some village Hampden, that with dauntless breast
     The little tyrant of his fields withstood;
   Some mute, inglorious Milton here may rest,—
     Some Cromwell, guiltless of his country's blood.

2. The applause of listening senates to command,
     The threats of pain and ruin to despise,
   To scatter plenty o'er a smiling land,
     And read their history in a nation's eyes,

3. Their lot forbade : nor circumscribed alone
     Their growing virtues, but their crimes confined;—
   Forbade to wade through slaughter to a throne,
     And shut the gates of mercy on mankind;

4. The struggling pangs of conscious truth to hide,
     To quench the blushes of ingenuous shame,
   Or heap the shrine of Luxury and Pride
     With incense kindled at the Muse's flame.

5. Far from the madding crowd's ignoble strife,
     Their sober wishes never learned to stray;
   Along the cool, sequestered vale of life,
     They kept the noiseless tenor of their way.

6. Yet e'en these bones from insult to protect,
    Some frail memorial still erected nigh,
With uncouth rhymes and shapeless sculpture decked,
    Implores the passing tribute of a sigh.

7. Their name, their years, spelt by the unlettered Muse
    The place of fame and elegy supply;
And many a holy text around she strews,
    That teach the rustic moralist to die.

8. For who, to dumb Forgetfulness a prey,
    This pleasing, anxious being e'er resigned;
Left the warm precincts of the cheerful day,
    Nor cast one longing, lingering look behind?

9. On some fond breast the parting soul relies;
    Some pious drops the closing eye requires;
Even from the tomb the voice of Nature cries,—
    Even in our ashes live their wonted fires.

10. For thee, who, mindful of the unhonored dead,
    Dost in these lines their artless tale relate;
If chance, by lonely Contemplation led,
    Some kindred spirit shall inquire thy fate,—

11. Haply some hoary-headed swain may say,
    "Oft have we seen him at the peep of dawn,
Brushing with hasty steps the dews away,
    To meet the sun upon the upland lawn;

12. "There at the foot of yonder nodding beech,
    That wreathes its old, fantastic roots so high,
His listless length at noontide would he stretch,
    And pore upon the brook that babbles by.

13. "Hard by yon wood, now smiling as in scorn,
    Muttering his wayward fancies, he would rove;
  Now drooping, woful, wan, like one forlorn,
    Or crazed with care, or crossed in hopeless love.

14. "One morn I missed him on the 'customed hill,
    Along the heath, and near his favorite tree;
  Another came,—nor yet beside the rill,
    Nor up the lawn, nor at the wood was he;

15. "The next, with dirges due, in sad array,
    Slow through the church-way path we saw him borne;—
  Approach and read—for thou canst read—the lay
    Graved on the stone beneath yon aged thorn."

### THE EPITAPH.

16. Here rests his head upon the lap of Earth,
    A youth to Fortune and to Fame unknown;
  Fair Science frowned not on his humble birth,
    And Melancholy marked him for her own.

17. Large was his bounty, and his soul sincere;
    Heaven did a recompense as largely send:
  He gave to Misery,—all he had—a tear;
    He gained from Heaven,—'twas all he wished—a friend.

18. No further seek his merits to disclose,
    Or draw his frailties from their dread abode,—
  There they alike in trembling hope repose—
    The bosom of his Father and his God.

THOMAS GRAY.

Thomas Gray was born at Cornhill, London, in 1716. His reputation as a poet rests, almost exclusively, on his "Elegy Written in a

Country Churchyard." It has been called "the corner-stone of his glory"; its keen descriptions of nature, its consummate taste, its exquisite beauty and finish, and the charming, easy flow of the verse make this a masterpiece of elegiac composition.

When Charles I. determined to govern England by his own will and contrary to the law of the land, John Hampden (1), born about 1594, refused to pay an illegal tax which the king tried to impose. He also opposed the king in many other ways, and became famous as one of the leaders of the Puritan party. He died in 1643 from a wound received at the battle of Chalgrove Field.

**Oliver Cromwell** (1), born in 1599, was the leader of the rebellion which drove Charles I. from the throne to the block. Cromwell became "Lord Protector" of England, and ruled the country with an iron hand until his death in 1658.

## LESSON XCI.

1. măn′ ôr; *n.* land belonging to a lord or nobleman.
1. rĕs′ pīte; *n.* the putting off of the execution; delay.
2. rĭg′ ôr oŭs; *a.* severe.
3. ăc quĭt′ tĕd; *v.* pardoned.
3. In′ trĭ ca çў; *n.* perplexity.
6. seōpe; *n.* intention.
7. frŭs′ trāt ĕd; *v.* defeated.
8. lau̇d′ả ble; *a.* worthy of praise.
8. măx′ ĭm; *n.* saying.
8. păt; *adv.* fitly.

### Sancho Panza's Government.

Sancho Panza is the squire or attendant of Don Quixote in the celebrated Spanish story of that name by Cervantes. The squire is represented as a middle-aged peasant, ignorant and credulous to excess, but of great good-nature; selfish and vulgar, yet attached to his master; occasionally shrewd, always amusing. Among other adventures he is appointed governor of the island of Barataria, and it is from the chapter which details his doings while in that office that this Lesson is taken.

1. The first case that occurred was a question put by a stranger, in presence of the steward and the rest of the assistants. "My lord," said he, "a certain manor is divided by a large river— I beg your honor will be attentive, for the case is of great consequence and some difficulty. I say, then, upon this river is a bridge, and at one

end of it a gibbet, together with a sort of court-hall, in which four judges usually sit, to execute the law enacted by the lord of the river, bridge, and manor, which runs to this effect: 'Whosoever shall pass over this bridge must first swear whence he comes and whither he goes; if he swear the truth, he shall be allowed to pass; but if he forswear himself, he shall die upon the gallows, without mercy or respite.'

2. "This law, together with the rigorous penalty, being known, numbers passed, and, as it appeared they swore nothing but the truth, the judges permitted them to pass freely and without control. It happened, however, that one man's oath being taken, he affirmed, and swore by his deposition, that he was going to be hanged on that gibbet, and had no other errand or intention.

3. "The judges, having considered this oath, observed: 'If we allow the man to pass freely, he swore to a lie, and, therefore, ought to be hanged according to law; and if we order him to be hanged, after he hath sworn he was going to be suspended on that gibbet, he will have sworn the truth, and, by the same law, ought to be acquitted.' I beg, therefore, to know of your honor, my lord governor, what the judges must do with this man, for hitherto they are doubtful and in suspense; and, having heard of your lordship's acute and elevated understanding, they have sent me to entreat your honor, in their names, to favor them with your opinion in a case of such doubt and intricacy."

4. To this address Sancho replied: "Assuredly, those judges who sent you to me might have spared themselves the trouble; for I am a man that may be said to be rather blunt than acute; nevertheless, repeat the business so that I may understand it fully, and who knows but I may chance to hit the nail on the head?"

5. The interrogator having repeated his story again and again, Sancho said: "I think I can now explain the case in the twinkling of an eye; and this it is: A man swears he is going to be hanged on such a gibbet; if he actually suffers upon that gibbet, he swore the truth, and, by the enacted law, ought to be allowed freely to pass the bridge; but if he is not hanged, he swore false, and for that reason he ought to suffer upon the gibbet."

6. "The case is exactly as my lord governor conceives it," said the messenger; "and, with respect to the scope and understanding of the matter, there is no further room for doubt or interrogation." "I say, then," replied Sancho, "that part of the man which swore truth ought to be allowed to pass; and that which told a lie ought to be hanged; and, in this manner, the terms or conditions of passing will be literally fulfilled."

7. "But, my lord governor," replied the questioner, "in that case it will be necessary to divide the man into two parts, namely, the false and the true; and if he is so divided, he must certainly die; therefore, the intent of the law will be frustrated, whereas there is an express necessity for its being accomplished."

8. "Come hither, honest friend," said Sancho; "either I am a blockhead, or this passenger you mention has an equal title to be hanged and to live and pass over the bridge; for, if the truth saves him on one side, his falsehood condemns him equally on the other. Now, this being the case, as it certainly is, I think you must tell the gentlemen who sent you hither that, as the reasons for condemning and for acquitting the culprit are equally balanced, they shall let him freely pass; for it is always more laudable to do good than harm; and to this opinion I would subscribe, if I could write my name. Nor, indeed,

have I spoken my own sentiment on this occasion; but I have recollected one among the many precepts I received from my master, Don Quixote, the night before I set out for the government of this island: he said that, when justice was doubtful, I should choose and lean toward mercy; and it pleased God that I should now remember this maxim, which falls so pat to the present purpose."

CERVANTES.

**Miguel de Cervantes Saavedra,** one of the greatest imaginative writers of Spain, was born in 1547. Although he wrote many works, Cervantes is remembered best as the author of "Don Quixote." This book, which has been translated into many languages, was intended to put an end to the absurd and affected romances which it was then the fashion to read. The work is regarded by the majority of readers as a burlesque, but the real aim of the author is to show that the disinterested, generous, kind-hearted, charitable man always commands our affections and esteem. Despite the fact that the works of Cervantes have had great circulation, he lived, the most of his life, in poverty.

## LESSON XCII.

3. In vĭş'ĭ blẹ; *a.* incapable of being seen.
4. strănd; *n.* shore or beach.
5. ăb'ā tĭs; *n.* large sharp-pointed branches of trees, used to prevent the approach of an enemy to a fortification.
5. plā teau'(plà tō); *n.* a plain.
7. Ĭm'mĭ nẹnt; *a.* threatening.
7. ăl tẽr'nā tĭvẹ; *n.* choice between two things.
9. pẽr fōrçẹ'; *adv.* of necessity.
10. Ĭn'tẽr vēnẹd; *v.* came between.

### Storming the Heights of Abraham. Part I.

During the reign of George II. of England the *Seven Years' War* (1756–1763) was waged between England and Prussia on the one side and France and Austria on the other. Between England and France the war became a struggle for colonial supremacy in America as well as India. The French had early colonized Canada, and threatened to check the spread of British dominion in that part of the world. The capture of Quebec, the capital, and the consequent surrender of Canada decided forever that the English, and not the French, were to rule in the New World.

1. Toward two o'clock the tide began to ebb, and a fresh wind blew down the river. Two lanterns were raised into the maintop shrouds of the "Sutherland." It was the appointed signal; the boats cast off and fell down with the current, those of the light infantry leading the way. The vessels with the rest of the troops had orders to follow a little later.

2. For full two hours the procession of boats, borne on the current, steered silently down the St. Lawrence. The stars were visible, but the night was moonless and sufficiently dark. The general was in one of the foremost boats, and near him was a young midshipman, John Robinson, afterward Professor of Natural Philosophy in the University of Edinburgh. He used to tell in his later life how Wolfe, with a low voice, repeated Gray's *Elegy in a Country Churchyard* to the officers about him. Probably it was to relieve the intense strain of his thoughts. Among the rest was the verse which his own fate was soon to illustrate—

"The paths of glory lead but to the grave."

"Gentlemen," he said, as his recital ended, "I would rather have written those lines than take Quebec." None were there to tell him that the hero is greater than the poet.

3. As they neared their destination the tide bore them in toward the shore, and the mighty wall of rock and forest towered in darkness on their left. The dead stillness was suddenly broken by the sharp "*Qui vive?*" of a French sentry, invisible in the thick gloom. "*France!*" answered a Highland officer of Fraser's regiment, from one

of the boats of the light infantry. He had served in Holland, and spoke French fluently.

"*À quel régiment ?*"

"*De la Reine*," replied the Highlander. He knew that a part of that corps was with Bougainville. The sentry, expecting the convoy of provisions, was satisfied, and did not ask for the password.

4. Soon after, the foremost boats were passing the heights of Samos, when another sentry challenged them, and they could see him through the darkness running down to the edge of the water, within range of a pistol-shot. In answer to his questions, the same officer replied in French, "Provision-boats. Don't make a noise, the English will hear us." In fact, the sloop-of-war "Hunter" was anchored in the stream not far off. This time, again, the sentry let them pass. In a few moments they rounded the headland above the Anse du Foulon. There was no sentry there. The strong current swept the boats of the light infantry a little below the intended landing-place. They disembarked on a narrow strand at the foot of heights as steep as a hill covered with trees can be. The twenty-four volunteers led the way, climbing with what silence they might, closely followed by a much larger body. When they reached the top, they saw in the dim light a cluster of tents at a short distance, and immediately made a dash at them. Vergor leaped from bed and tried to run off, but was shot in the heel and captured. His men, taken by surprise, made little resistance. One or two were caught, and the rest fled.

5. The main body of troops waited in their boats by the edge of the strand. The heights near by were cleft by a great ravine choked with forest-trees; and in its depths ran a little brook which, swollen by the late rains, fell

plashing in the stillness over a rock. Other than this no sound could reach the strained ear of Wolfe but the gurgle of the tide and the cautious climbing of his advance parties as they mounted the steeps at some little distance from where he sat listening. At length from the top came a sound of musket-shots, followed by loud huzzas, and he knew that his men were masters of the position. The word was given; the troops leaped from the boats and scaled the heights, some here, some there, clutching at trees and bushes, their muskets slung at their backs. Tradition still points out the place, near the mouth of the ravine, where the foremost reached the top. Wolfe said to an officer near him, "You can try it, but I don't think you'll get up." He himself, however, found strength to drag himself up with the rest. The narrow, slanting path on the face of the heights had been made impassable by trenches and abatis, but all obstructions were soon cleared away, and then the ascent was easy. In the gray of the morning the long file of red-coated soldiers moved quickly upward, and formed in order on the plateau above.

6. Before many of them had reached the top, cannon was heard close on the left. It was the battery at Samos firing on the boats in the rear and the vessels descending from Cape Rouge. A party was sent to silence it; this was soon effected, and the more distant battery at Sillery was next attacked and taken. As fast as the boats were emptied they returned for the troops left on board the vessels, and for those waiting on the southern shore under Colonel Burton.

7. The day broke in clouds and threatening rain. Wolfe's battalions were drawn up along the crest of the heights. No enemy was in sight, though a body of Canadians had sallied from the town and moved along the

strand toward the landing-place, whence they were quickly driven back. He had achieved the most critical part of his enterprise, yet the success that he coveted placed him in imminent danger. On one side was the garrison of Quebec and the army of Beauport, and Bougainville was on the other. Wolfe's alternative was victory or ruin; for if he should be overwhelmed by a combined attack, retreat would be hopeless. His feelings no man can know, but it would be safe to say that hesitation or doubt had no place in them.

8. He went to reconnoiter the ground, and soon came to the Plains of Abraham, so called from Abraham Martin, a pilot known as Maitre Abraham, who had owned a piece of land here in the early times of the colony. The Plains were a tract of grass, tolerably level in most parts, patched here and there with corn-fields, studded with clumps of bushes, and forming a part of the high plateau at the eastern end of which Quebec stood. On the south it was bounded by the declivities along the St. Lawrence; on the north by those along the St. Charles, or rather along the meadows through which that lazy stream crawled like a writhing snake. At the place that Wolfe chose for his battle-field the plateau was less than a mile wide.

9. Thither the troops advanced, marched by files till they reached the ground, and then wheeled to form their line of battle, which stretched across the plateau and faced the city. It consisted of six battalions and the detached grenadiers from Louisbourg, all drawn up in ranks three deep. Its right wing was near the brink of the heights along the St. Lawrence, but the left could not reach those along the St. Charles. On this side a wide space was perforce left open, and there was danger of being outflanked. To prevent this, Brigadier Townshend was sta-

tioned here with two battalions, drawn up at right angles with the rest, and fronting the St. Charles. The battalion of Webb's regiment, under Colonel Burton, formed the reserve; the third battalion of Royal Americans was left to guard the landing; and Howe's light infantry occupied a wood far in the rear. Wolfe, with Monckton and Murray, commanded the front line, on which the heavy fighting was to fall, and which, when all the troops had arrived, numbered less than thirty-five hundred men.

10. Quebec was not a mile distant, but they could not see it, for a ridge of broken ground intervened about six hundred paces off. The first division of troops had scarcely come up when, about six o'clock, this ridge was suddenly thronged with white uniforms. It was the battalion of Guienne, arrived at the eleventh hour from its camp by the St. Charles. Some time after there was hot firing in the rear. It came from a detachment of Bougainville's command attacking a house where some of the light infantry were posted. The assailants were repulsed and the firing ceased. Light showers fell at intervals, besprinkling the troops as they stood patiently waiting the event.

"*Qui vive?*" (kee veev) (3) is a French expression meaning "Who goes there?" "*À quel régiment?*" (ä kĕl' rā zhĭ mŏng) (3), "To what regiment?" "*De la Reine*" (duh lä rān) (3), "The Queen's."

---

There is a lesson in each flower,
A story in each stream and bower,
In every herb on which you tread
Are written words, which rightly read,
Will lead you from earth's fragrant sod,
To hope, and holiness, and God!

## LESSON XCIII.

3. quaint; *a.* odd and old-fashioned.
4. tär′ tạns; *n.* plaid woolen cloths, worn in Scotland.
7. vē′ he mẹnt; *a.* forcible.
8. feĭgnẹd; *v.* pretended.
10. pre çĭ′ şion (*pre sizh′ŭn*); *n.* accuracy; exactness.
11. cŭm′ bẽrẹd; *v.* crowded.
11. frăn′ tĭc; *a.* wild and disorderly.
11. clănş′ mẹn; *n.* belonging to particular clans, families, or tribes.
13. rĕc′ ŏg nīzẹd; *v.* knew the identity of.

### Storming the Heights of Abraham. Part II.

1. Montcalm had passed a troubled night. Through all the evening the cannon bellowed from the ships of Saunders, and the boats of the fleet hovered in the dusk off the Beauport shore, threatening every moment to land. Troops lined the intrenchments till day, while the general walked the field that adjoined his headquarters till one in the morning, accompanied by the Chevalier Johnstone and Colonel Poulariez. Johnstone says that he was in great agitation and took no rest all night. At daybreak he heard the sound of cannon above the town. It was the battery at Samos firing on the English ships. He had sent an officer to the quarters of Vaudreuil, which were much nearer Quebec, with orders to bring him word at once should anything unusual happen. But no word came, and about six o'clock he mounted and rode thither with Johnstone. As they advanced, the country behind the town opened more and more upon their sight, till at length, when opposite Vaudreuil's house, they saw across the St. Charles, some two miles away, the red ranks of British soldiers on the heights beyond.

2. "This is serious business," Montcalm said, and sent off Johnstone at full gallop to bring up the troops from the

center and left of the camp. Those of the right were in motion already, doubtless by the Governor's order. Vaudreuil came out of the house. Montcalm stopped for a few words with him, then set spurs to his horse, and rode over the bridge of the St. Charles to the scene of danger. He rode with a fixed look, uttering not a word.

3. The army followed in such order as it might, crossed the bridge in hot haste, passed under the rampart of Quebec, entered at the Palace Gate, and pressed on in headlong march along the quaint, narrow streets of the warlike town: troops of Indians in scalp-locks and war-paint, a savage glitter in their deep-set eyes; bands of Canadians, whose all was at stake—faith, country, and home; the colony regulars; the battalions of old France, a torrent of white uniforms and gleaming bayonets, La Sarre, Languedoc, Rouissillon, Béarn—victors of Oswego, William Henry, and Ticonderoga. So they swept on, poured out upon the plain, some by the gate of St. Louis and some by that of St. John, and hurried, breathless, to where the banners of Guienne still fluttered on the ridge.

4. Montcalm was amazed at what he saw. He had expected a detachment, and he found an army. Full in sight before him stretched the lines of Wolfe: the close ranks of the English infantry, a silent wall of red, and the wild array of the Highlanders, with their waving tartans, and bagpipes screaming defiance.

5. Vaudreuil had not come; but not the less was felt the evil of a divided authority and the jealousy of the rival chiefs. Montcalm waited long for the forces he had ordered to join him from the left wing of the army. He waited in vain. It is said that the Governor had detained them, lest the English should attack the Beauport shore. Even if they did so, and succeeded, the French might defy them,

could they but put Wolfe to rout on the Plains of Abraham. Neither did the garrison of Quebec come to the aid of Montcalm. He sent to Ramesay, its commander, for twenty-five field-pieces which were on the Palace battery. Ramesay would give him only three, saying that he wanted them for his own defense. There were orders and counter-orders; misunderstanding, haste, delay, perplexity.

6. Montcalm and his chief officers held a council of war. It is said that he and they alike were for immediate attack. His enemies declare that he was afraid lest Vaudreuil should arrive and take command; but the Governor was not a man to assume responsibility at such a crisis. Others say that his impetuosity overcame his better judgment; and of this charge it is hard to acquit him. Bougainville was but a few miles distant, and some of his troops were much nearer; a messenger sent by way of Old Lorette could have reached him in an hour and a half at most, and a combined attack in front and rear might have been concerted with him. If, moreover, Montcalm could have come to an understanding with Vaudreuil, his own force might have been strengthened by two or three thousand additional men from the town and camp of Beauport; but he felt that there was no time to lose, for he imagined that Wolfe would soon be reinforced, which was impossible, and he believed that the English were fortifying themselves, which was no less an error.

7. He has been blamed not only for fighting too soon, but for fighting at all. In this he could not choose. Fight he must, for Wolfe was now in a position to cut off all his supplies. His men were full of ardor, and he resolved to attack before their ardor cooled. He spoke a few words to them in his keen, vehement way. "I remember very well how he looked," one of the Canadians, then a boy of

eighteen, used to say in his old age; "he rode a black or dark bay horse along the front of our lines, brandishing his sword, as if to excite us to do our duty. He wore a coat with wide sleeves, which fell back as he raised his arm, and showed the white linen of the wristband."

8. The English waited the result with a composure which, if not quite real, was at least well feigned. The three field-pieces sent by Ramesay plied them with canister-shot, and fifteen hundred Canadians and Indians fusilladed them in front and flank. Over all the plain, from behind bushes and knolls and the edge of corn-fields, puffs of smoke sprang incessantly from the guns of these hidden marksmen. Skirmishers were thrown out before the lines to hold them in check, and the soldiers were ordered to lie on the grass to avoid the shot. The firing was liveliest on the English left, where bands of sharp-shooters got under the edge of the declivity, among thickets, and behind scattered houses, whence they killed and wounded a considerable number of Townshend's men. The light infantry were called up from the rear. The houses were taken and retaken, and one or more of them was burned.

9. Wolfe was everywhere. How cool he was, and why his followers loved him, is shown by an incident that happened in the course of the morning. One of his captains was shot through the lungs; and on recovering consciousness he saw the general standing at his side. Wolfe pressed his hand, told him not to despair, praised his services, promised him early promotion, and sent an aide-de-camp to Monckton to beg that officer to keep the promise if he himself should fall.

10. It was toward ten o'clock when, from the high ground on the right of the line, Wolfe saw that the crisis was near. The French on the ridge had formed them-

selves into three bodies, regulars in the center, regulars and Canadians on right and left. Two field-pieces, which had been dragged up the heights, fired on them with grape-shot, and the troops, rising from the ground, prepared to receive them. In a few moments more they were in motion. They came on rapidly, uttering loud shouts, and firing as soon as they were within range. Their ranks, ill ordered at the best, were further confused by a number of Canadians who had been mixed among the regulars, and who, after hastily firing, threw themselves on the ground to reload. The British advanced a few rods; then halted and stood still. When the French were within forty paces the word of command rang out, and a crash of musketry answered all along the line. The volley was delivered with remarkable precision. In the battalions of the center, which had suffered least from the enemy's bullets, the simultaneous explosion was afterward said by French officers to have sounded like a cannon-shot. Another volley followed, and then a furious clattering fire that lasted but a minute or two.

11. When the smoke rose, a miserable sight was revealed; the ground cumbered with dead and wounded, the advancing masses stopped short and turned into a frantic mob, shouting, cursing, gesticulating. The order was given to charge. Then over the field rose the British cheer, mixed with the fierce yell of the Highland slogan. Some of the corps pushed forward with the bayonet; some advanced firing. The clansmen drew their broadswords and dashed on, keen and swift as bloodhounds.

12. At the English right, though the attacking column was broken to pieces, a fire was still kept up, chiefly, it seems, by sharp-shooters from the bushes and corn-fields, where they had lain for an hour or more. Here Wolfe

THE DEATH OF WOLFE.

himself led the charge, at the head of the Louisbourg grenadiers. A shot shattered his wrist. He wrapped his handkerchief about it and kept on. Another shot struck him, and he still advanced, when a third lodged in his breast. He staggered, and sat on the ground. Lieutenant Brown of the grenadiers, one Henderson, a volunteer in the same company, and a private soldier, aided by an officer of artillery who ran to join them, carried him in their arms to the rear. He begged them to lay him down. They did so, and asked if he would have a surgeon. "There's no need," he answered; "it's all over with me." A moment after, one of them cried out, "They run; see how they run!" "Who run?" Wolfe demanded, like a man roused from sleep. "The enemy, sir. They give way everywhere." "Go, one of you, to Colonel Burton," returned the dying man; "tell him to march Webb's regiment down to Charles River, to cut off their retreat from the bridge." Then, turning on his side, he murmured, "Now, God be praised, I will die in peace!" and in a few moments his gallant soul had fled.

13. Montcalm, still on horseback, was borne with the tide of fugitives toward the town. As he approached the walls a shot passed through his body. He kept his seat; two soldiers supported him, one on each side, and led his horse through the St. Louis Gate. On the open space within, among the excited crowd, were several women, drawn, no doubt, by eagerness to know the result of the fight. One of them recognized him, saw the streaming blood, and shrieked, "*O mon Dieu! mon Dieu! le Marquis est tué!*" "It's nothing, it's nothing," replied the death-stricken man; "don't be troubled for me, my good friends."  
FRANCIS PARKMAN.

"*O mon Dieu,*" etc. (13), means "O my God! my God! the Marquis is killed!"

## LESSON XCIV.

1. shēavēṣ ; *n.* bundles. | 3. pĕr chânçe′ ; *adv.* perhaps.

### Sowing and Reaping.

1. Sow with a generous hand ;
    Pause not for toil and pain ;
   Weary not through the heat of summer,
    Weary not through the cold spring rain ;
   But wait till the autumn comes
    For the sheaves of golden grain.

2. Scatter the seed, and fear not,
    A table will be spread ;
   What matter if you are too weary
    To eat your hard-earned bread ;
   Sow, while the earth is broken,
    For the hungry must be fed.

3. Sow ;—while the seeds are lying
    In the warm earth's bosom deep,
   And your warm tears fall upon it—
    They will stir in their quiet sleep,
   And the green blades rise the quicker,
    Perchance, for the tears you weep.

4. Then sow ;—for the hours are fleeting,
    And the seed must fall to-day ;
   And care not what hands shall reap it,
    Or if you shall have passed away
   Before the waving corn-fields
    Shall gladden the sunny day.

5. Sow ;—and look onward, upward,
    Where the starry light appears,—
Where, in spite of the coward's doubting,
    Or your own heart's trembling fears,
You shall reap in joy the harvest
    You have sown to-day in tears.

ADELAIDE ANNE PROCTER.

    What is the meaning of this poem? Does it urge the reader merely to sow grain of wheat, corn, or barley, or is something better meant? Let the pupils explain as well as they can, in their own words, just what each stanza means.

    **Adelaide Anne Procter** was born in London, October 30, 1825. Her father was Walter Bryan Procter, better known as "Barry Cornwall." From him she inherited her gift of poetry. For many years she was a contributor to Dickens' "Household Words" without the editor knowing her identity, though he was a warm friend of her father's and a frequent visitor at the family residence. Her poems abound in deep Catholic feeling and are read wherever the English language is spoken. Her life, after her conversion to the true Faith, was spent in works of charity. She died February 2, 1863.

## LESSON XCV.

1. Ĭm pĕlled'; *v.* driven.
1. făc' ŭl tĭes; *n.* powers; talents; gifts.
1. de vĕl' ŏped; *v.* grow more and more perfect.
2. ăn' ärch ў; *n.* want of government; political confusion.
2. sŭb ôr' dĭ nate; *a.* inferior in order, nature, or dignity.
3. de bāsed'; *a.* lowered in dignity or worth.
3. dĕs pŏt' ĭc; *a.* tyrannical.
4. scāle; *n.* a ladder; a series of steps.

### The Necessity of Government.

    This Lesson is an extract from a speech delivered by John C. Calhoun in the United States Senate, June 27, 1848.

    1. Society can no more exist without government, in one form or another, than man without society. The political, then, is man's natural state. It is the one for

which his Creator formed him, into which he is impelled irresistibly, and the only one in which his race can exist and all his faculties be fully developed.

2. It follows that even the worst form of government is better than anarchy; and that individual liberty or freedom must be subordinate to whatever power may be necessary to protect society against anarchy within or destruction from without.

3. Just in proportion as a people are ignorant, stupid, debased, corrupt, exposed to violence within and danger without, the power necessary for government to possess, in order to preserve society against anarchy and destruction, becomes greater and greater, and individual liberty less and less, until the lowest condition is reached, when absolute and despotic power becomes necessary on the part of the government, and individual liberty becomes extinct.

4. So, on the contrary, just as a people rise in the scale of intelligence, virtue, and patriotism, and the more perfectly they become acquainted with the nature of government, the ends for which it was ordered, and how it ought to be administered, the power necessary for government becomes less and less, and individual liberty greater and greater. JOHN C. CALHOUN.

John Caldwell Calhoun was born at Abbeville, South Carolina, March 18, 1782. He served with distinction in Congress and the Senate, and was minister of war under President Monroe. The tariff of 1832 being unfavorable to the South, Calhoun advanced the doctrine that a State could nullify a law of the United States. The idea was taken up and passed as a law by South Carolina, and that state even threatened to leave the Union if the new tariff were carried out. The prompt action of President Andrew Jackson prevented any trouble. Calhoun died March 31, 1850.

## LESSON XCVI.

2. ŭn tĕn′ȧ blẹ; *a.* not capable of being held.
3. băs′tion (*băs′chŭn*); *n.* a projecting mass of masonry at the angle of a fortified work.
5. ăd′ȧ mănt; *n.* a stone of extreme hardness.
5. dĕç′ĭ mā tĕd; *a.* reduced.

7. gre nādẹs′; *n.* hollow iron balls, filled with explosives, and thrown among enemies.
7. făs çīnẹs; *n.* bundles of sticks used in raising batteries, and in filling ditches.
9. fŏ′ṣĭl lādẹ; *n.* a simultaneous discharge of fire-arms.

### How They Kept the Bridge at Athlone.

Though James II. was defeated by William at the battle of the Boyne, in 1690, and escaped to France, the Irish Jacobites still kept up the struggle. At Athlone, at Limerick, and at other places, they made a gallant defense; but at the battle of Aghrim, in 1691, St. Ruth, who led the Irish troops, was killed and his army totally defeated. The surrender of Limerick, two months later, brought the struggle in Ireland to a close.

1. On the 17th of June, 1691, the army of King William —" the ranks one blaze of scarlet, and the artillery such as had never before been seen in Ireland "—appeared in full force before Athlone. Ginkle summoned the town to surrender.

2. On a previous occasion when besieged, the governor had relinquished, as untenable, the Leinster (or " English ") side of the town, and made his stand successfully from the Connaught (or " Irish ") side. The governor on this occasion, Colonel Fitzgerald, resolved to defend both the English and Irish sides, St. Ruth having strongly counseled him to do so, and promised to reach him soon with the bulk of the Irish army from Limerick. Colonel Fitzgerald had not more than three hundred and fifty men as a garrison. Nevertheless, knowing that all depended on holding out till St. Ruth could come up, he did not wait for Ginkle to appear in

sight, but sallied out with his small force, and disputed with the Williamite army the approaches to the town, thus successfully retarding them for five or six hours.

3. But Ginkle had merely to plant his artillery, and the only walls Athlone possessed, on *that* side at least, were breached, and crumbled like pastry. Toward evening, on the 19th of June, the whole of the bastion at the " Dublin Gate," near the river, on the north side, being leveled, the town was assaulted. The storming party, as told off, were four thousand men, headed by three hundred grenadiers. To meet these, Fitzgerald had barely the survivors of his three hundred and fifty men, now exhausted after forty-eight hours' constant fighting. In the breach, when the assault was delivered, *two hundred* of that gallant band fell, to rise no more. The remainder, fiercely fighting, fell back inch by inch toward the bridge, pressed by their four thousand foes. From the Williamites shouts now arose from all sides of " The bridge, the bridge!" and a furious rush was made to get over the bridge along with, if not before, the retreating Irish. In this event, of course, all would be lost.

4. But the brave Fitzgerald and his handful of heroes knew the fact well. Turning to bay at the bridge-end, they opposed themselves like an impenetrable wall to the mass of the enemy; while above the din of battle and the shouts of the combatants could be heard sounds in the rear, that to Mackay's ear needed no explanation—the Irish were breaking down the arches behind, while yet they fought in front! "They are destroying the bridge!" he shouted wildly: "on! on! save the bridge—the bridge!" Flinging themselves in hundreds on the few score men now resisting them, the stormers sought to clear the way by freely giving man for man, life for life, nay, four for one.

5. But it would not do. There Fitzgerald and his companions stood like adamant; the space at the bridge-end was small; one man could keep five at bay; and a few paces behind, wielding pick and spade and crowbar, like furies, were the engineers of the Irish garrison. Soon a low rumbling noise was heard, followed by a crash; and a shout of triumph broke from the Irish side, a yell of rage from the assailants. A portion, but a portion only, of two arches had fallen into the stream; the bridge was still passable. Again a wild eager shout from Mackay. "On! on! now! now! the bridge!" But still there stood the decimated defenders, with clutched guns and clenched teeth, resolved to die but not to yield. Suddenly a cry from the Irish rear, "Back! back, men, for your lives!" The brave band turned from the front, and saw the half-broken arches behind them tottering. Most of them rushed with lightning speed over the falling mass; but the last company—it had wheeled round, even at that moment, to face and keep back the enemy—were too late. As they rushed for the passage, the mass of masonry heaved over with a roar into the boiling surges, leaving the devoted band on the brink in the midst of their foes.

6. There was a moment's pause, and almost a wail burst from the Irish on the Connaught side; but just as the enemy rushed with vengeance upon the doomed group, they were seen to draw back a pace or two from the edge of the chasm, fling away their arms, then dash forward and plunge into the stream. Like a clap of thunder broke a volley from a thousand guns on the Leinster shore, tearing the water into foam. There was a minute of suspense on each side, and then a cheer rang out, of defiance, exultation, victory, as the brave fellows were seen to reach the other bank, pulled to land by a hundred welcoming hands!

7. St. Ruth, at Ballinasloe, on his way up from Limerick, heard next day that the English town had fallen. He instantly set out at the head of fifteen hundred horse and foot, leaving the main army to follow as quickly as possible. On his arrival, he encamped about two miles west of the town, and appointed Lieutenant-General D'Usson governor, instead of the gallant Fitzgerald, "as being best skilled in defending fortified places." Now came the opportunity for that splendid artillery, "the like of which," Macaulay has told us, "had never been seen in Ireland." For seven long days of midsummer there poured against the Irish town such a storm of iron from seven batteries of heavy siege-guns and mortars, that by the 27th the place was literally a mass of ruins, amongst which, we are told, two men could not walk abreast. On that day a hundred wagons arrived in the Williamite camp from Dublin, laden with a further supply of ammunition for the siege-guns. That evening the enemy, by grenades, set on fire the fascines of the Irish breastwork at the bridge; and that night, under cover of a tremendous bombardment, they succeeded in flinging some beams over the broken arches, and partially planking them.

8. Next morning—it was Sunday, the 28th June—the Irish saw with consternation that barely a few planks more laid on would complete the bridge. Their own few cannon were now nearly all buried in the ruined masonry, and the enemy beyond had battery on battery trained on the narrow spot—it was *death* to show in the line of the all but finished causeway!

Out stepped from the ranks of Maxwell's regiment a sergeant of dragoons, Custume by name.

"Are there ten men here who will die with me for Ireland?"

A hundred eager voices shouted "Aye!"

"Then," said he, "we will save Athlone; *the bridge must go down.*"

9. Grasping axes and crowbars, the devoted band rushed from behind the breastwork and dashed forward upon the newly-laid beams. A peal of artillery, a fusillade of musketry from the other side, and the space was swept with grape-shot and bullets. When the smoke cleared away, the bodies of the brave Custume and his ten heroes lay on the bridge riddled with balls. They had torn away some of the beams, but *every man of the eleven had perished.*

10. Out from the ranks of the same regiment dashed as many more volunteers: "There are eleven more who will die for Ireland!" Again across the bridge rushed the heroes. Again the spot is swept by a murderous fusillade. The smoke lifts from the scene; nine of the second band lie dead upon the bridge—two survive—but the work is done; the last beam is gone! Athlone once more is saved.

A. M. SULLIVAN.

**Athlone** (1) a town built on both sides of the river Shannon, the "English" part being situated in Westmeath, in the province of Leinster; the "Irish" part in Roscommon, in the province of Connaught.

**Godard van Ginkle** (1), one of King William's Dutch generals, who won the battle of Aghrim and was made Earl of Athlone.

**St. Ruth** (2), a celebrated French general who fought on the side of James. He was killed at the battle of Aghrim.

**Mackay** (4), a general in William's army.

**Ballinasloe** (7) is a town in Galway and Roscommon counties, Ireland.

**Thomas Babington Macaulay** (7), one of the most brilliant but unreliable of English historians, was born in 1800 and died in 1859. The brilliancy of his style makes his writings very attractive.

## LESSON XCVII.

1. Gael; n. an Irish Celt.
1. lēa′ gūers; n. the men of the besieging army.
2. grĭm; a. fierce.
3. wrēnchĕd; v. forced by violence.
7. mōōr; n. marshy land; ground covered with coarse herbage.
7. hēath; n. a cheerless tract of country.
7. brĕast′ ĕd; v. opposed manfully.

### A Ballad of Athlone;

OR, HOW THEY BROKE DOWN THE BRIDGE.

1. Does any man dream that a Gael can fear,
   Of a thousand deeds let him learn but one!
   The Shannon swept onward, broad and clear,
   Between the leaguers and worn Athlone.

2. "Break down the bridge!" Six warriors rushed
   Thro' the storm of shot and the storm of shell;
   With late, but certain, victory flushed,
   The grim Dutch gunners eyed them well.

3. They wrenched at the planks 'mid a hail of fire:
   They fell in death, their work half done;
   The bridge stood fast; and nigh and nigher
   The foe swarmed darkly, densely on.

4. "Oh, who for Erin will strike a stroke?
   Who hurl yon planks where the waters roar?"
   Six warriors forth from their comrades broke,
   And flung them upon that bridge once more.

5. Again at the rocking planks they dashed;
   And four dropped dead, and two remained;
   The huge beams groaned, and the arch down-crashed—
   Two stalwart swimmers the margin gained.

6. St. Ruth in his stirrups stood up and cried,
   "I have seen no deed like that in France!"
   With a toss of his head Sarsfield replied,
   "They had luck, the dogs! 'twas a merry chance!"

7. Oh! many a year, upon Shannon's side,
   They sang upon moor, and they sang upon heath,
   Of the twain that breasted that raging tide,
   And the ten that shook bloody hands with death.

AUBREY DE VERE.

**Aubrey De Vere** was born at Currah Chase, county of Limerick, Ireland, in 1814. In 1851 he entered the Catholic Church, of which he has since been a devout member. His verse is smooth and melodious, and his inspiration springs from his faith and his patriotism, two qualities that are noticeable in most of his writings.

There is a difference of opinion as to the exact number of men who took part in this heroic act. The poet here says six, other authorities say eight or ten (see preceding Lesson).

**Patrick Sarsfield** (6), Earl of Lucan, was a famous Irish officer. He served under James II., and distinguished himself by his bravery and dash. He made a gallant defense of Limerick, and after its surrender crossed into France with the Irish Brigade. He fell at the battle of Landen in 1693. Catching the blood that trickled from his wound, he exclaimed, "Oh, that this had been for Ireland!"

LESSON XCVIII.

1. cŏŭrt; n. a yard; an inclosed space.
2. ăt tā\nĕd'; v. reached.
3. härd bȳ'; adv. not far off.
4. gŭīlĕ; n. deceit.
5. flĭŏk' ẽr; v. to waver, like a flame about to expire.
8. pā' tient (- shent); n. a sick person under medical treatment.

The Last Days of Colonel Newcome.

1. The old man must have passed a sleepless night, for on going to his chamber in the morning, his attendant found him dressed in his chair, and his bed undisturbed. He must have sat all through the bitter night without a

fire; but his hands were burning hot, and he rambled in his talk. He spoke of some one coming to drink tea with him, pointed to the fire, and asked why it was not made; he would not go to bed, though the nurse pressed him. The bell began to ring for morning chapel; he got up and went toward his gown, groping toward it as though he could hardly see, and put it over his shoulders, and would go out, but he would have fallen in the court if the good nurse had not given him her arm; and the physician of the hospital, passing fortunately at this moment, who had always been a great friend of Colonel Newcome's, insisted upon leading him back to his room again, and got him to bed. "When the bell stopped, he wanted to rise once more; he fancied he was a boy at school again," said the nurse, "and that he was going in to Dr. Raine, who was schoolmaster here ever so many years ago." So it was, that when happier days seemed to be dawning for the good man, that reprieve came too late. Grief, and years, and humiliation, and care, and cruelty had been too strong for him, and Thomas Newcome was stricken down. . . .

2. After some days the fever which had attacked him left him; but left him so weak and enfeebled that he could only go from his bed to the chair by his fireside. The season was exceedingly bitter, the chamber which he inhabited was warm and spacious; it was considered unadvisable to move him until he had attained greater strength, and till warmer weather. The medical men of the House hoped he might rally in spring. My friend Dr. Goodenough came to him: he hoped too; but not with a hopeful face. A chamber, luckily vacant, hard by the Colonel's, was assigned to his friends, where we sat when we were too many for him. Besides his customary attendant, he had two dear and watchful nurses, who were

almost always with him,—Ethel and Madame de Florac, who had passed many a faithful year by an old man's bedside; who would have come, as to a work of religion, to any sick couch,—much more to this one, where he lay for whose life she would once gladly have given her own.

3. But our Colonel, we all were obliged to acknowledge, was no more our friend of old days. He knew us again, and was good to every one round him, as his wont was; especially when Boy came, his old eyes lighted up with simple happiness, and, with eager, trembling hands, he would seek under his bed-clothes, or in the pockets of his dressing-gown, for toys or cakes, which he had caused to be purchased for his grandson. There was a little laughing, red-cheeked, white-headed gown-boy of the school, to whom the old man had taken a great fancy. One of the symptoms of his returning consciousness and recovery, as we hoped, was his calling for this child, who pleased our friend by his archness and merry ways, and who, to the old gentleman's unfailing delight, used to call him "Codd Colonel." "Tell little F—— that Codd Colonel wants to see him;" and the little gown-boy was brought to him; and the Colonel would listen to him for hours; and hear all about his lessons and his play; and prattle, almost as childishly, about Dr. Raine, and his own early school-days. The boys of the school, it must be said, had heard the noble old gentleman's touching history, and had all got to know and love him. They came every day to hear news of him; sent him in books and papers to amuse him; and some benevolent young souls—God's blessing on all honest boys, say I—painted theatrical characters, and sent them in to Codd Colonel's grandson. The little fellow was made free of gown-boys, and once came thence to his grandfather in a little gown, which delighted the old man hugely.

Boy said he would like to be a little gown-boy; and I make no doubt, when he is old enough, his father will get him that post, and put him under the tuition of my friend Dr. Senior.

4. So weeks passed away, during which our dear old friend still remained with us. His mind was gone at intervals, but would rally feebly; and with his consciousness returned his love, his simplicity, his sweetness. He would talk French with Madame de Florac, at which time his memory appeared to awaken with surprising vividness, his cheek flushed, and he was a youth again,—a youth all love and hope,—a stricken old man, with a beard as white as snow covering the noble, careworn face. At such times he called her by her Christian name of Léonore; he addressed courtly old words of regard and kindness to the aged lady; anon he wandered in his talk, and spoke to her as if they still were young. Now, as in those early days, his heart was pure; no anger remained in it; no guile tainted it; only peace and good-will dwelt in it.

5. The days went on, and our hopes, raised sometimes, began to flicker and fail. One evening the Colonel left his chair for his bed in pretty good spirits, but passed a disturbed night, and the next morning was too weak to rise. Then he remained in his bed, and his friends visited him there. One afternoon he asked for his little gown-boy, and the child was brought to him, and sat by the bed with a very awe-stricken face; and then gathered courage, and tried to amuse him by telling him how it was a half-holiday, and they were having a cricket-match with the St. Peter's boys in the green, and Grey Friars was in and winning. The Colonel quite understood about it; he would like to see the game; he had played many a game on that green when he was a boy. He grew excited; Clive dismissed

his father's little friend, and put a sovereign into his hand; and away he ran to say that Codd Colonel had come into a fortune, and to buy tarts, and to see the match out. *I, Curre*, little white-haired gown-boy! Heaven speed you, little friend!

6. After the child had gone, Thomas Newcome began to wander more and more. He talked louder; he gave the word of command, spoke Hindustanee as if to his men. Then he spoke words in French rapidly, seizing a hand that was near him, and crying, "Toujours, toujours!" But it was Ethel's hand which he took. Ethel and Clive and the nurse were in the room with him; the nurse came to us, who were sitting in the adjoining apartment; Madame de Florac was there, with my wife and Bayham.

7. At the look in the woman's countenance Madame de Florac started up. "He is very bad, he wanders a great deal," the nurse whispered. The French lady fell instantly on her knees, and remained rigid in prayer.

Some time afterward Ethel came in with a scared face to our pale group. "He is calling for you again, dear lady," she said, going up to Madame de Florac, who was still kneeling, "and just now he said he wanted Pendennis to take care of his boy. He will not know you." She hid her tears as she spoke.

8. She went into the room where Clive was at the bed's foot; the old man within it talked on rapidly for a while: then again he would sigh and be still: once more I heard him say hurriedly, "Take care of him when I'm in India;" and then, with a heart-rending voice, he called out, "Léonore, Léonore!" She was kneeling by his side now. The patient's voice sank into faint murmurs; only a moan now and then announced that he was not asleep.

9. At the usual evening hour the chapel-bell began to

toll, and Thomas Newcome's hands outside the bed feebly beat time. And just as the last bell struck, a peculiar sweet smile shone over his face, and he lifted up his head a little, and quickly said "Adsum!" and fell back. It was the word we used at school, when names were called; and lo, he, whose heart was as that of a little child, had answered to his name, and stood in the presence of The Master.

THACKERAY.

The character of Colonel Newcome is one of the most beautiful in English fiction, and had Thackeray written nothing else he might rest his reputation on that. Madame de Florac, too, is charmingly drawn, and is a fine type of a noble-hearted Catholic woman.

*I, Curre* (5), is a Latin expression which, freely translated, means *speed thee! Toujours* (tōō zhūr) (6) is the French for *always; adsum* (9) is equivalent to our *I am here!* or *present!* that is, *not absent.*

# Benziger Brothers' School Books.

*Benziger Brothers' Catholic National Readers are universally acknowledged the best, and they are as cheap as the cheapest. . . . .*

**CATHOLIC NATIONAL READERS.**
    The New Primer, with slant or vertical script. 12mo, paper covers.
    The New Primer, with slant or vertical script. 12mo, cloth.
    The New First Reader, with slant or vertical script. 12mo, cloth.
    The New Second Reader, with slant or vertical script. 12mo, cloth.
    The New Third Reader. 12mo, cloth.
    The New Fourth Reader. 12mo, cloth.
    The New Fifth Reader. 12mo, cloth.
    The Sixth Reader. 12mo, cloth.
    The Primary Speller. 12mo, cloth.
    The New Speller and Word Book. 12mo, cloth.
    The Catholic National Charts. 22 numbers, slant or vertical script.

*Points of Superiority of the Catholic National Readers.*
    The literary character and Catholic tone of the lessons.
    The easy and natural grading of the series, and its general adaptation to the demands of the school-room.
    The mechanical execution, including the quality of the paper, the type, the binding, and the beauty and number of the illustrations.

**GRAMMAR.**
    Easy Language Lessons. Illustrated. 12mo, cloth.
    Bone Rules; or, keleton of English Grammar. By Rev. John B. Tabb. 16mo, cloth.
    English Grammar. 12mo, cloth.

**ARITHMETIC.**
    Table Book and Introductory Arithmetic. By L. Nash. 16mo, cloth.

**CATECHISM.**
    Klauder's Revised Edition of the Baltimore Catechism. Complete in 3 numbers. No. 1, paper; No. 2, paper; No. 3, boards.
    Catechism of the Third Plenary Council of Baltimore. *Edition with Word-Meanings*, and the Questions numbered to correspond with Rev. Thos. L. Kinkead's "Explanation of the Baltimore Catechism". Abridged, No. 1, and Large, No. 2. Paper and flexible cloth. *Edition without Word-Meanings:* Abridged, No. 1, and Large, No. 2. Paper and flexible cloth.
    Groening's Large Catechism. 12mo.
    Groening's Small Catechism. 12mo.
    Deharbe's Large Catechism. 12mo.
    Deharbe's Small Catechism. 12mo.
    Explanation of the Baltimore Catechism. By Rev. Thos. L. Kinkead. 12mo, cloth.
    Hand-book of the Christian Religion. By Rev. W. Wilmers, S.J. 12mo, cloth.
    Instructions for First Communicants. By Rev. Dr. J. Schmitt. 16mo, cloth.
    Short Stories on Christian Doctrine, A Collection of Examples illustrating the Catechism. 12mo, cloth.

# Benziger Brothers' School Books.

## HISTORY.

Bible History. By Right Rev. Richard Gilmour, D.D. With 145 illustrations. 12mo, cloth.
New Testament Studies. The Chief Events in the Life of Our Lord. By Right Rev. Mgr. Conaty, D.D. 12mo, cloth.
Bible Stories for Little Children 16mo, cloth, and paper covers.
Illustrated Church History. By Rev. Richard Brennan. 8vo, cloth.
School History of the United States. Illustrated. 12mo, cloth.
Primary History of the United States. Illustrated. 12mo, cloth.

## PENMANSHIP.

Benziger Brothers' New Slant Penmanship. Complete in six numbers.
Benziger Brothers' New System of Vertical Penmanship. Complete in six numbers.
Vertical Penmanship Charts. Complete in two numbers.

## ELOCUTION.

Aids to Correct and Effective Elocution. With Select Readings. 12mo, cloth.
Select Recitations for Catholic Schools and Academies. 12mo, cloth.
Readings and Recitation for Juniors. 16mo, cloth.
Elocution Class. A Simplification of the Laws and Principles of Expression. 16mo, cloth.

## MISCELLANEOUS.

The English Reader. Edited by Rev. Edward Connolly, S.J. 12mo, cloth.
Catechism of Familiar Things. Their History, and the Events which Led to their Discovery. 12mo, cloth.
Hints on Letter-Writing. 16mo, cloth.
New Sunday School Companion. Containing the Catechism, Devotions and Prayers, Hymns and Simple Music. 16mo, cloth.
Hymn-book of the New Sunday School Companion. 12mo, cloth.
Sursum Corda. A Manual of English Hymns and Prayers. 32mo, paper.